Fulfillment in Adulthood

PATHS TO THE PINNACLE OF LIFE

Fulfillment in Adulthood

PATHS TO THE PINNACLE OF LIFE

Calvin A. Colarusso, M. D.

Plenum Press • New York and London

Library of Congress Cataloging-in-Publication Data

Colarusso, Calvin A.
Fulfillment in adulthood : paths to the pinnacle of life / Calvin A. Colarusso.
p. cm.
Includes bibliographical references and index.
ISBN 0-306-44769-X
1. Adulthood--Psychological aspects. 2. Maturation (Psychology) 3. Developmental psychology. 4. Midlife crisis. I. Title.
BF724.5.C594 1994
155.6--dc20 94-30372
CIP

ISBN 0-306-44769-X

Plenum Press is a Division of Plenum Publishing Corporation
233 Spring Street, New York, N.Y. 10013-1578

Printed in the United States of America

To my present grandchildren Caitlin, Michael, and Christopher Colarusso, and Angela Stieber, and to those future wonders who have not yet come on the scene.

For them my wife, Jean, and I have to thank our three children Mike, Mary Ann, and Tom, and their wonderful spouses Paula, Rob, and Betsy.

These four little ones have added a dimension to our lives which we can barely comprehend, but I do know they have brought my wife and me the purest form of love we have ever known, and true fulfillment.

Preface

This book is written for those who are entering and traversing midlife, and for their loved ones who are affected by the pleasures and travails of the journey. A period of profound, often perplexing, and troublesome physical and psychological change, the years between 35 and 65 should be rich and fulfilling, bursting with the very best that life has to offer. But they can be filled with disappointment and disaster—anxiety about sex and intimacy, disappointment on the job, serious physical illness, and problems with growing children and elderly parents.

Drawing on the latest scientific concepts from the rapidly expanding field of adult development, the information in these pages will provide the reader with the thorough understanding of the biological, psychological, and environmental factors required to maximize the pleasure and avoid the pitfalls of this most fascinating time of life.

In addition to the factual information, which outlines

the smoothest, most direct paths to adult fulfillment, these pages are filled with brief clinical vignettes and seven detailed case histories which demonstrate that it is never too difficult, or too late, to reach for and achieve happiness and fulfillment.

Contents

1

Fulfillment through Maturity

Understanding the Nature of Development

Though we travel the world over to find the beautiful we must carry it with us or we find it not.

RALPH WALDO EMERSON

Like it or not, sooner or later, kicking and screaming or with dignity and grace, each of us enters those years in the middle of life when we are expected to be grown up, responsible, even act as adults. What an odd sounding word, *mature.* Despite the negative connotation attached to the word by many, particularly those on the cusp of forty, mature rolls off the tongue easily, full of richness and texture. And that's about as good a definition as any. Maturity signifies the richness and texture of life, human existence at its zenith of complexity and fullness, pulsating with pleasure, pain, and possibilities.

Those who have achieved a sense of selfhood as adults, most likely someone on the cusp of fifty, will tell you that it is a mental state to be desired, even striven for passionately, because of the encompassing sense of self-awareness, understanding, and fulfillment it brings.

The Knowledge Needed to Become Fulfilled: Understanding Development

The knowledge needed to experience fulfillment in adulthood is contained in a large, rapidly expanding field of study on normality and pathology in the second half of life. Most commonly called *adult development,* this science is populated by psychiatrists, psychologists, cultural anthropologists, gerontologists, and sociologists, among others, who have studied the uncharted waters beyond the horizon of childhood and adolescence.

Let us join them by focusing first on the concept of *development.* Development may be defined as the emergence and evolution of the human mind from birth until death as the result of the constant interplay of biological, psychological, and environmental influences. This definition suggests several critically important ideas. First, development, which focuses on the study of the mind, is not synonymous with growth and physical aging; these are reference terms for the changes which occur in the body over time. However, mental functioning is profoundly influenced by the condition of the body, particularly in midlife. Conversely, neither is development the study of the effect of environment alone. As used here environment refers to all external influences on the mind, particularly the effect of interactions with other human beings. Both biological and environmental influences must be understood within the context of the third factor in this confluence of forces which shape the developmental process; namely, the mind itself as it exists at a particular point in the life cycle, be it one of relative immaturity in infancy and early childhood or one of sophistication and complexity in midlife. Thus, in attempting to understand mental functioning at any age, we must consider biological, environmental, and intrapsychic influences as they exist at that moment in time.

Two other basic assumptions follow. First, the developmental process is always in a state of dynamic flux and change. In more formal terms, this is a reference to the constant interplay of this trilogy of influences on each other, which continually produce new, more complex mental forms.

Equally important, and inspiring, for our consideration of adulthood, development is life-long, continuing into old age. Thus, it is never too late to change, to grow, to mature, to find new paths to fulfillment.

Developmental Tasks and Phases

In order to provide a framework in which to consider this highly complex process, the lifelong course of development has been broken down into blocks of time called *developmental phases.* Although there is no single universally accepted nomenclature, most students of development combine the phases for childhood proposed by Sigmund Freud with those for adulthood suggested by Erik Erikson, the psychoanalyst who directed his attention to the entire lifecycle. This combination is illustrated below.

PHASES OF DEVELOPMENT

First Phase	Oral	Ages 0–1
Second Phase	Anal	Ages 1–3
Third Phase	Oedipal	Ages 3–6
Fourth Phase	Latency	Ages 6–12
Fifth Phase	Adolescence	Ages 12–20
Sixth Phase	Young Adulthood	Ages 20–40
Seventh Phase	Middle Adulthood	Ages 40–60
Eighth Phase	Late Adulthood	Ages 60–80
Ninth Phase	Late Late Adulthood	Ages 80–

These artificially determined divisions are organized around basic themes and issues, which are specific for any particular phase, called *developmental tasks.* Engagement and mastery of each of the tasks at the appropriate time strengthens and expands mental structures and capabilities and provides the tools needed to engage the next set of developmental tasks—and so it goes, throughout life.

Although most of our attention in this book will be focused on the sixth and seventh phases—young and middle adulthood—as we study the steps to fulfillment in adulthood, we will also consider the childhood phases in the context of the impact of the past on the dynamic present and future. Because we are the product of both past and present, we continually interact with the child and adolescent within us. The chorus of voices from the past, our own and those of significant others, particularly siblings and parents, cannot be denied. Consciously and unconsciously, they affect every present thought and action. Awareness of personal history, particularly when coupled with a detailed knowledge of child development, is the key to controlling the effect of the past on the present, amplifying those memories and feelings that produce joy and fulfillment, muting those that bring pain and sadness. This is why we begin our study of the paths to fulfillment in adulthood with a consideration of childhood.

A Definition of Maturity

Success and happiness in adulthood are made possible by achieving a modicum of maturity—a reference to a mental state, not an age. Webster suggests that maturity refers to "complete and finished in natural growth or development . . . maturation plays a large role in emotional development . . . the state or quality of being fully grown."(1) While disputing the "complete and finished" suggestion, a developmental definition of maturity contains some of the same elements. *Maturity refers to that mental state found in healthy adults which is characterized by a detailed knowledge of the parameters of human existence; a sophisticated level of self-awareness based on an honest appraisal of one's own experience within those basic parameters; and the ability to use this intellectual and emotional knowledge and insight caringly in relationship to one's self and others.*

Thus, the path to fulfillment in adulthood is clearly outlined. Learn as much as possible about the basic stuff of life through experience and study. Determine your success or failure with the major developmental themes of life through a searingly honest appraisal. Then, building on this increased understanding, think, feel, and act accordingly, enhancing your life and the lives of those around you.

The Challenges of Adulthood

A detailed knowledge of the parameters of human existence could also be defined as a thorough understanding of the developmental tasks of childhood and adulthood. In subsequent chapters we will explore how the developmental past and present determine the ability of the adult to think and act maturely. But for the moment let us expand the definition of maturity by suggesting that the ability to live a full and satisfying life grows out of the successful engagement and mastery of most, if not all, the major developmental tasks of adulthood.

As they leave childhood and adolescence behind and journey along the paths through young adulthood and middle life, men and women attempt to:

1. Separate psychologically from the parents of childhood and achieve self-sufficiency in the adult world.
2. Find a gratifying place in the adult world of work.
3. Experience sexual and emotional intimacy within a committed relationship.
4. Become a biological and psychological parent.
5. Forge a new relationship with parents, one that is based on equality and facilitates the mid- and late life development of the progenitors.
6. Accept the aging process in the body.
7. Integrate the growing awareness of time limitation and personal death.
8. Maintain physical and emotional intimacy in the face of the powerful physical, psychological and environmental pressures of midlife.
9. Facilitate the emergence of children into adulthood by letting go, accepting an equal relationship, and integrating new family members.
10. Care for aging parents and prepare to accept their deaths.
11. Exercise position and power in the workplace. Become a mentor.

12. Develop and sustain friendships with individuals of different ages and backgrounds.
13. Continue to play throughout adulthood.
14. Leave a legacy for future generations by facilitating the development of younger individuals.

Implications for the Present and Future

Those who expand their knowledge of development through the information presented in this book and emerge from an assessment of their level of maturity with an overall feeling of satisfaction will certainly find some areas for contemplation and change, since the developmental process is never totally mastered. Those young and middle-aged adults who are less satisfied with their self-appraisal can make an effort to change while they have the luxury of abundant time. Ahead for all, lies the Eighth Stage, Late Adulthood, when, as Erik Erikson put it, the choice is between integrity and despair. Integrity is the reward for having lived life with meaning, fully, and well. For Erikson that means balancing the certainty of death "with the only happiness that is lasting; to increase by whatever is yours to give, the good will and higher order in your sector of the world."(2) However, if the life review reveals a series of missed opportunities, bungled relationships, or personal misfortune, the result is a sense of bitter despair and a preoccupation with what might have been. Then death is to be feared, for it symbolizes a life of personal emptiness.

Striving for maturity and fulfillment throughout the second half of life insures that old age, as well as the adult years which precede it, will be filled with a deep, sustaining sense of integrity, the awareness that one's life has been lived fully and well, with pleasure, purpose, and meaning.

2

The Importance of Childhood Experiences

General Principles of Child Development

All roads to fulfillment in adulthood begin in childhood. Some are as smooth as the Indianapolis Motor Speedway, others are rough as a pothole-scarred, big-city street. Most individuals experience some of both as they traverse the six stages of development leading to midlife. Indeed, it is the enormous variety of human experience which adds texture to the broad expanses of daily living and sparkle and uniqueness to the individual personality.

The information on child development presented in the next few chapters is intended to provide the curious adult with some of the conceptual tools needed to ask, and answer, the central questions posed in this book: What is adult fulfillment and how do I achieve it? Although the answer to the first question is highly individual, the answer to the second is not. Fulfillment is within the reach of those men and women who have acquired a detailed understanding of the human condition through study and experience and have then applied it to appraising their own lives with searing honesty and compassion.

The dread of conducting such a self-examination may be cushioned by the following: In our daily lives each of us meets individuals who were raised in seemingly ideal circumstances and went astray, and others who transcended the most horrendous backgrounds to become remarkably "together" adults. How did they do it?

The answer lies partly in an understanding of two aspects of developmental theory. First, maturity in adulthood is not based on childhood experience alone. Freud's focus on the first several years of life as the primary source of adult psychopathology (unlike his early disciple Carl Jung and others) and his relative neglect of subsequent experience delayed the study of adulthood by others for several decades. Contemporary adult developmental theory does not diminish the importance of childhood but suggests that normality and pathology in adulthood are an amalgam of experience from *all* phases of the life cycle, up to and including the present. Thus, those who were damaged by an emotionally impoverished beginning may have overcome the handicap and learned from it in adolescence and adulthood.

Second, we know that not all aspects of development are explained by a continuous, lock-step progression model. Some features appear to result from *discontinuous* experience, arising seemingly de nova, thus providing a second, third, or fourth chance. The resulting kaleidoscope is a picture of a developmental process in a continuous state of flux and turmoil, dynamic and multipotentiated. In short, the paths to adult fulfillment are open to almost everyone.

An Historical Overview

Prior to the twentieth century, children were thought of as miniature adults, physically smaller and asexual but mentally the same as their progenitors. Over the centuries this misconception became the rationale for the misunderstanding and maltreatment of children. Almost inadvertently, Freud shattered this belief when his interest in childhood was peaked by the discovery of the relationship between infantile sexual experience and adult symptomatology. "As long ago as in the year 1896, I insisted on the significance of the years of childhood as the origin of certain important phenomena connected with sexual life, and since then I have never ceased to emphasize the part played in sexuality by the infantile factor."(1)

The thought that children were sexual was shocking to the Victorian Viennese—and still is to some. Despite a hundred years of dissemination of information, some adults still react to the obvious sexual play of children with surprise and dismay because of unresolved conflicts about their own early sexuality. Coming to terms with one's sexual past and present, and understanding—and then comfortably accepting—the role of human sexual experience across the broad expanse of the life cycle, is an indispensable component of maturity which enhances one of life's greatest pleasures.

In 1909 Freud attempted to apply his new insight to the treatment of a child. Immortalized in the case of "Little Hans," this was the first attempt to treat a child using psychological techniques.(2) Freud did not actually meet with Hans. He talked with his father, a student who then imparted "the professor's" ideas to the boy. It was not until the 1920s and 1930s that the actual treatment of children began, spearheaded by the pioneering efforts of Freud's daughter, Anna, who followed in her famous father's footsteps. As the clouds of World War II gathered in Europe, many therapists sought refuge in the United States, where they introduced analytic concepts and became part of the rapidly expanding number of therapists treating children.

As strange as it may seem today, because the idea is so completely accepted, the importance of the mother–child relationship for normal infant and early child development was not fully recognized before the 1940s and the 1950s. Then psychoanalyst Rene Spitz's work on "hospitalism" revolutionized contemporary thought.(3) In orphanages and foundling homes around the world he was shocked to find row after row of listless, hollow-eyed infants. Although fed and clothed, they received little stimulation and love from their starchly dressed nurses. Doomed by the ignorance of their well-intentioned caregivers, many died before they were a year old. In startling contrast were the happy babies cared for on a continuous basis by their unwed mothers who were relegated to institutions because of their disreputable status.

After fleeing to England in the 1930s with her famous father to escape Nazi persecution, Anna Freud studied the effects of trauma and separation on children who were caught in the London blitz.(4) Those who remained with their parents, huddled each night in the cramped, womblike security of the subways, often fared better than those who were sent away to the physically safe but emotionally barren countryside.

The treatment of children with psychotherapy and psychoanalysis, which became commonplace in the 1950s, opened a rich vein of research data that increased knowledge of normal and pathological development exponentially. The relationship between fathers and their children, relegated to the scientific back-burner for decades because of the all-consuming interest in mother–child studies, is currently commanding center stage and producing intriguing insights into what is now recognized to be a critically important factor in normal development.

The Nature of Development in Childhood

Backward, turn backward, O Time in your flight
Make me a child again, just for to-night.
ELIZABETH AKERS ALLEN, *Rock Me Sleep, Mother*

As described in Chapter 1, development is the study of the evolution of the mind which results from the continuous, lifelong interactions among three sets of variables: (1) the body as it grows during childhood and ages during adulthood; (3) the mind itself, qualitatively different at different points in the life cycle; (3) and external influences, consisting primarily of the family of origin in childhood and the family of procreation in adulthood. As indicated by this definition, physical maturation, limited to childhood, and development, which is lifelong, are not the same. Physical maturation is a more circumscribed concept, referring to the unfolding of genetically controlled potentials in childhood, such as the emergence of the abilities to walk at about one year of age, to read and write during the elementary school years, and to become sexually mature in adolescence. Understanding these concepts sets the stage for a discussion of the unique way in which the three sets of variables interact in childhood and a consideration of some basic differences between the child and the adult.

Children Are Different at Different Ages

Children differ at different ages because mind and body evolve so rapidly in childhood. This seemingly simplistic idea has far-reaching consequences for understanding children because it suggests that similar behaviors have different meanings at different ages. The ubiquitous temper tantrum of the two-year-old is normal, but the unbridled thrashing about of a six-year-old is not. The terrified response of a four-year-old (to a frightening nightmare) is an age-appropriate response to an intense struggle with feelings of anger and competition, but the frequent occurrence of nightmares in a ten-year-old is a likely indication of pathology. Infants change from minute to minute, toddlers from hour to hour, and adolescents overnight. By contrast, the pace of development in adulthood is leisurely, almost luxuriously slow, with basic themes emerging over decades rather than days. At first glance, nature's division of life into childhood and adulthood appears capricious and inequitable, since we have but twenty years in which to crowd the experiences of childhood, but three times as long to struggle with the great issues of adulthood. However, a more studied consideration suggests that the temporal distribution may be just right. The passion of youth must recede before the unhurried contemplation of adulthood can begin.

Parenthood: The Power of the Potter's Wheel

When they are very young, children are amorphous and unformed, responsive to the touch of their parents who shape and mold them like wet clay. But as time passes and the clay hardens, children become less malleable but still responsive to the potter's wheel. Once fired in the kiln of adolescence, the artist's influence diminishes, reduced to the role of connoisseur admiring his or her creation.

Parents are nature's substitute for the instincts which provide newborns in the animal kingdom with the survival skills needed to evade predators. Human infants are not so equipped; they do not survive in life's jungle without caretakers. Healthy parents recognize their awesome power and exercise it judiciously, remaining steadfast and firm when necessary. Then gradually, joyfully, they relinquish control to the toddler's messy demand to feed him- or herself, to the seven-year-old's insistence on bathing in private while undoubtedly forgetting to wash behind the ears, and to the impetuous adolescent who wants it all—now! After all, active parenthood is meant to be a time-limited activity. The successful practitioner of the art is out of business when the young ones reach eighteen or so, but not out of the role of parent. Fortunately, or unfortunately, as the case may be, the relationship between parent and child continues. Their lives remain tightly intertwined as they march through the second half of life, anxiously anticipating the arrival of the next generation, who will assign them the new roles of parents and grandparents and further transform their lives.

The Power of Innate Forces: The Quality of the Clay

In spite of their power, parents are not the only, or sometimes even the dominant, influence on a child's development. Biological processes, sometimes referred to at the psychic level as drives or impulses, may be equally or more potent. This is particularly true when nature throws a curve, as, for example, when an infant is born with a birth defect or develops a debilitating disease. The potter has to work with the clay he or she is given. But even when nature is kind and the clay has no perceptible flaws, the wise potter recognizes his limitations.

He watches in awe as the clay shapes itself, developing textures, mental and physical capabilities which could not be anticipated or controlled. And then there are times, like the early adolescent years, when the clay seems totally foreign, unfamiliar, despite the fact that it had worked for years. Nurture or nature, the chicken or the egg, biology or environment, never either, always both; the end-product an amalgam, a blend, but always a work of art.

Developmental Differences between Children and Adults

The developmental differences between children and adults are huge. They are physical and mental, qualitative and quantitative. Understanding them encourages generativity, caring for the next generation, that indisputable facet of maturity. As one gets older, although cushioned by the warmth, understanding, and empathy that maturity brings, one cannot help but be in awe of the child, jealous of his or her potential, protective of his or her vulnerability, and aware of his or her limitations.

Developmental Differences between Children and Adults
Egocentricity
The immaturity of the genitals
The irrationality of childhood
A different sense of time
The frequency of regression

Egocentricity

The first area of difference is egocentricity. During infancy mother is not perceived by the child as having an existence of her own. Rather, she is an extension of the child's needs and wishes, the source of satisfaction and frustration. Every preoccupation of the mother—her concerns with other family members, with work or outside interests, illnesses and absences, even her death—is transformed into an experience of rejection and desertion. This means that the infant and toddler misinterprets the actions of significant adults. Under normal circumstances, these repeated inevitable slights are compensated for by innumerable interactions of assurance and pleasure.

As parents help the young child to engage the developmental tasks of early life such as weaning and toilet training and accept the frustrations involved therein, he or she gradually develops the capacity to control raging wants and desires. Then, too, as intellect develops, the toddler begins to *understand* that he or she is not the center of the universe and that all actions which frustrate wishes are not intentional. Slowly, ever so slowly, as adulthood approaches, the egocentricity of childhood is partially transformed into enlightened self-interest and a growing concern for others. But as muted as infantile egocentricity may be in the mature adult, it is never totally absent, constantly lurking beneath a facade of civility, ready to reassert itself at a weak moment's notice. The mature person recognizes, accepts, and occasionally befriends the beast within, occasionally satisfying the wish to be special.

The Immaturity of the Genitals

The physical immaturity of the genitals and the qualitative differences between their sexual capabilities and those of adults ensures that the young child will misinterpret adult sexuality, distorting it to fit his or her physical experience and limited mental capabilities.

As Anna Freud expressed it, "This accounts for parental intercourse being misunderstood as a scene of brutal violence and opens the door for all the difficulties of identifying with either the alleged victim or alleged aggressor which reveal themselves later in the growing child's uncertainty about his own sexual identity."(5)

The achievement of a mature, comfortable adult sexual identity is a life-long process, growing in complexity as each developmental phase, in both childhood and adulthood, adds new elements. It cannot be instantly instilled into a young child through education or experience. The confident adult empathizes with the child and tenderly contemplates the dilemma which consciously and unconsciously resonates with his own infantile notions, now tempered by physical maturity and experience. We will trace this lifelong line of sexual development through each of the developmental phases until we explore it in the full bloom of maturity.

The Irrationality of Childhood

The ability of the young child to think in logical, rational terms does not exist in infancy and increases slowly over the first decade of life. Even the adolescent will be discovered to harbor infantile misconceptions beneath a thin veneer of rational thought (masturbation causes pimples and girls can get pregnant from toilet seats). This qualitative difference in the nature of thinking between the child and the adult means that the former must, will, misinterpret events and adult intentions, creating considerable frustration in those grown-ups who do not understand.

For example, I was asked to do an emergency consultation on a four-year-old boy who had been admitted to a pediatric ward with a broken arm. When awakening from surgery, he began to cry and could not be consoled by the increasingly anxious and frustrated nursing staff. When I asked him why he was crying, he sobbed in miniphrases, watered by alligator tears, that his arm was gone. He wanted it back. What he couldn't see wasn't there, creating a hole in his body image similar to that caused by a missing piece in a puzzle. After he and I wrapped, unwrapped, and reapplied a "cast" to the arm of his favorite GI Joe, our wounded warrior began to calm down, reassured that his arm was "safe" inside the cast, now decorated by us with images of Tony the Tiger, his favorite cartoon character.

Just as the wise adult enjoys the child's sexual immaturity, so does he or she feel compassion for the child's inability to understand the world. This empathy is heightened by the mature recognition that the child is not alone in the inability to understand; both adult and child are constantly in touch with the unknown and the incomprehensible, as the older imperfectly shield the younger from life's uncertainties.

A Different Sense of Time

To the one-year-old left by his or her parents for a much needed weekend of R&R, time stretches out endlessly. This is so because of the limited cognitive understanding of time which exists during infancy and early childhood and even more important, the manner in which it is experienced subjectively. Possessing little ability to tolerate frustration and delay gratification, the child experiences time in relationship to basic needs.

These are the factors which determine whether the intervals set for feeding, the absence of the mother, and the duration of nursery school attendance will seem to the child short or long, tolerable or intolerable, and as a result prove harmless or harmful in their consequences.

In addition, young children are not yet equipped with the sustaining capacity for *object constancy,* the ability to maintain memories and mental images of the needed and desired person in their absence. Without the internal organization of experience provided by the primary caretakers, the passage of time is often associated with pain and frustration. Like all other capacities, the ability to understand and organize temporal experience gradually increases as the child grows.

Differing needs and a lack of knowledge about time sense in childhood create painful dilemmas for adults. "My husband and I want to take a two week vacation. We plan to leave Sharon (18 months of age) with her grandparents. What do you think?" The determined tone in Sharon's mother's voice indicated that there was only one correct answer. Screwing up my courage, I explained why Sharon might have difficulty tolerating such a long absence. "Oh," said her mother with resignation, "you're telling me that at this point in her life, I have to put her needs before mine." Her response had the ring of maturity. Unspoken but understood was the recognition of the qualitative difference in cognitive development, time sense, and frustration tolerance between adult and child. "Lucky girl," I thought.

Regression as a Normal Phenomenon

Regression—the abandonment of recently acquired functions and abilities for patterns and behaviors from earlier phases—is a ubiquitous phenomenon in childhood. Normally, such behavior is temporary and self-limiting, related to some identifiable stress such as fatigue, illness, jealousy, parental absence, or facing a daunting new challenge such as riding the school bus for the first time or going out on a date with the most popular boy or girl in the class. When pathological processes dominate, however, regressions become pronounced, long lasting, and involves more mental functions and behaviors, sometimes resulting in an inability to bounce back to more age appropriate behavior. This is called *fixation.*

Backward moves accompany all developmental progression in childhood including control of bowels and bladder, the growth of frustration tolerance, language acquisition, and conscience formation. Indeed, the ability to achieve a higher level of functioning is no guarantee that such performance will be stable or continuous.

In fact, occasional returns to more infantile behavior is a normal sign. Thus, nonsense talk or even babbling have a rightful place in the child's life, alongside rational speech. Clean toilet habits are not acquired instantly, but take the long back-and-forth way through an interminable series of successes, relapses, and accidents.

Adults regress, too, although not as frequently as children. The middle finger-pointing temper tantrum on the freeway when cut off by another driver or the second martini after a tough day at work are somewhat problematic examples. Mature adults legitimize the need to regress and pepper their work time with vacations, play, and free intervals, thus creating a balance which promotes mental and physical health and infuses life with the qualities of richness and variety.

CASE REPORT: Mother, Is That You?[6]

Sometimes life throws a curve, even in childhood. The following detailed case report of a patient of mine describes how an adopted boy dealt with the sudden, totally unexpected, appearance of his biological mother. Her presence threatened him and complicated his life, but also provided an opportunity for present and future fulfillment.

Ron, a small, wiry 10-year-old, had been referred because of fighting in school, particularly with younger children. He lacked friends and was the subject of ridicule by his peer group. Bed wetting had been a continuous problem since toddlerhood. He expressed a vivid, violent fantasy life, had frequent nightmares, and was afraid of being alone day or night.

Ron's natural parents had been unmarried teenagers at the time of his birth. At four weeks of age he was adopted through an agency by a couple I shall call Ed and Jean Long. Ron was told of his adoption as soon as he was old enough to understand. Although he did not ask many questions, the subject came up frequently over the years.

Mrs. Long was the primary caretaker. Efforts at toilet training were inconsistent and casual, and as a result, Ron was never dry at night and was wet during the day until age seven. He was very close to his adoptive parents, particularly his mother.

During the diagnostic interviews, Ron seemed a somewhat subdued, sad youngster who related well and readily told me of bad dreams in which people tried to kill and eat him. He also spoke of his loneliness and lack of friends, a consuming interest in war games, and a deep love for his adoptive mother. When asked about his adoption, he expressed little interest; the subject was apparently unimportant to him.

Psychological testing revealed an IQ in the bright normal range and the presence of intense anger. Ron felt continually threatened by others, whom he saw as hostile and uncaring. His lack of self-esteem was pronounced, leading to a growing preoccupation with odd, hostile figures living on the fringes of society.

Treatment began just before Ron's tenth birthday.

Initial Course of the Treatment

During the first two years and three months of therapy, the work centered on Ron's nightmares and lack of friends. Gradually he revealed an intense interest in vampires, horror movies, and war games. These preoccupations and his dressing and behaving like a hostile guerrilla fighter made his absence of friends readily understandable. As these themes emerged in the playroom, I was often the victim of attacks by vampires, monsters, and Rambo-like characters.

The adoption was a frequent topic of conversation between us. Ron manifested many of the themes typically seen in adopted children. After an interval of seeming disinterest, he began to describe fantasies about his natural parents. They were young students who gave him away because they could not afford to raise him. More conflicted were thoughts that he had caused their abandonment. As Ron grew more attached to me, he became very curious about my family. "I'll bet you have seven kids," he said. "I think you're a good father." His wish to be my son was first revealed in dreams and later in less disguised ways in fantasy and play.

The Appearance of Ron's Biological Mother

Ron's therapy was radically changed soon after his biological mother walked into his adoptive father's office and asked to see her son. When he called me at home that evening, Mr. Long's understated question was simple and dramatic: "I'll bet you never ran into this one before. Ron's biological mother showed up in my office today. She wants to see him. What do I do?"

After thinking the matter through, I advised Ron's father to meet again with the boy's biological mother, whom I shall call Sue, to assess her motivation and reliability. He discovered that she lived in the area, was married, and had a family. After several years of trying, she had traced the Longs with the help of a searcher and an organization of women who had given their children for adoption and now wished to reestablish contact.

Sue had been under great stress when Ron was born because neither the baby's father nor her family were supportive. The last time Sue had seen her lover was just before the birth, when he drove her to the hospital and left, never to be heard from again. She deeply regretted the decision to give up her baby, and her intention now was to get to know Ron without disrupting the twelve-year relationship he had with his adoptive parents. Mr. Long felt she was sincere, bright, and reliable. He was prepared to take the next step. I suggested that both parents meet with me prior to telling Ron about his biological mother's appearance.

Because of their individual strengths and the rapport built during the two years of Ron's analysis, the Longs were able to face their fears that Sue would try to displace them and/or that Ron would prefer her to them. Recognizing that neither they nor I could completely determine the future course of events, they decided to permit a meeting between Ron and Sue because it would be in Ron's best interest. Both of them were reassured by the fact that the boy would be able to bring his thoughts and feelings into his therapy. With considerable trepidation, they told Ron what had happened. He met with me a day later.

January 25: "My mom and dad are more nervous than I am," he said. After finding out the night before, he had wet the bed. "I do want to meet my birth mother, I think. At worst I can find out more about myself. At best I can make a good friend." From the moment he found out about his natural mother's presence on the scene, Ron was concerned about his adoptive parents' feelings. "My mom is worried that my birth mother will want to take me away. She won't. Mom and Dad are the only family I have."

His mind raced from subject to subject: "I have a new brother, I mean half-brother, and a stepfather, and maybe new grandparents too. Wow!" Later his thoughts turned to his biological father. "Maybe I'll find out about him. Maybe I'll look like him." Then, motivated by guilt, he began to discuss his "real" (adoptive) father. "I walk like him. I even talk like him. I don't try to. I don't even want to, but I do." As he worked furiously to integrate the profound changes taking place in his real and intrapsychic worlds, Ron's ambivalence toward his fantasized, but now a bit more real, birth mother emerged. "She must have had a good reason to give me up . . . but she'll have to earn being a parent." He readily agreed with my suggestion that he take as much time as he needed to analyze his feelings about this big change in his life before he met her.

Three weeks were to pass before Ron decided that he was ready. A sequential summary of some of the work done during that period follows.

January 28: Ron was anxious about the first meeting. "If she doesn't like me, it's her fault, not mine." He was less willing to talk about his thoughts and feelings than he had been in the previous session when words and feelings had rushed out in a torrent. Ron wondered how tall she would be, fearing that both his biological parents were short. He was just experiencing the pubertal growth spurt and was keen on becoming as tall as his adoptive father.

Sue had told the Longs that her baby's father had dropped her off at the hospital and then left. Ron was incensed by that information but had avoided analyzing thoughts and feelings about his natural father. I interpreted the resistance. "Do you sense that you're having more trouble talking about your birth father than your birth mother?" "Yeah, I wonder where he is, the jerk. He dropped her off at the hospital and left." Then he built a house, filled it with toy soldiers, and blew it up.

"Could your birth father be one of the people inside that bombed house?"

"I'll find him some day and I'll give him hell for leaving my Mom."

"And you?" I added.

"Yeah, me too [sadly]. He probably didn't have any choice in giving me up. It's the woman's choice, you know."

January 31: "I haven't thought about my mother since last time . . . I wet the last two nights. I'll bet its related to [in baby talk] 'Mommy, Mommy.' "

"You don't talk in baby talk. I think that's a wish that your birth mother had been around to take care of you when you were a baby."

Later Ron expressed the fear that his "new" mother would steal him away. "I'd be scared she might try and make me part of her family. Then I'd lose my own. She might try and steal me illegally. She'd toss me in the car and drive away." Yet he wanted to talk to her alone so he could "get to know her as a friend." The prospect of the meeting was overwhelming. "For all I know I may faint when I see her."

February 2: The fantasy that Ron would be stolen took several sessions to work through. This day it was elaborated more fully.

"She says to me, 'Ron, how would you like to live with

me?' I say, 'No, I like my family the way it is!' Then she grabs me and pushes me into a box in the back of her car. I dive out while the car is going and do a couple of rolls to break the fall. She drives away thinking I'm in the car. Then I call my mom and she comes and gets me."

Later, Ron expressed concern about the impression he would make on Sue and was thankful for the analytic work we had done. "I'm glad she didn't meet me before when I was a self-centered asshole. She wouldn't have liked me then."

He continued to struggle with the painful issue of why she gave him up. "Mothers who can't afford their kid shouldn't feel bad because if they can't afford him he'd be better off. But they should keep in touch [with emphasis] and the kid should know why he was adopted. I'm not mad at her. She was pressured into it. I'm mad at her family for making her."

February 4: Ron's attempt to relate his emerging sexuality to his biological parents continued, as did the intense struggle with anger at his biological father. "Some day I'll make Sue a grandmother. Oh my God, my kid will have three grandparents."

"Why not four? What about your birth father?"

"He's dead."

"Not likely."

"If he's not dead, I'll kill him." The direct expression of the rage was too powerful and had to be displaced. "What do you call a person with leprosy in a hot tub?"

"I don't know. What?"

"Stew!" The sick jokes continued for some time.

"Why do you think your mind went to sick jokes just now?"

"I don't know."

"I think it's a way of continuing to express anger at your birth father. You still feel guilty when you do it directly."

February 10: Ron wanted to meet Sue as soon as possible. He'd decided when and how—in McDonald's restaurant after school. That way he'd be safe until his mom picked him up. His biggest worry was hurting his mom by telling her he was ready to meet Sue.

February 12: Jean Long had called Sue, and the two mothers agreed to meet to arrange details. "Yippee! I'm finally going to get to meet her, that is [soberly], if the two of them get along." He felt his mom was "real nervous" about this. "Up to now, she's been my only mother."

"I think your mom is worried about the same things you are, that Sue will take you away from her."

"Or try. She doesn't have to worry."

February 18: Ron tried to make light of his first meeting with Sue, but his thoughts and feelings soon rushed out. "When she came to the door, I thought, 'Oh my God, is this really happening?' She looked sorta like me. The same kind of face and hair." They drove to a nearby shopping center and ate. "I found out how and why I was adopted. She was still under the anesthesia when she signed the papers and didn't know what was going on. She thought she was signing papers to take me home. It was basically an illegal adoption. My brother, I mean my half brother's name is Sam. . . . I told her how little she would have liked me three years ago [before analysis]."

Ron asked Sue to meet again the following weekend, this time at her house. She agreed. She told Ron that his parents were wonderful to let them meet. She knew that a lot of adoptive parents refuse. "My parents are cool. They knew I wouldn't go nuts."

Ron reported, "She asked me how I feel about having two mothers. I said, 'Fine.' I'm really lucky to have such nice people for mothers."

February 22: In this session Ron dared to feel pleasure and joy over being loved by Sue, and he began to find a place for her intrapsychically as he replaced fantasy with reality. "She cares about me a lot! She loves me very much. She told me she's waited twelve years to tell me that. She tried for a long time to find me." His increased self-esteem was almost palpable. "It's amazing that we found each other. It's kind of like 'E.T., phone home.' My parents have been great. I knew they wanted to know what was going on, but they didn't make me say anything. I think I like my mothers in the order they came into my life. Jean first and Sue second."

February 26: A subtle but distinct difference was apparent after Ron's second meeting with Sue. He was full of details about her house and family, but more subdued. He seemed to need to distance himself, to allow time for integration. Although she hadn't said so, he felt his mother didn't want him to see Sue all the time. He felt she was still worried, unnecessarily. "I really like Sue, and I plan to keep seeing her, but I'm not going to jump up and say, 'Mom, let's go.' I'm sort of like a dog. I'm real loyal."

Later I asked if Ron had found out anything about his birth father. With mild annoyance, he said that he hadn't asked. "I don't want to know. I know I have to sometime and I will. There's nothing nice to say about a guy who leaves his kid at the hospital."

March 4: A pattern began to emerge for future meetings between Ron and Sue. Ron planned to see Sue, "when I want to. My mom and dad say it's okay as long as I plan ahead."

Intrapsychic integration continued. Ron joked, "I think I'll keep Sue around for a while. She ranks right up there, just behind my mom and my dad, in about the same place you are."

Ron and Sue met once or twice a month for the next several months and talked occasionally on the phone. In that time he met her extended family, commenting primarily on similarities in appearance.

Eventually Ron did ask Sue about his birth father. They had been students together, but she knew few details of his life and nothing about his whereabouts since the day Ron was born. Ron's anger continued unabated, but near the end of the analysis, long after his presenting symptoms had disappeared, he did express sadness about not knowing "this guy who made me. There's a hole inside me that only he can fill." We were able to analyze some of his fantasies about physical resemblance and sexual functioning.

Discussion

Adopted children must include two separate sets of parents in their world. Even under the best of circumstances, they may have difficulty differentiating between the "real" and the "false" parents, ascertaining which is which.

All children deal with the issue of real and imagined or false parents through what Freud called the family romance. In an attempt to compensate for real and fantasized disappointments, the biological child imagines having been adopted into an inferior family—the "real" parents are important, all-loving people who will find him or her some day. But the fantasy solution of the biological child's conflict—adoption—is a *fait accompli* for the adopted child. The adoptee's wish is to deny adoption, fantasize a blood tie to the adoptive parents, and thereby erase the rejection adoption implies. Further complications occur in adolescence when the adopted child attempts to organize his or her childhood past and experiences intense curiosity about his or her biological origins. Such is the enormity of the task facing the adopted child as he or she moves developmentally from phase to phase, working and reworking the idea of two sets of parents. (In the case of divorce, three or more sets of parental figures, real and imagined, may be involved.)

Before and during the first two years of his analysis, Ron went about the business of dealing with the idea of adoptive and fantasized biological parents much the way any adopted child would. He first expressed a lack of interest in his adopted state, but gradually began to speculate. What were his natural parents like? Why had they given him up? Did he cause it? Did he have any siblings? And so on.

The sudden appearance of Ron's natural mother shattered this ongoing work and precipitated a major psychic reorganization. Unlike the typical adopted child who experiences *curiosity* about early life as conflictual and dangerous, this boy had detailed factual information thrust upon him. For him, actual *knowledge,* not fantasy, was the threat.

At first Ron was unclear about his feelings about all three parent figures, but gradually achieved a new, more comfortable, and lasting integration as he came to the conclusion that his adoptive parents were his "real" parents. They had raised him, taken care of him, loved him. They were at the center of his life in the past and present. They would remain there in the future. This case material also demonstrates how an older adopted child can think abstractly enough to differentiate the functions of progenitor and parent, roles performed in his case by different people.

Although he already had a "mother," his progenitor's determined effort to find him, her intactness and interest, allowed him to develop a more pleasing picture of her, replacing the ambivalent one that preceded it and that still existed for his biological father. Still, she remained less important than his adoptive parents.

What made this integration possible? The analysis facilitated the process but undoubtedly did not determine the outcome. Ron's solid, lifelong relationship with his adoptive parents was clearly an important factor. So was the age at which his biological mother appeared and her desire to occupy a constant but secondary position in his life.

At age twelve Ron had developed considerable capacities for reason and judgment and thus was able to compare the impact of each parent on his development. For instance, he recognized that his adoptive parents were a proven commodity. They had demonstrated over twelve years that they loved him and could take care of him. Further, he reasoned (correctly) that they were well educated, financially secure, and in a better position than his biological mother to further his development.

But probably the most important factor was the changed awareness of the biological mother. She was no longer the forlorn, unmarried teenager forced by circumstances to give him up; that predominant, persisting fantasy had been based on the scrap of information he had been given that his natural parents were young and unmarried. That fantasized mother had been much like him: young, vulnerable, a victim of circumstances beyond her control—a figure to be cherished and protected as well as hated for rejecting him. This image could not be sustained in the presence of a real, not too pretty, middle-aged woman, who, although she had sought him out, had also, disloyally, found time to find a husband and have another child. In some way the fantasized mother was more gratifying than the real mother, for her image could be manipulated without fear of contradiction by reality. The luxury of such intrapsychic manipulation was rudely taken away from Ron by the presence of the woman who suddenly appeared in his life.

The power of such fantasized constructions remained obvious where Ron's biological father was concerned. The image of him as an unloving cad who abandoned both mother and infant (confirmed by the biological mother) was now intensified and unyielding. There was no actual contact to modify the fantasies. The fact that his biological mother had no knowledge of his father's whereabouts further fueled Ron's increasingly hostile feelings. In addition, the boy resisted learning more about his progenitor because of a strong sense of loyalty to his adoptive father.

Ron tackled the challenge of his biological mother's sudden appearance with great courage and determination. I felt privileged to have been there to help him and pleased that his experience is available to demonstrate that obstacles and unexpected shifts in life may be blessings in disguise, opening up new pathways to fulfillment in childhood and adulthood.

3

Early Childhood

Laying a Firm Foundation

The mansion of maturity rests upon the solid foundation of childhood. During the first decade of life, concrete, brick, and lumber are collected and assembled. Then, under the loving, discerning eye of the architect-parents, the building of a structure begins. When the building is complete, the work of these early phases—studding, wiring, and plumbing—is hidden, silently supporting the magnificent house of glittering lights, elegant wallpaper, and draped windows.

The insightful adult becomes his or her own tradesman and architect, possessing detailed knowledge of his or her dwelling, understanding the connections between past and present, visualizing the unseen studs behind the wallpaper and able to trace life from phase to phase throughout childhood and adolescence into the present. The result is a sense of authenticity and joy, an unshakable conviction about the integrity of individual experience.

Stage 1: The Oral Phase (Ages 0–1)

Early infancy is a time of psychological mastery, shadowy bits and hidden images in the nonverbal mist. Because infants cannot speak, we can only guess about when they begin to think or what they know. The subject has been the cause of great controversy for decades, and still is. However, most experts agree that the ability to understand words begins to develop during the second half of the first year of life and the ability to speak begins at about a year of age. Both are reflections of the appearance of that miraculous quintessential human capacity, the ability to think. Then, like a rocket lifting off from Cape Canaveral, the course of human thought and speech is straight up, reaching ever-increasing heavenly heights of nuance, sophistication, and complexity throughout the remainder of life. Descartes said "I think, therefore I am." I would add, "I think, therefore I can explore the deepest recesses of my inner being and the world of which I am a part."

In infancy and early childhood, the external evidence of the emergence of this grandest of human capacities—thinking—is the occurrence of single words at approximately one year of age and short sentences by age two.

The Emergence of the Self: When Do I Know I Am Me?

But when does the human infant become aware of who he or she is, develop a sense of self, or perceive where he or she ends and others begin? The answers are contained in the large and rapidly expanding body of "object relations" theory. Like most other development concepts about infancy, the theory postulates a gradually increasing ability to differentiate self from others, particularly from the primary caretakers, culminating in a well-established sense of self by age three.

The intrapsychic process is illustrated most clearly in the work of two psychiatric theoreticians of infancy, Rene Spitz and Margaret Mahler, whose theories are outlined below.

SPITZ	MAHLER
Psychic Organizers	*Separation–Individuation Theory*
Smile response (0–3 months)	Pseudoautistic subphase (0–3 months)
Stranger anxiety (8 months)	Symbiotic subphase (3–12 months)
Negativism (18 months)	Separation–individuation substage (12–36 months)
	Object constancy (by 3 years)

Spitz's Psychic Organizers

Let us begin with a consideration of Spitz's theory because his work preceded and influenced Mahler's. Spitz used the term *psychic organizer* to explain the importance of the smile response, stranger anxiety, and negativism. He borrowed the term from embryology, where it is used to describe a set of agents and regulating elements which direct subsequent change. Before the emergence of the organizer, transplanted cells assume the structure and function of the organ into which they are placed. After the emergence of the organizer, they retain the structure and function of the tissue from which they came and can no longer be changed. In an analogous way, the three psychic organizers are indicators that a new, irreversible level of psychic organization and complexity has been reached which pushes mental development forward(1).

The Smile Response. Normal infants smile by four to eight weeks of age, lighting up their parents' eyes and producing a similar response of even greater magnitude. But what does it mean? Is it a response to a gas pain, as some relatives are sure to suggest, or a thank you for changing that dirty diaper? In his research, Spitz discovered that the infant is responding, as other human infants have for millions of years, to a gestalt—not to a person but to an outline of the forehead, eyes, and nose seen straight on and in motion. Since cardboard "faces" would elicit a smile, Spitz concluded that the infant was not yet capable of responding exclusively to another human being. But the first smile did indicate that profoundly important mental processes were beginning to appear—differentiation of the inner world from the outer world, reality from fantasy, past from present, and self from other. The absence of a smile response by three months of age usually indicates a major abnormality in the central nervous system.

Stranger Anxiety. Nearly everyone is familiar with what is known as eight-month or stranger anxiety. Dear Aunt Martha travels across three states for her first visit with eight-month-old Johnny, the firstborn of her very favorite niece. Rushing into the house, she sweeps him up in her arms, smothering him with kisses only to be rudely disappointed when he pulls away and begins to bawl. Turning to her embarrassed niece, she whimpers pathetically, "Oh, he doesn't like me!"

Not necessarily, Aunt Martha; he doesn't *know* you. Johnny is displaying a newly emergent capacity that indicates a quantum leap forward in his development, namely, the ability to distinguish one human being from another, to separate the familiar from the unfamiliar. In a few short months he has progressed from indiscriminate smiling in response to any face to the ability to relate to specific individuals. He is becoming a social being, human in the truest sense of that word.

Negativism. To parents and grandparents who love to hold and cuddle infants, the second year of life is a bittersweet time. Gone is the passive creature who molded to your chest and arms, content to be hugged for hours on end, replaced by an ever-exploding bundle of energy who wants to be *free* to crawl, walk, run, and explore. And as Susie plows into life, her increasingly weary and frustrated parents frantically try to follow. Like Sherman marching through Georgia, she is capable of destroying everything in her path. But unlike Sherman, Susie is in great danger herself since she has no judgment, understanding of cause and effect, or sense of danger.

These newly emergent abilities to walk, climb, and explore dramatically change the bucolic relationship between parent and infant that existed during the first six months of life to one of contention and confrontation. Increasingly, parents are forced to curb the toddler's initiative out of concerns for safety. Increasingly, they must say "No," shaking their heads from side to side.

In the healthy toddler these prohibitions cause great frustration, which is not readily tolerated. Caught in monumental conflict between the need for physical and emotional closeness and the undeniable drive for autonomy and independence, Susie solves the dilemma by developing a new defense mechanism, *identification with the aggressor.* By using the disciplinarian's word and gesture, she remains identified with her caregivers, feels stronger, and is still free to attack the world. Once this mechanism is established, the stubbornness of the second year begins in earnest and Spitz's third organizer is in place. Putting words into Susie's mouth which she does not yet possess, her "No" eloquently says, "Watch out world, here *I* come, ready or not. *I'm* going to have it all and don't try to stop me. *I have arrived.*"

Some parents are insulted and enraged by the toddler's negativism and respond with hostility and insults, squashing initiative and self-esteem. Mature parents accept, even enjoy, their toddler's challenge, recognizing within it the healthy roots of self-confidence, curiosity, and autonomy. They protect the toddler from their frustration and his or her transparent vulnerability by not responding with anger and by guarding his or her physical safety.

Erikson described the toddler's dilemma at this point in the life cycle as *autonomy versus shame and doubt.*(2) Physical maturation pushes the toddler to experiment with two sets of action and reaction, holding on and letting go. Because he or she has little ability to discriminate or control these new expressions of assertion and aggression, the environment must provide a supportive, benevolent firmness. If this support is lacking, Erikson suggests that the results are dire, "for if denied the gradual and well-guided experience of the autonomy of free choice (or, if indeed weakened by an initial loss of trust), the child will turn against himself all his urges to discriminate and to manipulate. He will overmanipulate himself, he will develop a precocious conscience."(3) The result will be the emergence of shame and doubt, emotions which smother the child's drive for autonomy. Once in place, these attitudes squelch the developmental course by interfering with the comfortable engagement of the developmental tasks of each subsequent stage, right into adulthood. The paths to fulfillment are many—but so are the detours. Forks in the road leading in very different directions are encountered early in life, before one is able to navigate. A benign, loving, backseat driver is indispensable at such junctures.

Mahler's Separation–Individuation Theory

Based on Spitz's ideas, Margaret Mahler asked the question, how are human beings born *psychologically*?(4) How do they come to understand the concepts I and You, Self, and Other. Her research suggested that these capacities develop gradually during the first three years of life, springing from the rich, nurturing soil of the mother–child dyad. As we see in the table on page 37, she divided her theory into three substages; the pseudoautistic (0–3 months), symbiotic (3–12 months), and separation–individuation (1–3 years). The third substage, confusingly, is given the same name as the complete theory.

The Autistic and Symbiotic Substages. During the earliest months of life, the infant appears to be autistic, out of touch with reality. Although the infant is actually quite responsive to the world in a reflexive way, Mahler used the term autistic to describe the relatively undeveloped state of higher mental functions at the time of birth and shortly after. Exquisitely tuned to respond to her infant's needs by the genetic wisdom passed on to her by millions of predecessors, mother provides what her child needs—nourishment, stimulation, and protection. She becomes, in Mahler's words, the *external executive ego,* the child's interpreter of the world.

As the early months of life melt into one another, through thousands of repetitions of prompt relief of frustration, gratification, and stimulation, the infant gradually becomes aware of a "need-satisfying object." But unable yet to differentiate self from others, he or she behaves as though infant and mother (or mothering person) were an "omnipotent system," a dual entity, cozily coexisting within a common boundary or membrane; hence the term symbiotic.

Picking up each other's signals, mother and infant amplify each other's needs. Securely wrapped in the symbiotic blanket, the infant comes to feel that living is a safe and gratifying experience, feeling what Erikson called "basic trust." But when the time is right, fully nourished and prepared for metamorphosis, the infant, just like the caterpillar, emerges from the cocoon, sheds the protective skin of the symbiotic partner, and radiates the perpetuating glow of selfhood. In Mahler's terms, he or she has begun to separate and individuate.

The relationship between infant and parent is by no means one-sided. As they minister to their creation, both parents are lifted to a new level of fulfillment and awareness. They share a depth of intimacy with each other and their child hitherto unknown. And as their child moves from developmental phase to developmental phase they are stimulated to rework, to master, infantile and childhood experience. Parenthood is a royal path to maturity, providing travelers with a panoramic view of the beginnings of life and a retrospective view of their own.

The Separation–Individuation Subphase. Locomotion has a great catalyzing influence on human development. As he or she first crawls, then walks and finally runs away from mother, the toddler snaps the symbiotic cord between them and begins to experience the joy—and terror—of separation and individuation. Indeed, psychological separation from the symbiotic partner is as inevitable as biological birth, both processes having been programmed into each individual by genetic imperatives. The fact that speech and language develop simultaneously is not by chance. Increasingly separated from the source of all comfort, the toddler develops the powerful communicative instrument, language, to leap across the ever-widening void to mother.

When parental acceptance of the toddler's determination to leave the nest is present, the toddler is at the "peak of elation," free to explore the world, encounter the twin imposters of victory and defeat, and return to the unambivalent acceptance of the parental embrace. Consistent parental presence ensures that the toddler will use this emotional recoupling only as a brief pit stop. Once the gas tanks are filled and the battery charged, he or she roars away again eager to reengage with fascination and awe the ever-expanding universe.

Object Constancy: Captured Forever. By approximately age three, the separation–individuation process culminates in the emergence of a capacity which is at the core of all human interaction for the remainder of life. Called *object constancy* by Mahler, the term refers to the ability to maintain mental images and memories of others for extended periods of time in their absence. So equipped, the young child is capable of providing himself or herself with emotional sustenance and relatedness. Those who provide definition and meaning to life are captured intrapsychically where they can be loved, hated, and manipulated through fantasy. Frequent references to them and their activities at home were clear indications to the preschool staff that three-year-old Roberta has brought her mother, father, and brother with her. Their intrapsychic presence sustained her during school hours and colored her interaction with others.

In the preschool years the ability to maintain this newly emergent capacity is tenuous, jeopardized by prolonged separation which can produce anxiety and regression. As childhood and adolescence progress, this danger diminishes because the function becomes fully autonomous, no longer dependent upon external sources of support. In adults the ability to maintain images of figures from the past is almost unlimited. For example, think about your last class reunion or chance encounter with a childhood friend whom you had not seen for years. Remember that uncomfortable, jarring sense of dissonance that occurred when you compared the real person in front of you with the mental picture from the past, frozen in time at the age of your last encounter? That is object constancy. So is the continuous alteration and updating of the mental picture which takes place with those individuals whom we see frequently. It is the bedrock on which all adult relationships exist. Those who possess object constancy are bonded together forever with those they know and love. Seriously disturbed individuals who never obtained object constancy or lost the capacity live in a barren, internal hell; their mental representations of others resemble torn photographs or puzzles with the most important pieces missing.

Self constancy is the complement to object constancy. By the middle of the second year of life, toddlers begin to think of themselves as semiseparate beings, often referred to in the third person. By about age two, the word "I" begins to creep into the vocabulary, reflecting a growing sense of individuation. As the toddler is transformed into a young child, the sense of self becomes firmly entrenched and unshakable. Self constancy has been established. Then as individuals proceed along the developmental path, experiencing what life has to offer, their sense of self is elaborated and embellished, reflecting both who they were and who they are becoming.

Now the stage is set, the characters identified, the drama of human interaction about to begin. In an oversimplified way, maturity may be defined as the detailed awareness of self and other gained on the journey from childhood and adolescence to midlife.

Feeding and Weaning: The Role of Frustration and Gratification

Feeding. Dining—that is, pampered care and excellent food in a delightful setting—is the adult equivalent of a gratifying, infantile feeding experience. Feeding is one of the most important early interactions which stimulates and organizes development. Spitz called the mouth "the cradle of perception," and both he and Mahler suggested that the beginning differentiation of self from other as well as the basic attitude toward life—sweet and optimistic or sour and pessimistic—originates in early feeding experiences. The sucking reflex is highly organized at birth, allowing the infant to take nourishment and begin to organize experience, to symbolically drink in the outside world. For instance, visual perception begins during nursing as the infant repeatedly gazes at the mother's face. When mother promptly relieves disorganizing hunger pangs and responds emotionally with tenderness and love, feeding becomes the basis of relatedness and the world is experienced as a congenial place, warm, fuzzy, gratifying—the first experience with fulfillment. Mature adults maintain this basic sense of optimism and gratification which they first experienced at mother's breast, broadening the base of such experience far beyond, but never exclusive of, that wonderful adult equivalent, dining.

In today's complex society other family members or caretakers may perform the maternal function of feeding. The important thing is that they stand in for mother with similar feelings of love and affection, providing the infant with the same kind of physical and emotional nourishment which she would provide, as is illustrated by the following example. Laying at her mother's breast, half asleep, half awake, perfectly secure in her state of satiated bliss, baby

Angela is learning that the world is a safe, gratifying place. She is beginning to experience Erikson's basic trust, the foundation on which her future experience of fulfillment will be built.

Satisfaction of hunger is the first experience of instinctual gratification in a child's life. Because the demands of a hungry belly are so urgent and cannot be controlled by the limited mental structures which exist in early infancy, mother limits the degree of pain and frustration which her baby experiences by *feeding on demand.* But no matter how responsive mother may be, baby Angela will inevitably experience nagging pangs of hunger and direct rushes of rage at her imperfect provider who does not always respond instantly on cue. Consequently, it is not the presence or absence of frustration which determines the long-term effect on development; rather, it is the *pattern* of parental response leading to either rapid satisfaction or repeated delays.

Breast-feeding is nature's way of promoting normal growth and development, providing instant milk shakes of just the right temperature and texture and ensuring mother's emotional involvement, magnetically drawn to her offspring by the pleasurable relief of emptying breasts and the hypnotic power of those dramatic eyes, which demand a response.

All of these built-in growth promoting aspects of breast-feeding can be matched by bottle feeding if loving parents understand the critical emotional components involved. But the possibilities for benign neglect are multiplied since TV programs, microwaves, and other demanding humans may drain away the intensity of the parent–infant interaction, resulting in propped bottles and vacant stares.

A well-nourished—physically and emotionally—baby is a happy baby, learning to churn the milk of human kindness into an enduring sense of self-love and self-esteem.

Weaning. Toward the end of the first year of life, mother, assisted by Mother Nature, will gently nudge baby Angela to give up her tenacious attachment to the breast or bottle. The urging may not be so gentle since Angela's soft gums are now populated with razor sharp teeth. The combination of biting and the return of the menstrual cycle explodes the nursing dyad and pushes both mother and child in new developmental directions. The rapturous closeness of infancy is gone, never to return, a victim of the infant's overwhelming urge to break the symbiotic bond and explore the ever-expanding world—and mother's desire to get on with her own life, as well.

Weaning stimulates developmental progression because it pushes the toddler toward the next set of developmental challenges. Diminished dependency on mother facilitates the separation–individuation process and increases the ability of the child to tolerate frustration and control impulses, all important first steps on the long road to maturity.

Some parents, often because of unconscious conflicts with their own aggression, finesse weaning. "He'll give up the bottle when he's ready," they say. "What's the rush?" As a child psychiatrist, looking through that famous retroscope, used when evaluating an immature five-year-old who is having difficulty adjusting to nursery school or kindergarten, the answer to "What's the rush?" is: failure to wean Johnny is usually the beginning of a pattern of difficulty in actively presenting the child with appropriate developmental challenges. Johnny is not doing well in kindergarten because he wasn't actively weaned, or toilet trained, or limited during his "terrible two's." He tends to be whiny, regressed, demanding, unable to comfortably leave mother, and prone to temper tantrums. He has not been able to develop the *internal* control of his feelings and actions which are demanded by the harsh, cruel world outside of the overindulgent cocoon of the nuclear family. Now he must play catch-up, shoring up the weak timbers which are the foundation on which his future development rests.

The Transitional Object: Linus's Blanket

Why do infants and toddlers become attached to blankets and teddy bears? The British psychoanalyst, D. O. Winnicott suggested that these soft fuzzies begin to have a special significance during the second half of the first year of life because they come to represent aspects of the relationship to the mother.(5) By choosing to use a transitional object, as Winnicott called them, the toddler feels connected to mother during periods of separation. Transitional phenomena—sounds, words, and songs—may be used for the same purpose.

Probably the most famous transitional object in the world is Linus's blanket from the comic strip *Peanuts.* His fanatical attachment to his blanket illustrates a common problem faced by parents and clinicians. As one parent put it, "How do I get her to give up that damn thing? It's ugly and it smells, but she thinks it's the cat's meow!"

Linus's blanket may be the most famous one in the world, but certainly not the only one. A patient of mine named Shelley had difficulty relinquishing her poor tattered blanket. When she was four years and seven months old, much too old for a blanket, her mother sent me a frantic S.O.S. What should she do? The blanket was gone and Shelley was hysterical. As I asked questions, the following story emerged. As time passed, out of self-defense, Shelley's mother had taken to washing the blanket. On such occasions, Shelley would stand longingly under her precious possession as it hung on the clothesline to dry, tantalizingly out of reach. The immediate crisis was precipitated by the fact that the blanket, reduced by years of constant use to a tattered rag, had disintegrated in the washing machine. It had gone in and not come out. It had ceased to exist!

Shelley survived the loss of her blanket and went on to become a lawyer. But her parents could have saved her, and themselves, much distress if they had helped her give up the blanket when it was no longer helpful developmentally. Just as sucking on the breast or bottle does not further the developmental process as the second year progresses, neither does tenacious attachment to a transitional object after object constancy. By actively weaning the child from the transitional object sometime after age three, parents provide the child with a gentle developmental push. With the initiation of benevolent parental expectation, the battle is joined. Gradually, child and teddy bear retreat before superior parental forces, restricting the bear army first to the bedroom and then to a drawer or closet shelf. There the bruin resides, permanently, ready to be rediscovered many years later as a remnant of a distant past, the conflict surrounding its surrender forgotten.

In adulthood we continue a clandestine relationship with objects that signify a special degree of closeness and warmth. A favorite sweater or scarf, silk sheets and flannel pajamas, even an irreplaceable jogging suit or a sweat-stained tennis cap—all may be the key to reopening a pathway to a soothing, nurtured past. More ethereal stimuli such as music may also invoke the same feelings. A man of forty was puzzled by his deep love for a particular Chopin etude. When I asked when he first heard it he immediately told me, eyes shining, about the first concert he ever attended with his mother, at age eight. The red velvet seat cushion was warm and fuzzy against his bare, short-panted legs. As mother smiled, the music, particularly that etude, had transported him.

Sexual Development in Infancy: The Core Gender Identity

Although the proud father doesn't know it when he brings a ballerina doll or a football to the hospital for his particularly precious newborn, he is contributing to the infant's *core gender identity*—the basic, primitive sense of maleness or femaleness that is the foundation on which later sexual attitudes and understanding are built. According to psychiatric researcher Robert Stoller, this complex phenomenon results from a confluence of biological, environmental, and psychological factors and attitudes.(6) In utero, an admixture of female and male hormones bathe the brain and determine the appearance of the external sex organs. At the moment of birth, all eyes are riveted on the genital area, ready to exclaim "It's a boy" or "It's a girl." Instantly, powerful conscious and unconscious forces are set in motion in the primary caretakers which cause them to continually bombard the infant with the message "you are a girl" or "you are a boy." Under normal circumstances, this process continues into the second year of life, resulting by eighteen months in a deeply engraved, unalterable sense of maleness or femaleness. The first step into adult sexuality has been taken.

The Developmental Residue of Infancy in Later Life

The internalized residue from the engagement of the developmental tasks of infancy continues to exert an influence throughout childhood and into the adult years. Many of the basic developmental issues which originated during infancy, such as the direct relationship between mother and food, and weaning, spill over into the years between one and three. Propelled by locomotion, language, and the drive for autonomy and independence, the docile infant disappears, suddenly replaced by that would-be master of the universe, the toddler. Feeding an infant can be dignified and restrained, like a Japanese tea ceremony. By contrast, watching a toddler feed him- or herself is akin to being caught in the crossfire of a food fight in a junior high school cafeteria. Food is accepted or refused with the exclamation "Me do it!," a clamped jaw, turned head, and inevitable messiness. Strong food preferences appear overnight, associated with texture, temperature, and taste. Parents who understand will take heart and endure, recognizing that dirty floors, messy faces, and sticky fingers are the price to be paid for joyous eating. Today's gourmand is tomorrow's gourmet.

Later, the young child builds his theory of sexuality with oral timbers, the resulting architecture strange and faulty by adult standards. Mommies get pregnant by swallowing seeds. Babies grow in the "tummy" and come out through the belly button or anus. Adults who attempt to counter these misconceptions with the truth run into the stone wall of intellectual and physical immaturity; the young child lives in a world of misconceptions and half-truths. Only as mind and body mature do the secrets of adult love and intimacy become clear.

The American Advertising Council understands latency (ages 6–11). Companies sell millions of boxes of cereal, candy, underwear, and toys to unsuspecting children who will eat, wear, or play with anything that is hawked by their cultural icons who represent the newly emergent quest for athletic superiority and masculine or feminine identity.

In adolescence food fads, inconsistent attitudes toward eating and the rejection of favorite family recipes and togetherness at mealtime are all reflections of the tumultuous intrapsychic reshuffling which accompanies physical maturity and the breaking of infantile attachments to the parents.

Adults eat for nourishment and pleasure. A balanced diet maintains body integrity. Sharing food with friends and loved ones continues to be an intimate experience, resonating with the biopsychological rapport that existed between mother and child in the dawn of life. The mature adult effortlessly meshes past attitudes and current realities about food, transforming eating into a nonconflictual, highly pleasurable oasis.

The importance of a healthy, solid beginning in life is not lost on the mental health professional who knows from experience that the sickest patients usually have had very chaotic and troubled childhoods. Conversely, healthy individuals were usually blessed with physical health and strong environmental support during their early years. The seeds of maturity are planted in the rich, nourishing soil of a healthy infancy. In early childhood, they begin to bud.

Stage 2: The Anal Phase (Ages 1–3)

Internalizing Expectations: The Terrible Twos

The "terrible twos" aren't really so bad when you understand their developmental purpose. Using the newfound ability to locomote, the toddler ramrods into life. Unfortunately, the equipment is a little out of balance. As Anna Freud put it, the manifestations are expressed directly through destructiveness, messiness, and motor restlessness; and reactively through clinging, inability to separate, whining, and chaotic affective states (including temper tantrums).(7) For all of its severity and pathological appearance, such behavior is short-lived. It remains in force while there are no other than motor outlets for the child's energies and disappears or decreases in intensity as soon as new pathways for expression appear, especially the acquisition of speech.

Thus, for a brief interval there is a natural imbalance between the powerful, maturing body, exploding with new potential, and the limited ability of the mind to contain and channel newly emergent feelings and functions. Once that untamed energy is harnessed by the appearance of language, which replaces action with words, the imbalance is redressed. This will not be the last time we will encounter such unevenness. Ahead lies adolescence. Then the body of the child vanishes overnight, trapping the innocent mind of the child in the awkward, hairy Frankenstein body of adolescence. This imbalance takes longer to redress; the mind doesn't catch up for several years.

From Wetting and Soiling to Bowel and Bladder Control: A Giant Step toward Maturity

The immediate goal of the toilet-training process is the consistent deposit of urine and feces in the toilet. However, the long-term effect is to put in place flexible, adaptive mental attitudes about the body and its products which last a lifetime. Spanning the first four developmental phases, the developmental line from wetting to soiling to bowel and bladder control results in nothing less than personality growth and transformation.

The complete freedom to wet and soil lasts until the parents decide it's time to do otherwise. Usually around age two, the child is ready physically and psychologically for the next step, the toilet-training process itself. Often tested by stubborn resistance and refusal, parents attempt to contain their frustration and mediate sympathetically between the environmental demands for cleanliness and the child's desire to wet or soil without restraint. When parents are clear, consistent, and kind about their expectations—sometimes after weeks or months of wet beds, soiled pants, and crossed legs—as soon as parent and child are out of range of a toilet, a significant change begins to occur.

Gradually the child accepts and takes over the environment's attitudes toward cleanliness and through identification makes them an integral part of the personality. What was outside now is inside. Pleasure in or indifference to being dirty is replaced by a desire to be clean. The child's mind is stronger, more capable of complying with the standards of cleanliness and behavior demanded as the price for entering society.

But the story doesn't end here. That occurs sometime during the elementary school years when bowel and bladder control lapses no longer occur, even in times of stress, and the use of the toilet is completely disconnected from parental knowledge, dictates, or support. In the physically and psychologically healthy individual, this state continues into adulthood, becoming one facet of the comfortable competence in regard to the control of body and mind which characterizes maturity.

Character: The Core of Strength Emanating from the Toddler Years

As a result of love and limits, particularly in regard to control of the body and its products, character emerges. The tough, responsible integrity that is found in abundance in every mature adult originates here. As Anna Freud put it: "Disgust, orderliness, tidiness, dislike of dirty hands guard against the return of the repressed; punctuality, conscientiousness, and reliability appear as by-products of anal regularity; inclinations to save, to collect, give evidence of high anal evaluation displaced to other matters. In short, what takes place during this period is the far-reaching modification and transformation of the [personality] which—if kept within normal limits—supply the individual personality with a backbone of highly desirable, valuable qualities."(8)

So armed, with strength and determination our young Samsons and Amazons are prepared to enter the next phase of development where they set their sights on bigger game. Their view of the larger world is limited by their mental and physical immaturity, and like Saddam, they expect to take by force what cannot be theirs.

Stage 3: The Oedipal Phase (Ages 3–6)

Understanding Sex and Competition

Three-year-old Mike was happy and bouncy prior to bedtime, wrestling playfully with his dad. As he lay in bed while his contented father read him a story, he seemed peaceful and serene. Suddenly, his countenance changed to one of anger. "Why do you get to sleep with Mommy and I sleep alone?" he thundered, as much as a three-year-old can thunder. Whereupon he leaped out of bed, ran into his mother's bedroom, and buried himself under the covers—on his father's side. When somewhat startled Dad caught up with him, Mike had taken possession of the bed and looked like the cat who had swallowed the canary.

Five-year-old Mary Ann, her face and hands sticky from the ice cream cone dripping like a leaky faucet because of the heat of a late summer evening, had just returned from a lovely outing with her very tolerant mother. The two had laughed and played together at the park and had walked home in leisurely intimacy. Suddenly, Mary Ann bounded ahead of her mother, jumping up the steps which lead to the front door, and whirled around, towering above her progenitor by a foot or two. "I could kill you if I wanted to," she scowled. Then as if frightened by the intensity of her words and feelings, she smiled and added gently, "but I don't want to." Before her startled mother could respond, Mary Ann raced through the front door and was gone, undoubtedly to her adoring daddy.

Freud based his theory of development during this phase on the myth of Oedipus. In Sophocles' tragedy, Oedipus unknowingly kills his father and marries his mother. What we observe in young children between the ages of three and six is a persistent competition with the parent of the same sex for the attention and affection of the parent of the opposite sex. That is the essence of the Oedipal Complex, nothing more, nothing less. However, Mike's and Mary Ann's rather puzzling behavior must be understood from the vantage point of the physical and mental development of the three-year-old, not the adult.

Children at this age are just beginning to think about relationships, particularly their own, with the two most significant figures in their lives, mother and father. This newly emergent capacity springs from the attainment of object constancy, the ability to create and hang onto mental images of others in their absence. Now parents can be engaged on a continuous basis through *fantasy,* the outcome of any interaction manipulated as the child chooses. This quantum leap forward in the child's ability to relate to others and the world is the sturdy foundation on which the Oedipal Complex rests.

Erikson described the newly emergent vistas and potentialities of the three-year-old in terms of a struggle between initiative and guilt.

> While autonomy concentrates on keeping potential rivals out, and therefore, can lead to jealous rage most often directed against encroachments by younger siblings, initiative brings with it anticipatory rivalry with those who have been there first and may, therefore, occupy with their superior equipment, the field toward which one's initiative is directed. Infantile jealousy and rivalry, those often embittered and yet essentially futile attempts at demarcating a sphere of unquestioned privilege, now come to a climax in a final contest for a favored position with the mother; the usual failure leads to resignation, quiet, and anxiety. The child indulges in fantasies of being a giant and a tiger, but in his dreams he runs in terror for real life.(9)

Some of the child's fantasies and preoccupations are sexual, but not in the adult sense. In order to understand children and the sexual child within ourselves, we must face the frequently maligned, sometimes dreaded bugaboo of *infantile sexuality.* By doing so, we take the third step on the path to mature sexuality, building upon the establishment of core gender identity in the first year of life and the recognition of genital difference in the second and third. Most adult explorers of infantile sexuality travel blind, their path shrouded in the mist of the near universal repression of memories from the first five or six years of life. Freud postulated that this amnesia was a necessary mental maneuver, needed to squash the continued conscious preoccupation with oedipal wishes which would drag the ship of development into incestuous waters. Many adults never become aware of their infantile sexual pasts but the mature adult does, first with some apprehension, then with humor and acceptance of this fascinating aspect of the human condition. The combination of a childhood sexual past, unblemished by seduction or punitiveness, and the experience of being on the receiving end of infantile love as a parent can add a new measure of richness to adult sexuality, rekindling long lost or muted feelings of passion, naiveté, and seduction.

Infantile Sexuality: The Case of "Little Hans"

Infantile sexuality refers to the nature of the sexual thought and action in childhood *as experienced and understood by the child.* This was first recognized and described by Freud, a remarkable feat of genius considering the prudish atmosphere which prevailed in Victorian Vienna and the failure of anyone before him to describe ubiquitous behavior which is strikingly obvious and universal.(10) Freud became familiar with "Little Hans" when his father, a student of Freud's, sought help for the boy's fear of horses, a most debilitating phobia in the horse and buggy Vienna of 1909. As Hans's father brought material from the boy to "the professor," Freud made suggestions which the father carried out. In his "Analysis of a Phobia in a Five-Year-Old Boy," the first psychotherapeutic treatment of a child, Freud gave many examples of the nature of the infantile sexual mind, examples which have been confirmed innumerable times by parents and professional observers of children in the last 85 years. Although the case material is about a boy, little girls are every bit as curious and intense about their quest for sexual knowledge and gratification.

Curiosity about the Nature of the Genitals. Not quite three, Hans was "showing a quite peculiarly lively interest in that portion of his body which he used to describe as his 'widdler' " (p. 7). Hans was becoming enamored with the highly pleasurable sensations which he could produce in his penis and nowhere else in his body. This supercharged interest in his phallus caused him to wonder about the presence or absence of widdlers in the world around him.

HANS: Mummy, have you got a widdler too?
MOTHER: Of course. Why?
HANS: I was only just thinking.(11)

As we shall see, mother was not always the most honest or empathetic observer of infantile sexuality, reflecting a bias which exists to some degree in all of us.

Hans' interest in widdlers extended far beyond his mother and himself, quite indiscriminately by adult standards. After seeing a cow being milked, he exclaimed, "Oh look! There's milk coming out of its widdler!" Locked into the world of concrete thinking characteristic of early childhood, he concluded that anything that hangs down and squirts must be a widdler. Several months later, Hans saw some water being let out of an engine. "The engine's widdling," he said. "Where's it got its widdler?" Trying to sort it all out, he added reflectively, "A dog and a horse have widdlers, a table and a chair haven't."

The Inseparable Connection between the Thirst for Knowledge and Sexual Curiosity about the Parents. As Hans moved through the Oedipal years, he continued his voyeuristic assault on his parents' privacy.

HANS: Daddy, have you got a widdler too?
FATHER: Yes, of course.
HANS: But I've never seen it when you were undressing. (Hans watched his mother like a hawk, particularly at bedtime.)
MOTHER: What are you staring like that for?
HANS: I was only looking to see if you've got a widdler

too. (Obviously he did not believe her previous positive declaration.)

MOTHER: Of course, don't you know that?

HANS: No, I thought you were so big you'd have a widdler like a horse.(12)

In his expectation of bigness, Hans displays another aspect of infantile sexuality, a preoccupation with size.

Hans, like all Oedipal-aged children, is stunned by the realization that he is small and disadvantaged in a world controlled by large adults. This painful realization is so powerful, so agonizing, that some men and women never abandon the idea that when it comes to penises, size, and not function, is all important. Mature adults gradually abandon this notion in the course of post-Oedipal development and eventually come to the realization that fulfilling sensuality is based on successful function and appreciation of the interlocking, complementary roles of the male and female genitals.

Infantile Masturbation. Freud was not afraid to address with scientific detachment this most controversial, albeit undeniable, aspect of infantile sexuality. When Hans was three and a half years old, Freud commented, "Meanwhile, his interest in his widdler is by no means a purely theoretical one; as might be expected, it also impelled him to touch his member." By the time Hans was four years old, he was an old hand at self-stimulation. As those of us who treat children and adults know, the physical act is accompanied by elaborate fantasies which reveal much about the sexual life of the person involved.

Hans was no exception. In his fantasies, and in action as well, he took aim on his chosen sexual target, using techniques not so different from those employed by adolescents and adults.

> This morning Hans was given his usual daily bath by his mother and afterward dried and powdered. As she was powdering his penis and taking care not to touch it, Hans said, "Why don't you put your finger there?"
>
> MOTHER: Because that'd be piggish.
> HANS: What's that? Piggish? Why?
> MOTHER: Because it's not proper.
>
> Undaunted by her insensitivity, Hans replied:
>
> HANS: [*laughing*] But it's great fun.(13)

Oedipal Development in the Boy: David and Goliath

Although the nature of infantile sexuality is essentially the same in boys and girls, there are differences which must be considered separately.

During infancy and toddlerhood, mother is the center of the boy's world, nourishing and bathing, enhancing psychological individuation and teaching him about the world. Building upon his dawning understanding of sexual difference and curiosity about male–female relationships, our budding Oedipus gradually transforms his mother into a beguiling sexual being and, like any infatuated lover, builds an elaborate fantasy life about her.

His ingrained sense of maleness and his growing awareness that his father has a privileged relationship with his mother—they sleep together, he sleeps alone; they go out together, he stays home—gradually draws him into competition with his dad. The battle is joined, but not easily, since the son loved his father before he began to challenge and fear him. The external blustering is but a reflection of the mental war raging inside.

Young adult parents, facing this sudden onslaught and brazen seduction from one so young, are thrown off balance. They don't know whether to laugh or cry, succumb or fight back. Usually they do all of the above and more, riding an emotional roller coaster which stirs up long forgotten memories from their own infantile past, now reexperienced and reordered in the crucible of young adult parenthood. Parenthood is a path to maturity *because* it reexposes mothers and fathers to infantile feelings of rage and sex—both from within themselves and their child—which can now be examined and responded to, unlike the child, in a reasoned, tempered manner.

Father's ongoing presence and response to his son's hostility is critically important in determining the outcome of the boy's march toward masculinity. If he is tolerant and accepting without being either seductive or punitive, father creates an atmosphere in which his boy can struggle with conflicted thoughts and feelings, utilizing the limited, but sufficient, psychological resources available to him. And struggle he does, particularly with fantasies. Every wish to attack, wipe out, even kill Dad is frightening as well as gratifying. After all, Dad is bigger and stronger than he and has used his clout many times to restrict, punish, and deprive: David and Goliath and Remember the Alamo. Thus, every wish to attack the father boomerangs, producing increased fantasies of retaliation and heightened anxiety. The inability to sharply distinguish fantasy from reality creates a painful mental state from which there is no escape, short of oedipal "resolution." For these reasons, the bravado and competitiveness directed toward the parent of the same sex (by both boys and girls) should not be punished or encouraged; even when Junior uses his head as a battering ram aimed at father's most private, and potentially painful parts. Broad limits on behavior obviously need to be set, but the time-limited, phase-specific challenge so essential to normal developmental progression should be understood and accepted. Indeed, the healthy parent, secure in his or her sexuality, will find the pseudochallenge and the wish to be emulated and displaced highly enjoyable.

As his investment in his penis becomes more focused and valued, our young challenger is flooded with phallic pride, that bedrock component of male sexuality. But having something so wonderful puts you at risk, particularly from that other bull in the house whose incredibly big member you've envied and coveted for yourself. In the concrete mind of the little boy, such a danger is real, not symbolic, heightened by the erroneous but understandable misconception that females had penises and somehow lost them. Thus is born the most dreaded fear of the male species, castration anxiety, and it's not limited to childhood. Within the protected sanctuary of the therapeutic relationship I have heard more than one man tell me, with conviction, that he would rather die than lose his penis. Phallocentricity dies hard, even in the mature male, who claims there is more to life than sex.

Because of their curiosity and love for their mothers, boys, at about age three, admire the female body and sometimes verbalize the wish to have breasts and babies. Parental panic often follows, precipitating frantic calls for professional help to squash this provocative symptom of homosexuality. Responding to the unmistakable environmental pressure and the inner need to consolidate their masculine identity, most boys quickly repress these feminine strivings until a later developmental day when they can more comfortably experience the feminine side of themselves through identification with wives and lovers. Mature males, unencumbered by parental concerns and deeply secure in their masculinity, come to understand the bisexual nature of all human beings and comfortably move toward what the cultural anthropologist, David Guttman called the normal androgyny of life.(14)

Masturbation, that normal, necessary oedipal experience, heightens fantasy production by adding the physical sensation of intense genital pleasure, and later assists in the resolution of the Oedipal Complex by stimulating castration anxiety since something so pleasurable is highly valued and not to be lost. The typical masturbatory fantasy at this age has not changed since the days of Little Hans; it involves sexual play with mother, particularly the touching and exploration of sexual parts and masturbation, but not penetration or ejaculation. These hallmarks of male sexuality, driven by an outpouring of testosterone, make their first appearance in adolescence.

As the fear of castration permeates the boy's psyche, supplanting sexual wishes for the mother as the dominant force, the Oedipal Complex is gradually "resolved." Other forces also push the boy, now about age six, in that direction, particularly the growing realization of his relative weakness and impotence in a world controlled by adults and the now intense desire to be *like* his father and other men and boys. As Jimminy Cricket whispers, "no," and shouts in his ear "You can't beat 'em, join 'em," the disappointed would-be lover turns his attention away from his intense fantasy world and precious penis. He avoids his mother and feminine interests, which he begins to loudly devalue. Then, like a good soldier he marches resolutely into latency, the next phase of development, there to learn what his father, friends, and culture consider to be masculine.

Oedipal fantasy and experience continue to influence

sexual thought and action well into adulthood. Some infantile fantasies are eventually actualized, particularly in foreplay, while others are incorporated into or replaced by more complex wishes from adolescence and adulthood. Mature sexual thought and action is an amalgam, a fulfilling expression of the sexual past and present.

Oedipal Development in the Girl: The Source of Feminine Intuition

The sugar and spice, if not the everything nice, the little girl's core gender identity, like the boy's, is firmly in place by eighteen months of age. Then the girl is confronted with a very challenging task, that of conceptualizing her not so easily seen genitals with the limited cognitive abilities of the age and comparing it with the very obvious penis and testicles of her brother or father. "Something" versus "nothing" is the initial mental picture of the two-year-old as she struggles to understand the nature of her genitalia. Gradually, as a result of self-exploration, this simplistic idea is replaced by an awareness of labia, clitoris, and vagina, places of mystery and intriguing sensation, a wellspring of wonderment and pride. The mental work involved in the construction of the genital body image is considered by many to be the source of feminine intuition, sensitivity, and complexity.

Another difficult and painful task awaits the girl as she begins her Oedipal journey. Unlike the boy, who remains zeroed in on his mother with laser-beam intensity, she must partially abandon her deep attachment to mother and redirect her sexually determined interest and affection toward her father. Once this is accomplished, the girl's Oedipal development proceeds on a parallel course with the boy's. She covets her father's attention and affection and continually plots the overthrow of the queen who sits at his side.

Like her male counterpart, she is a determined seductress, using all of her beguiling charm to entice the man she desires to love her physically and mentally. But even in moments of triumph, she glances over her shoulder, sadly, to the regal rival from whom she emerged body and soul.

Eventually, the girl "resolves" (resolves, in quotes, because, as we shall see, it is a recurring theme throughout the life cycle) the Oedipal Complex in the same manner as the boy. Because of her love of her mother and the fear of retaliation by the bigger, more powerful parent; she gradually mutes her sexual desires for her father and wishes to replace her mother. Then through identification with Mom and the other important females in her life, she dips into the lake of latency, there to expand her sense of femininity to include cultural values.

The Meaning of Some Typical Oedipal Behavior: "Mommy, I'm Afraid"

As four-year-old Caitlin sleeps, she shakes in terror as two shadowy arms reach in the window to grab her. "Mommy, Daddy," she screams, "save me!" After the eternity it takes for a parent to arrive, she cries, "A monster was trying to take me. Stay here, please!"

The groggy parent, half asleep, has been a player in this scenario many times during the past year. He or she mechanically responds, "No, honey, there are no monsters, it was just a bad dream. You're fine. I'll stay here until you fall asleep." "I'm afraid to sleep. What if he comes back?" "He won't, dear. He won't."

Caitlin had a nightmare; her parents, another night of interrupted sleep. Like her chronological counterparts, Caitlin also has other fears—of the dark, of ghosts and goblins, of monsters in the closet and in her dreams. These are *normal* phenomena at this stage of development, indications that the child is actively engaged in the Oedipal conflict and resorting to the formation of phobias, a sophisticated form of mental gymnastics, in a semifutile attempt to control the raging sexual and aggressive feelings which are barely contained behind the mental dam being built to regulate them. The emergence of the abilities of the mind to construct phobias and nightmares, which occurs for the first time during the Oedipal phase, is a quantum leap forward because it disguises the true target of the aggressive impulses (the parent of the same sex), thus protecting the child from conscious awareness of the hostility, and permits a more comfortable relationship with the progenitor—but not without a price, nightmares and fears in the case of Caitlin and a fear of horses (but no longer of his father) for Little Hans.

Freud called these fears and phobias the *infantile neurosis,* indicating the similarity between these normal childhood experiences and the abnormal fears of later life. The Oedipal phase is the only time in life when persistent fears, phobias, and nightmares are considered to be normal. Their ongoing presence at later stages in life may call for therapeutic intervention. This is a good example of the principle stated in Chapter 1 that what is normal at one stage of development may be abnormal at another. As the child moves into latency, the symptoms of the infantile neurosis "magically" diminish on their own, indicating the resolution of the Oedipal Complex and the dawn of a whole new developmental era.

Big Is Better

Sitting in the living room after dinner, engrossed in the paper, Mother was relaxed and vulnerable and, therefore, startled and shocked when five-year-old Ann pinched her breast and commanded in a severe voice "When I get big, *my* breasts are going to be big, bigger than yours, and you won't have any."

Oedipal-aged children are preoccupied with size. Big is better. Small is bad. In the all-or-none world of Oedipal rivalry, only one person can be big—winner take all. Ann will have breasts, which somehow make Mother more attractive to Father. Mother will have none.

As illustrated, sometimes the attack on the parent's body is direct, sometimes thinly veiled as accidental, and other times more benign. As his father lingered over dessert, five-year-old Tom gently rested his hand on Dad's palm. Disappointed when his entire appendage was contained in Dad's, he sighed sadly, "I wish I was big." Empathic parents understand and encourage, "You'll be big as me some day, Tom. Maybe even bigger."

"Daddy, Where Do Babies Come From?" The Thirst for Sexual Knowledge

JOSEPH: Daddy, where do babies come from?
DADDY: From inside the mommy.
JOSEPH: (*after a long, thoughtful silence*) How do they get out? Through the belly button?
DADDY: (*after a brief, thoughtful pause*) No, there's a special opening between the mommy's legs.
JOSEPH: (*satisfied response as he runs off to play*) Oh.
DADDY: (*relieved response to himself*) Whew!

Oedipal-aged children ask lots of sexual questions. Answering them honestly and matter-of-factly in language the child can understand provides just enough information to satisfy curiosity and convey an attitude of benign acceptance without overstimulating the child. In other words, adults facilitate sexual development in children by not imposing their own physical experience and mental set on the child and following the child's verbal lead.

Oedipal resolution is based on the comfortable management of feelings and sensations, some factual information, and numerous misconceptions that persist into adolescence and adulthood. Despite the introduction by parents of "Everything you Wanted to Know about Sex" during the Oedipal and latency years, facts about adult sexuality are repeatedly distorted and the most imaginative misconceptions continually created (to the exasperation of the well-intentioned teacher) because the infantile mind cannot integrate more.

Questions are one thing, actions another. Little Hans and Lolita will make every attempt to learn from experience as well, prancing around the house nude, shamelessly displaying their genitals, or climbing into the parental bed whenever it is occupied. The practicing child psychiatrist frequently hears examples of unwitting unconscious collusion on the part of the parents. One young father, in therapy for unrelated matters, described with relish his pleasure and pride in taking showers with his four-year-old daughter. They never seemed happier, or closer, than during the moments when beads of water were cascading from father to child. Their rendezvous continued until one day when she, just about crotch high, suddenly grabbed his penis. "Daddy," she said, clutching it with glee, "this is *so big*." That marked the end of their watery trysts.

When young children are allowed to express their infantile sexuality within the bounds of a *pattern* of relatively neutral parental response, they develop a nonconflicted curiosity toward their sexuality which becomes the basis for a rewarding sexual life in adolescence and adulthood.

The Plight of the Single Parent: "I Don't Live with My Daddy"

Separation and divorce can be significant, but no insurmountable, obstacles to Oedipal development. Cooperation between the parents can smooth the way. Regular access to both parents in a noncritical atmosphere helps. So does resisting the temptation to use the child as a source of solace for parental pain and loss by elevating him or her to the role of pseudospouse. A parade of new parental partners observed in casual dating or sexual situations is sure to be confusing. So is the introduction of a potential stepparent before the relationship is likely to be lasting. Stepparents who are kind and loving can greatly enrich a young child's life—as an additional source of adult involvement, not as a replacement for a sometimes present parent.

Children are amazingly resourceful. When suitable replacements for absent parents are not readily available, they will seek them out in the extended family or neighborhood, or create them by resorting to fantasy and fairy tale.

The Transition to Latency: All Grown Up

At three, the world of the family is all that is needed and almost all that is known. At six, one stands poised on a high plateau contemplating a horizon that appears to stretch forever. Out there is the unexplored world of school, new friendships, families different from your own; the thrilling world of knowledge, opened up by reading and writing; and last, but not least, a rapidly expanding inner universe of ideas and values. As the child mutes Oedipal strivings and adheres to parental expectations because of the triple threat of bodily harm, narcissistic injury, and loss of love, he or she becomes aware that parents not only enforce behavioral standards, but themselves live by a set of moral and ethical codes.(15) As these values and standards are internalized and integrated, they become a powerful inner voice which first whispers, then commands that thought and action be judged. No longer can Oedipal fantasies be entertained without *inner* judgment and recrimination. No longer can the world of reality be subordinated to selfish desires. Pushed by this new and imposing psychic structure, this superego, this conscience, our young charges turn their backs on infancy and all of its gratifications and limitations and bravely, and naively, march toward the next way-station on the road to maturity—latency.

4

Latency and Adolescence

Stage 4: Latency (Ages 6–12)

Opening to the World

> When I think of elementary school children, I see them rushing and tumbling at recess, balancing on railings, sliding, swinging with zest, chanting their rhymes, sucking lollipops, comic books in their hands, tearing around chasing one another. I hear the sounds of roller skates on the pavements, hopscotch chalked on sidewalks, the girls skipping ropes to chants.(1)

Latency signifies calm. In this instance mental calm in the midst of frenetic physical activity, as described in the quote above by psychiatrist Elizabeth Bremner Kaplan. Freud introduced the term to describe the *relative* mental calm and slow but steady physical growth that characterize the years between the hurricane of the Oedipal phase and the cyclone of adolescence. Latency begins with a soothing psychological event, the resolution of the Oedipal complex, and ends with a physiological upheaval, the onset of puberty.

Early latency is a time of transition, characterized by two events, one actual, the other internal, which radically alter the relationship to parents and family. As John and Susan place that first tentative step onto the school bus they begin life on their own, entering a world which does not include their parents. Paradoxically, at the same time that they leave Mom and Dad waving at the curb, our young adventurers do the impossible and take their parents along, captured forever, in a new mental structure, the conscience or, as Freud called it, the superego.

The Developmental Tasks of Latency: A Taste of Freedom, Capability, and Responsibility

Like all developmental phases, latency is defined by work in progress, that series of new challenges which must be faced and mastered if the mind is to continue to expand in capability and complexity. In the elementary school years, the challenges revolve around freedom, capability and responsibility; molding a conscience, broadening a sense of masculinity or femininity, forming friendships, learning new mental and physical skills; all important additions to the growing mosaic of maturity.

THE DEVELOPMENTAL TASKS OF LATENCY

Forming a conscience
Becoming a friend
Consolidating a masculine or feminine identity
Becoming a student

Conscience Formation: The Beacon of Morality

The conscience or superego has a bad name, associated as it is with the restriction of thought and action and the feeling of guilt. The criticism is undeserved. Conscience formation during the latency years provides the personality with indispensable attributes of restraint, consideration, kindness, and morality. When the child acts and thinks in harmony with the dictates of the conscience, he or she is flooded with a sense of approval and love from within. When the bounds of acceptable thought or behavior are breached the instant response is guilt, that most uncomfortable of feelings.

Freud related the formation of the superego to the resolution of the Oedipal complex because an inner force was necessary to direct the child away from sexual and aggressive preoccupations. Conscience formation is a gradual process, begun in infancy and expanded each time parents set limits, respond to the toddler with the ubiquitous "No," actively initiate toilet training, and gently temper the sexual and aggressive thrusts of the Oedipal years. Thus, the critical impetus to the formation of this highly valuable and adaptive judgmental aspect of the personality is parental criticism which has been gradually internalized and then expanded on as the child is exposed to formal education and cultural values.

Adult maturity is impossible without that strong sense of morality, tempered and refined in the years beyond latency. With its crystallization in latency, the child becomes *civilized* because thoughts and actions are constantly and automatically monitored and controlled from within. No longer dependent on parents' physical presence to control behavior the young child is free to explore the world, which demands that he or she exercise judgment and restraint.

With parental prohibitions and morality safely locked inside, the latency-aged child is able to relate to his or her progenitors in a new way. No longer consciously preoccupied with stimulating and disturbing fantasies, he or she manages a calmer, more modulated interaction based on mutual interests and realistic considerations. Competitiveness is largely replaced by identification and admiration—"I want to be just like you when I grow up, Mom." Sexual preoccupations diminish, their intensity transformed into a burning desire to learn—"Please, Dad, pitch to me again. Just ten more minutes." Basking in such admiration, healthy parents reap the rewards of parenthood. Latency is the golden age of childhood for the parents as well as the child.

The Emergence of the Capacity for Friendship: Pristine, Pure, Extrafamilial Love

A good friendship with another child is like a thick fur coat on a cold gray day, providing warmth and protection against life's wintry blasts. With the consideration of the emergence of the capacity for friendship in latency we begin a journey down one of life's most rewarding paths, studying relationships which are an indispensable part of the lives of all mature individuals, who recognize the uniqueness of this extremely fulfilling form of human love.

Freud saw friendship as a form of love. "We do not separate from this—what in any case has its share in the name 'love'—on the one hand, self love, and on the other, love of parents and children, friendship and love for humanity in general. . . . "

Ah, if the story was only that simple. But, unfortunately, human beings are aggressive as well. "As a result their neighbor is for them not only a potential helper or sexual object, but also someone who tempts them to satisfy their aggressiveness on him, to exploit his capacity for work without compensation, to use him sexually without his consent, to seize his possessions, to humiliate him, to cause him pain, to torture and to kill him."(2)

Watch the wolf pack of pre- and early adolescent girls attack the "friend" singled out for sacrifice to the gods of unbridled aggression on any particular day and you will know that Freud was not exaggerating the nature of the dark side of the force. Friendships are complex relationships, requiring a constant titration of feeling and restraint, sex and aggression, love and hate. Based on mutuality, equality, and freedom of choice, they flower for the first time in early latency when children have developed the capacity to control behavior, delay gratification, separate from mother and father, and comfortably relate to others.

Latency-aged children of both sexes form intense friendships. These are the years of Tom Sawyers and Nancy Drews, of lazy afternoons in the sun, of pranks and adventures. Siphoning off some of the infantile affection for Mom and Dad, now redirected away from the parents by the conscience, this excess love is channeled into sexually defused friendships. Together, friends explore the world, accept the dictates of the superego, and provide solace for the lost and now forbidden intimacy with parents. A pattern is set in motion here which will be repeated throughout the life cycle, namely, the use of friendships as a vehicle for growing and maturing.

The Elaboration of Sexual Identity and Friendship: "Boys Have Cooties," "I Hate Girls"

As we traced the developmental line of sexual identity through the first three developmental stages we noted the establishment of core gender identity in the first year of life, the recognition of genital difference during the second and third, and the preoccupation with the role of sexuality in relationships during the Oedipal phase. In latency one learns about being a boy or a girl from parents, teachers, Cub Scout and Brownie leaders, coaches, and, as Art Buchwald put it, guttersnipe friends.

Masculinity and femininity become highly subjective concepts, defined by family, friends, and culture; stringent standards which are applied to all thought, action, and activity. Involvement with the opposite sex is taboo, the better to keep those recently repressed, rampant Oedipal feelings in check. All hail to the Oedipal victor, the parent of the same sex and his or her gender-related friends. There will be no fraternizing with the enemy. Well, at least none that the peer group knows about. A solid front of masculine disdain or feminine aloofness are the best ways to hide the second-grade engagements and fourth-grade crushes that continue to exist clandestinely.

In the rush to be more masculine or feminine, nearly every activity is assigned to one sex or the other, without rational rhyme or reason but with clear developmental purpose. Eight-year-old Jack, youngest member of a tough coal-mining family in West Virginia, wouldn't think of taking music lessons. That was for "girls and sissies." But in a distant city, eight-year-old Bob couldn't spend enough time practicing the trumpet; he wanted to be as good as his brother and father, both of whom were professional musicians. Blowing that horn was the highest expression of manliness, something "no sissy girl can do."

The peer group is the arena in which the internal and external battle against the opposite sex is waged. Strongly supported by her friends, fourth-grade Anna publicly denounced the boys in her class. They were gross, crude, and obnoxious, she shouted to the satisfaction of her Greek chorus of girlfriends who echoed her views. Taunted as they were, the boys responded verbally and physically, punching and running, pulling hair and jeering. The undertone of sexual excitement was obvious to the adult observers and appeared to be fleetingly recognized by both sexes as they giggled and laughed behind their self-imposed barricades.

As the developmentally wise observer knows, this normal, phase-specific need to exaggerate the difference between the sexes is short lived, swept away by the flood of estrogen and testosterone which demolishes latency mental structures and signals the onset of adolescence. Although mature men and women bask in the warmth of their relationships with each other, both sexes reserve a spot, occasionally a prominent one, for same-sex friendships which satisfy needs that no one of the opposite sex could possibly understand.

School Days, School Days, Good Old Golden Rule Days

The transition from home to school may appear to the casual adult observer as simple as "Beam me up, Scotty" since most children accomplish it without great difficulty. In actuality successful adjustment to school is a significant achievement indicating that development is progressing nicely in multiple ways. Happy campers in kindergarten and first grade can control bowel and bladder, sit still for long intervals, and possess the cognitive maturity to begin readiness activities, the forerunners of reading and writing. They can also separate easily from parents and relate to strange adults, sharing their interest and affection, forge friendships and tolerate the rough-and-tumble politics of the peer group, and accomplish all of the above with a modicum of impulse control and a minimum degree of regression.

Erikson packaged the essence of latency under the banner of industry. Like the passing of the baton in a relay race, family and school must work hand in hand. "Many a child's development is disrupted when family life has failed to prepare him for school life, or when school life fails to sustain the promises of earlier development."(3) The result of such failure and disruption is an ingrained sense of inferiority which grievously undermines future development. Critical components of adult maturity are self-confidence and industry, the legacies of the latency phase.

As the elementary school years progress, the latency child acquires the intellectual, social, emotional and physical skills, and knowledge that are the cultural keys needed to unlock the doors to adulthood. Knowledge of these cultural norms are absolute prerequisites for the attainment of maturity in any adult society in the world.

Play in Childhood

Rushing, tumbling, sliding, swinging with zest, chanting, dashing about are words used by Elizabeth Bremner Kaplan at the beginning of this chapter to describe latency-aged children and their play. Although play begins earlier and continues throughout life, latency-aged play is unique because it is during this phase of development that the games of a particular culture are learned. They continue to influence development throughout adulthood.

"When they're at recess, I can't stop them from playing," said one elementary school principal. Indeed, play is a major preoccupation which consumes huge chunks of the child's physical and mental energy and time. Why? Not because Mom or Dad say "Go out and play. I'll call you when dinner is ready." The romanticized sense of play as random, carefree activity is far removed from its purposeful, psychically determined nature. Children play endlessly because they need to, constantly working over and assimilating experiences too overwhelming for their immature psyches to digest and integrate quickly. Adults have more mental resources available to cope with the pressures of everyday life, hence, they play less. This basic urge to repeat is an attempt at mastery, surging activity to wash away the pain and discomfort of being in a world which is often incomprehensible and overwhelming.

Four-year-old Susan was jabbed twice by a "mean" nurse at her pediatrician's office. Upon returning home she rushed to her doll house and assaulted her favorite doll verbally and physically. "Don't cry, you bad girl. This won't hurt you."

Eight-year-old Matthew's play was generated by a fantasy, not a real event. In the dual roles of announcer and basketball star, racing about the Madison Square Garden court which was his driveway, he repeatedly exclaimed to the imaginary audience, "And Jordan scores again! The World Championship is his!" Never mind that most heaves didn't reach the basket, or that he was barely able to dribble. In the world of play his painfully small stature and lack of skills vanished when he crawled inside Michael Jordan's skin and soared to a slam dunk.

Like almost everything else as we develop, play changes from phase to phase. Toddlers play at practicing physical skills and dealing with Mommy's unnerving comings and goings. Peek-a-boo is an example. Play as most adults conceptualize it refers to the activities of Oedipal and latency-aged children. Oedipal-aged play is highly idiosyncratic, based on individual fantasies, but the themes involved are very consistent, reflecting the sexual and aggressive preoccupations of the day. For example,

> FIRST CHILD: Let's play house, I'll be the mommy. You'll be the daddy. You be the baby.
> SECOND CHILD: I want to be the mommy.
> FIRST CHILD: You can't. This is my game.

As the psychiatrist Lili Peller put it, the basic anxiety in Oedipal-aged play is "I am small and left out of adult pleasures and prerogatives;" the compensatory fantasy, "I am big and can do what adults do."(4) This identification with adults lends a charming quality of triumph and naive invincibility to the play. For example,

> FIRST CHILD: I'm Superman. You can't hurt me.
> SECOND CHILD: Oh, yes I can. I'm Batman. He's stronger than Superman.

With the onset of latency, play changes dramatically. Complicated physical actions are possible because coordination is greatly enhanced. The ability to read and write unlocks the door to board and card games. Because the conscience insists on monitoring play as well as everything else, rules are everywhere. "Three strikes you're out!" "Do not pass go, do not collect $200." "You're penalized ten yards." No longer is play based on individual fantasies. Games are learned from older children who in turn were introduced to them by their predecessors. Some have endured for decades. They are an expression of the culture, a powerful link to past generations. As we shall see, adolescents and adults play the same games they were taught in latency, but for very different reasons. Play is a source of great fulfillment for adults as well as children—even more so when they understand its psychological purposes and intricacies.

The Literature of Latency

Just as each society passes on its games from generation to generation, so does it perpetuate its myths, providing not only generational continuity but also a powerful sense of connectedness between adult consciousness and the sometimes misty memories of childhood. Many a Sunday afternoon has been spent by parent and child "happily" watching Walt Disney's Bambi—until Bambi's mother is killed during one of the most violent scenes in childrens' movie history! After getting over the initial shock and dabbing away a tear or two, the usual adult response is: "I'll be damned. I thought this was a fun movie. Why am I putting my kid through this? Why didn't I remember how awful it was when I saw it when I was a child?" Why? Just because it was so painful. The need to forget, to repress much of the pain of childhood, was strong.

The beloved literature of latency is an absolute reflection of development to this point in life, dealing with the delightful childhood themes of murder, mayhem, and sex, all thinly disguised, to be sure, to "fool" the superego and unsuspecting adults. "Mirror, mirror on the wall, who's the fairest one of all?" "You are, oh Queen, except for your lovely daughter, Snow White." "Then we'll knock her off," replies the loving mother. And she tries, with a vengeance. The sex is more disguised than the aggression, stripped of its hot, primitive characteristics and replaced by pristine or innocuous images. The Handsome Prince prefers Snow White to her mother and destroys the evil spell by giving her the sweetest, most asexual kiss imaginable. The good stuff is left for the place where "they live happily ever after." Peter Pan, Alice (in Wonderland), and Dorothy in *The Wizard of Oz* are examples of heroes who possess magical powers or associate with those who do in order to compensate for the child's sense of apprehension and impotence in the mysterious, dangerous adult world.

Aspects of narcissism and egocentricity are reflected in the absence of siblings, those unwelcome guests who don't know enough to leave. In many classics, such as Cinderella, they are sheared of their birthright, ugly beyond words, and certain losers.

Good and bad, black and white are the dichotomous characters of latency; no vagueness here, no quasiheroes. The superego demands that the heroes, such as Superman and Wonder Woman, be very good, and the villains, such as Captain Hook and the Wicked Witch of the West, be very bad. Heroes use their superhuman powers in the service of justice and the American way and never deviate from the straight and narrow, at least until Superman used his X-ray vision in the movie version to see the color of Lois Lane's underwear. The scrupulosity of the superego is reflected in Wonder Woman's lasso, which surrounds perpetrators with the rope of morality and compels honesty, and quite literally in Jimminy Cricket, who sits on Pinocchio's shoulder and whispers advice and admonitions in his ear. Protected by their naiveté, immature cognitive capacities, and vigilant superego—and, hopefully, a life filled with a lot of love and little actual violence—healthy latency-aged children use classic literature to integrate their emotional development and cultural identity. Those children who are abused and/or neglected may not fare so well. For them the violence in movies, fairy tales, and television is too close to reality, a painful and traumatic reflection of their daily lives.

By late latency and early adolescence the literature reflects the winds of developmental change. The heroes are often real people, such as Benjamin Franklin (despite his illegitimate children and bed hopping in the Court of France) and Helen Keller. Anticipating the fall of the icons of childhood during the adolescent years, child heroes, such as Nancy Drew and the Hardy Boys, use their intelligence and wit to demystify the formerly inscrutable adult world and vanquish the villains.

The literature of adulthood incorporates the myths of childhood, packaging them in more sophisticated metaphors which express both the physical, sexual, and emotional maturity of the adult and the primitiveness and vulnerability of the child. Great literature taps into the childhood past so deeply that the seventh-stage reader is flooded with conscious and unconscious memories and feelings which heighten awareness when reading. Despite increased understanding and maturity, he or she, like the child, lives in a world filled with sudden vulnerability and incomprehensible and unsolvable mysteries.

Stage 5: Adolescence (Ages 12–20): The Gateway to Adulthood

It's easy to tell when adolescence begins, with the maturational event, puberty, but not so easy to determine when it ends. Some say twenty, thirty, or even forty; others say never. One thing is clear: The emergence of the physically mature adult body, seemingly overnight, far outpaces the ability of the mind to keep up. For a number of years a child's mind is trapped in an adult body. The study of psychological development in adolescence is the story of how the mind catches up, becoming again the master of the body, and acquires the skills needed to make the transition to adulthood.

The Developmental Tasks of Adolescence

Accepting the physically and sexually mature body
Utilizing friendships in the service of development

Separating from parents
Beginning an active sexual life
Preparing to work

Erikson characterized adolescence as a time of struggle over identity.

> The growing and developing youths, faced with this psychological revolution within them, and with tangible adult tasks ahead of them are now primarily concerned with what they appear to be in the eyes of others as compared with what they feel they are and with the question of how to connect the roles and skills cultivated earlier with the occupational prototypes of the day.(5)

If the adolescent is unable to master the developmental tasks of this phase, role confusion results—confusion over individuality, sexuality and adult identity.

Puberty: Accepting the Physically and Sexually Mature Body

Gangly arms and legs, breasts, pubic hair, pimples, angles and curves, jumbled parts, sweat and fluids—puberty refers to the biological and psychological events which surround the first menstrual period in the girl and the first ejaculation in the boy. Like the Vandals invading Rome, puberty leaves the golden order of latency in ruins and results in a long, medieval night of psychological upheaval and uncertainty.

Regression is the order of the day. Silliness, immaturity, and unpredictability abound. Thirteen-year-old Johnny, formerly a quiet, somewhat mousey kid, became a bundle of nervous energy. He walked around the house making farting noises with his mouth and asking inappropriate questions. Although John became an even-tempered, serious adult, his parents never forgot the day he embarrassed them by asking a family friend why her nose was so big.

Like turtles curling up in their protective shells, teenagers withdraw from their puzzled parents, hiding their embarrassing disarray in body and mind from inquiring, concerned eyes. Secretiveness replaces openness at home but leads to the formation of cliques and "best" friendships in which sexual information (and misinformation) is pooled and debated with others who are in the same boat.

Suddenly strange hairdos, designer jeans, and namebrand sneakers become extremely important, reflecting the tremendous investment in, and insecurity about, the new body. Clothes make the man, or woman, accentuating or hiding bulges, curves, cavities, and emotional disarray.

A thirteen-year-old patient of mine paraded around in steel-tipped shoes, ripped jeans, and a tee-shirt which heralded "Hitler's Triumphant Tour across Europe." This dress and a menacing countenance were meant to disgust peers and adults alike, a goal easily accomplished. Behind the bravado was a frightened, insecure youngster who had been rejected by both his natural and adoptive parents. As he and I faced these underlying issues, his appearance softened and he began to tackle the adolescent issues of social acceptance, sexual involvement, and separation from parents.

Another young man hid his "98-pound weakling" body by wearing the bulkiest of sweaters, even on the hottest, soggiest August days. As the adolescent compares his or her body with peers and adults, real or imagined differences are magnified. Legs, arms, and noses are too long; pimples too gross and obvious; breasts and penises too small or too large. Potential prom queen or plain Jane, musclebound jock or scrawny egghead—all must tolerate the universal feelings of embarrassment, doubt, and inadequacy that accompany the metamorphosis from physically immature child to physically mature adult.

As these changes are gradually accepted and integrated, the body once again becomes a source of pride and pleasure, stronger, more capable, and for a brief time in late adolescence and young adulthood a Stradivarius, flawlessly expressing its master's physical and sexual wishes. Often taken for granted and abused by its preoccupied owners, its fleeting perfection unappreciated, adults in the seventh stage watch with envy, mourn what they no longer have, and take solace in George Bernard Shaw's somewhat bitter insight that youth is wasted on the young.

Adolescent Friendships: Love and War, Refuge and Disappointment

During the latency phase friendships were fun, best friends viewed the world through the rose-colored glasses of physical and sexual immaturity. Friendships in adolescence can be another matter, fragile unreliable supports for surging impulses, serious relationships and significant separations, or sturdy buttresses against the winds of change. At no other point in the life cycle do friendships play such a prominent role.

Nowhere is the jarring impact of the peer group more noticeable than in early adolescence. Thirteen-year-old Laura sat in my office crying her eyes out. Between sobs she managed to tell me that her best friend, Jane, wasn't talking to her anymore. In a Byzantine plot of immense proportions, Amy, her worst enemy, had sent a note to Jane, her best friend, through Sally, who was at the moment friends with everybody. Amy told Jane that Laura has said that Jane looked awful in the pink sweater that she had worn to school that day. "It's not true!" she sobbed. "I would never say that. Jane is my best friend." Dozens of phone calls among the main characters and their respective claques resolved the matter and lead to a rapprochement between Laura and Jane. Amy was once again their worst enemy, but in the course of the electronic roundtable negotiations, several vassals changed sides, forming new but hardly reliable alliances.

Pre- and early adolescent boys, who mature physically a year or so later than the girls and tend to be less tempestuous about their masculine rivalries, are quite threatened by these increasingly fascinating young Amazons. They maintain the latency attitude of "hating" girls or cover their emerging sexual feelings and fears with taunts and bravado. Group activities such as Boy Scouts and organized sports help the boys separate from parents and channel sexual and aggressive energies into nonsexual directions until they are ready to approach the girls more directly.

The reasons for such behavior are multiple. They include the displacement of powerful, ambivalent feelings about parents onto the peer group, insecurity about the rapidly changing body (hence the reaction to the alleged remark about the sweater), and the loosening of dependent ties to the family of origin. The loosening of alliances and shifting ties within the peer group are external reflections of an analogous internal process.

In midadolescence friends provide validation for feelings and opinions without much concern or objectivity; support against impossible and oppressive parents, regardless of the validity of their stance; and unconditional acceptance to cushion the blows from demanding teachers, social superiors, and rejecting lovers. On those occasions when Antarctica seems more hospitable than home or school, best friends are there, faithful as Saint Bernards, always to the rescue.

In late adolescence and early young adulthood friends become family. Having left the nest for college or apartment, alone in the world for the first time, temporary families are created. Fraternity brothers and sorority sisters assume the title as well as the functions; roommates do the same in less formal ways. Like Columbus and his crew who left home to explore the unknown, late adolescent friends band together for courage and companionship as they venture forth to search for a new personal world in adulthood.

The Second Individuation: "This Time I'm Leaving for Good . . . I Think"

Pushed along by the inevitability of physical maturation, all vestiges of early childhood gone, the sometimes eager, sometimes reluctant adolescent must physically and psychologically separate from parents. At the beginning of this transition phase the child is physically and sexually immature and content within the supportive embrace of the family. At the end of it the young adult is sexually active, independent, and autonomous—or trying to be! Referring to Mahler's separation–individuation theory, Blos called the psychological steps from A to B the "second individuation."(6)

Just as toddlers venture away to explore the world and return for refueling, so do adolescents. They break away by fighting curfews, questioning parental values, and retreating to the monastic safety of the bedroom, which is isolated from the outside world by "Keep Out—Parents, This Means You!" signs on the door. They hide behind house-shaking stereo noise, but sometimes shyly seek love and rapprochement through an occasional hug or kiss, agree to go to Grandma's, or watch a movie at home on a Saturday night.

Sometime it's easier to experience strong emotions for

family members by making war, not love. One 17-year-old senior, about to go off to college in several months, became more surly and impossible as spring approached. Sooner or later he managed to draw his parents into verbal battles and recriminations. In the midst of one heated exchange his underlying ambivalence burst through as he stormed out the door. "This time I'm leaving for sure . . . I think!"

As the second individuation progresses, the child who was dependent and secure within the safe harbor of the family slowly fades away. In his or her place is the unpolished late adolescent who feels confident and insecure, capable and anxious, strong and vulnerable, increasingly aware of entering a strange but exciting new world—alone. If childhood has achieved its developmental purposes, what stands on the threshold of adulthood is a diamond in the rough, lacking polish and definition, but possessing the inner character and luster needed to find fulfillment in the seventh stage.

Accepting Sexual Maturation and Preparing for an Active Sexual Life

"I'm Ready." Sexual development during the first decade of life is like a slowly meandering river, quiet and serene. The establishment of core gender identity in infancy, the recognition of two sets of genitals and sex within the context of relationships during the anal and Oedipal phases, and the addition of a cultural measure of masculinity and femininity during latency all occur while the river runs deep.

A distant rumble grows louder as the rapids of puberty signal the approach of the sexual Niagara of adolescence, an awesome, thrilling, and potentially dangerous plunge into the world of adult sexuality. During adolescence the developmental task is to accept the sexually mature body and establish an active sexual life. First the sexually mature body must be explored and accepted, leading to familiarity and appreciation of such new phenomena as vaginal wetness and ejaculation. Then, through repeated experience with fantasy and masturbation, psychological preparations are made to take those exquisitely thrilling and painful first steps toward the opposite sex. By late adolescence most individuals are psychologically prepared for an active sexual life which includes intercourse.

One sixteen-year-old boy, his strong desire to have intercourse already practiced a thousand times while masturbating, announced to me with determination, "I'm ready! And I don't care who knows it. I'm ready for that, too." The "who" referred to his parents and peers. Having endured the physical and psychological tumult and uncertainty of puberty and early adolescence, internally sure of his sexual desires and ambitions, he was prepared to declare his sexual maturity to the external world.

"Isn't this timeline a bit retarded?" you may be thinking. "Don't kids nowadays become sexually active much earlier?" Some do, but such precocious behavior is often a sign of pathology, not normal developmental progression, indicating a lack of impulse control and occurring before psychological separation from parents has taken place. As at all other stages in the life cycle, the tortoise who covers every inch of developmental ground is more likely to win the race for fulfillment than the hare who leapfrogs obstacle after obstacle without ever learning what they were about.

"I'm in Love." In order to appreciate fully the adolescent sexual transformation we must consider a second, quite familiar component. Sometime during the wonder years of midadolescence most people are lucky enough to enjoy one of life's memorable experiences. When one's affections are reciprocated, the occasion immortalized in song and verse is called falling in love. From a more objective standpoint a better term is adolescent infatuation. Infatuation implies an overwhelming preoccupation with a creature of total perfection who is possessed mentally and sometimes physically as well. All other interests and activities fade into the background. Time is measured by the endless intervals until he or she reappears. Cutting through the rhapsodic illusions to reveal the developmental purposes of adolescent infatuation requires substituting reason for feeling, shining sunlight on images intended to be remembered by moonlight.

A necessary prerequisite to, but quite different from, mature adult love, infatuation furthers developmental progression by temporarily transferring loving, sexually charged feelings for parents onto nonincestuous others. Briefly illuminated by the displaced love for the parents of childhood, the new loved one glows in the light of false perfection. Sooner or later the new relationship fails to provide the sustenance provided by the old and it collapses abruptly, with great pain and disillusionment. Bruised by the experience, licking their wounds, our young Romeos and Juliets retreat and, like the toddler, reconnect, if ever so briefly, with Mom and Dad. The more resilient adolescents stake a ride on this emotional roller coaster more than once, each time abandoning a bit more of the infantile ties to the parents and becoming more familiar with nonincestuous love.

By the end of adolescence the healthy individual has accepted the sexually mature body and loosened the infantile sexual ties to his or her parents. No longer preoccupied with function, the sexual adventurer then sets out to find partners, in the process sometimes trampling on the bodies and feelings of others in order to gain sexual experience. The rush for satisfaction and misinformation often results in inappropriate and dangerous sexual activity, particularly unprotected sex, which sometimes results in unplanned pregnancy, venereal disease, and AIDS. As cruel and insensitive as such behavior may be, sexual experience, with or without love, lays the foundation for the emergence in emotionally intact individuals of that wondrous human capacity, mature sexual intimacy, one of the crown jewels of young adult development.

Preparing to Work

Adolescence is the phase of development in which decisions are made about work and career which dramatically affect the quality of adult life. In a sense nature plays a cruel joke by forcing adolescents to make such vital decisions at a time in life when their most pressing interests are "broads, booze, and bopping around," as one sixteen-year-old expressed it.

Five-year-old Ben stopped his play and stood motionless, obviously deep in thought. After a pregnant silence he announced to his attentive parents, "When I grow up I'm going to be an astronaut (another pause) or maybe a garbage man." As he returned to his play, Ben's bemused parents smiled benignly at each other, knowing they didn't have to worry about that one for some time to come; actually only about 10 years. But when seventeen-year-old Jim sheepishly announced that he was getting three F's, two D's, and one C on his first-semester report card in his junior year despite a high I.Q., his parents were frustrated and dismayed. The realistic consequences were considerable if Jim continued to undermine their efforts, and his own, to achieve a grade point average which would get him into a good college.

Those fortunate individuals who had a solid developmental experience in the preadolescent years are usually able to temper the internal and external pressures for instant gratification with the need to prepare for the future. Those who screwed up royally in adolescence need not despair because second and third chances to scramble and succeed will be available in young adulthood when mentors and maturity point out pathways to fulfillment and career success.

The Cognitive Bridge to Adulthood

An increased ability to think abstractly molds, orders, and transforms the adolescent mind. As every parent and therapist knows from experience, adolescents develop the ability to critically assess and logically evaluate ideas—their own, and others. In late adolescence, in particular, freed of the shackles of childhood and not yet burdened by the realistic limitations and responsibilities of adulthood, the emotional fervor of youth and the cognitive abilities to abstract and criticize result in the idealism and determination to produce social change which are so characteristic of the age. Although young adult experience usually tempers these attitudes, it thankfully does not extinguish the optimism and activism begun in late adolescence, for these are beliefs and motivations which enhance and encourage social responsibility in the seventh stage.

CASE REPORT: The Treatment of a Severe Learning Disturbance in a Bright Adolescent Boy[7]

In 1901, Freud described similarities between the formation of neurotic symptoms and errors in speaking and writing. Considerably later, he described how thoughts and feelings may inhibit various mental functions. In the adult such restrictions and inhibitions frequently diminish the capacity to work; in the child they may primarily diminish the capacity to learn (the child's work).

During the psychoanalysis of a very intelligent adolescent boy, I was able to study the reasons why this young man was unable to excel academically. The following case report illustrates how he and I worked together to overcome the obstacles to his learning and return him to the path leading to academic success and emotional fulfillment.

History

The second oldest of five children, Bob was referred for treatment when he was thirteen years old because of continuous academic failure and a lack of drive and confidence. His father described him as "without hope," while his mother feared he would never be able to compete successfully with his active father and siblings. Bob was bitter. He considered himself a failure at school, isolated from his peers, and in need of help.

Bob had enjoyed elementary school, but had done little academically despite persistent pressure from his parents to achieve. "I was intolerant of his mistakes and impatient with him," said his father. "I would reduce him to tears." His mother had worried about Bob from the time of his birth. When Bob was in the first grade, she realized that she had identified him with her mentally retarded, brain-damaged brother. During Bob's preschool years his mother had apprehensively pushed him to learn. Then during his first years in school she had spent hours hovering over him, insisting that he practice his reading and writing. Her anxiety was such that during the first grade Bob was "patterned." This questionable procedure consisted of various body exercises and the use of multicolored eye pieces and patches which were intended to correct a theorized organic imbalance in the central nervous system. As the years passed, Bob became known as a poor student who put forth little effort.

Despite his barely passing grades, psychological testing revealed a verbal IQ of 124, a performance IQ of 133, and a full-scale IQ of 131 (100 is average). No organic or perceptual evidence for the learning difficulties was found. The tests revealed a sense of helplessness and defeat. Bob feared that successful behavior would result in retaliation from his father whom he saw as powerful and successful beyond what he could ever hope to achieve. He saw himself as helpless and at the mercy of forces beyond his control.

Bob's early development was uneventful. He was wanted and loved. His mother was actively and lovingly involved in his care, both nurturing and structuring developmental tasks like weaning and toilet training. During latency and adolescence, Bob tried to accomplish on the athletic field what he could not achieve in the classroom. His family regarded sports highly and competition was strongly encouraged. But here, too, Bob's problems with aggression interfered and he was more often than not the loser. His friends were much like himself—boys who did poorly academically and were on the fringes of the peer group. By the time he reached adolescence, Bob was a thoroughly crushed, frustrated young man who stood out like a sore thumb in a family of successful people.

Bob's father was an impressive, powerful man who was outstanding in business and constantly on the go athletically. He played a very active part at Bob's private school, and was often competitive with Bob and his other sons. Bob's mother was a stately, sensitive woman with considerable insight into his problems. As a child she was very close to her retarded brother whom she often cared for—thus the identification with him. After college she worked for a time in a mental institution where another close male relative was a patient. These experiences were funneled into her relationship with Bob.

The Analysis

Vignettes of the major themes that arose in the psychoanalysis of Bob's learning inhibition are contained in the following subsections, essentially in the order in which they emerged: (1) identification with a defective uncle; (2) learning as an expression of conflict with the father; (3) learning as homosexual submission; (4) avoidance of learning; and (5) refusal to learn as a means of punishing the parents.

Identification with a Defective Uncle. After visiting his maternal grandmother's home, Bob described how grandmother ruled the family. Bill, his mother's defective brother, lived there. He was "crazy about football." Bob talked of Bill's difficulty in holding a job. I asked what the problem was and Bob immediately began talking of Bill's "prematurity." He was "possibly brain-damaged, and he didn't get the training he needed when he was young." When I asked what his reaction had been when he found out about his uncle, Bob replied with pain and anxiety. "I wasn't astonished, just surprised. My mother told me a few months ago."

Dr. C.: It's tough to come to see your family the way they are with their strengths and weaknesses, but it would be even harder to continue to see things the way you did when you were little.

Bob: Yeah, it is tough, but maybe that's what happened to Bill. He never changed.

A week later, Bob talked of Bill's children, who, he said, were "bright as whips."

> Dr. C.: Were you surprised that they were smart?
> Bob: No, my mother explained that Bill's problem was from prematurity, not inherited. I guess he inherited the ability to be smart.
> Dr. C.: Did you wonder about this with your mother?

After commenting that he had wondered, but always knew that his mother was smart, Bob began to rattle off the things he had inherited: tallness, blue eyes, light skin, long fingers.

> Dr. C.: You mentioned everything but your IQ.
> Bob: I hadn't thought of it. I think it's high, about 125. What's average?
> Dr. C.: About 100. In a way, knowing your IQ must have relieved one potential worry but confronted you with another.

Warming to the analytic process, Bob asked if he could guess.

> Bob: It relieved the worry that I might have a low IQ and need special help.
> Dr. C.: Right, I meant that you might have worried that . . .

Bob interrupted and completed the sentence, ". . . that I was like Bill." He smiled, seeming to have a dawning realization that his ability to analyze was proof that he was not like Bill.

Several sessions later Bob felt we were making progress because he was reading twice as much as he had in the past. He had not read much before because of his reading problem. He then told me what he remembered of the patterning experiences when he was in the first grade, particularly the placement of a green glass on one eye to help him read.

Dr. C.: What did you think of that at the time?
Bob: Just that I needed it to read.
Dr. C.: I think you know enough about how the mind works to know that it must have stirred up a lot of thoughts in little Bob's mind.
Bob: You mean like he was defective or had crazy eyes or something like that? Or that I had an IQ like Bill's. . . . That patterning place had the thickest walls I've seen lately.
Dr. C.: What do you think brought that to mind now?
Bob: (*smiling knowingly*) To keep crazy people in?
Dr. C.: I think you can see how scared you must have been that something was wrong with you.

Five days later, after a discussion centered around his fear of injury from sports and worry about being "damaged," Bob asked, with considerable apprehension, if anything were physically wrong with him.

Dr. C.: As far as I know there is nothing that would cause you to have problems in learning, reading, or any other area. You certainly are not damaged or defective like Bill.

Bob sighed with relief, sat quietly for a moment, and then in a tone of voice that said, "Now I understand," commented, "I do remember my mother getting nervous about me when I was little and angrier and angrier when I would not read, but I never understood why. Now I do."

Learning as an Expression of Conflict with Father. Having dealt with his feelings of defectiveness, Bob began to talk increasingly of wanting to do well in school, but he was afraid. What if he tried and still failed? Over a year had passed since the hours described in the previous section, and much of the naïve, little-boy quality had disappeared. His study habits and performance in school improved slightly but were still borderline. Then some real improvement began to occur in a math course. Bob earned a 95 on a math test. He was very pleased and not as interested as he had been in knowing what the other class members got on the test; he was satisfied with his own mark and it did not matter.

His next association was to a problem with another course. He had been assigned a book to read for a test but had not read it even though the test had been postponed for a week.

Dr. C.: What are your thoughts about why you don't seem able to read it?

Bob: Well, it was assigned before Christmas, and I hadn't decided to try then. So I let it slide. (*He smiled.*) That would be an easy way out, wouldn't it?

Bob was beginning to be able to laugh at himself. Becoming more serious, he added:

Bob: Doing well in math is enough. If I do well in everything, I'll be open to attack.

Dr. C.: What kind of attack?

With intense, controlled feeling he told of his anger at the five or six boys in his class who were the "brains." They were always elected president of the class or to the student council. He resented them very much. I reacted to his comment as follows: "Are you saying that if you were on top and people were as angry at you as you are at these guys, it would be pretty scary?" The interpretation allowed two fantasies into his consciousness. Bob said, "I can picture myself on a big pedestal. The guys are all around throwing tomatoes at me. I'm smiling. I'm not hurt." The second fantasy involved making a speech after becoming valedictorian of the class. In his speech, Bob tongue-lashed his teachers for not helping him when he needed it. He pounded the lectern with his fist and shouted that his improvement was his own. No one deserved credit for his success, including his parents and me.

The next day, Bob described "failing" as his way of attacking, controlling, and rendering his teachers impotent. He said, "You have more power over teachers when you get bad grades. With good grades they can enjoy your doing well." A week later, this theme was dealt with again. The following remark was made with the most determination he had ever manifested:

> Bob: I don't want my teachers to get *any* credit for my improvement. I don't want anybody to think that they helped. I want to remain hostile.
>
> Dr. C.: I'm sure that I'm included in that everybody along with your teachers. Likely your parents are too. If you weren't in analysis, no one could get the impression that I had anything to do with your improvement either.

Agreeing heartily, Bob felt the list should also include the doctors and tutors who got credit for working with him when he was a child. He could not imagine a little child getting credit for learning.

> Dr. C.: Let's look at the reality. Of course, if a first-grader reads well, he gets the credit. Sure the teacher helps him, but she can't read for him. The same is true in twelfth grade or analysis or if you become a lawyer, doctor, or Indian chief in later life. But this isn't the idea contained in your fantasies. There it's you or the teachers, you or me, you or your parents, a battle.

BOB: (*pausing for a moment*) I could never imagine myself in a room full of microphones and people and having to say "I owe it all to my father." I could never say that.

Bob was not able to sustain his academic improvement. His B average in math became a D by the next grading period. The conflict was still too strong to allow the success to continue without the expectation of retaliation. Much more work needed to be done on the themes of attacking the father-teacher and depriving him of his potency—the ability to teach.

Learning as Homosexual Submission. Early in the analysis Bob made occasional veiled references to homosexual material. He mentioned that his friends had told him of being picked up by two "queers," and that one of his teachers in grammar school was supposedly homosexual. These and several other statements were made almost in passing; it was clear that he was not ready to deal with this material in depth. In fact, additional thoughts were withheld for almost two years and, before he approached the subject, he dealt extensively with conflicts over heterosexuality.

As Bob's conflicts over heterosexuality were analyzed, he began tentatively to reach out to a girl who had shown interest in him, and, in the second year of his analysis, he began to date her. Their relationship progressed slowly but steadily both emotionally and sexually. Within six months the sexual play had reached the point of mutual masturbation and intercourse was contemplated. Bob's confidence in himself grew by leaps and bounds. He became less hostile toward teachers and was then able to approach the homosexual material.

During elementary school Bob had a teacher who

brought up sexual topics and on occasion showed his students explicit pictures of nudity and intercourse. He saw to it that Bob and a friend "won" a contest and got to go on a trip with him. All three stayed in the same room, and it appeared that the teacher seduced Bob's friend while Bob slept on a cot next to a double bed occupied by friend and teacher. In retrospect, Bob felt that the teacher was more interested in his friend and engineered things so that the friend would end up in the double bed with him. (Obviously, heterosexual teachers, both male and female, also seduce students.)

During one hour Bob complained of being disorganized, particularly in school, where he had lost an important notebook—it was the third thing he had lost recently. As he talked of various ways of organizing himself, he mentioned the possibility of carrying a briefcase but immediately rejected the idea. When I asked why he rejected the idea so strongly, he replied that in junior high it would mean that he was a "fag"—he would stand out—"It would be like walking around with a ribbon on your penis." Later in the hour he began talking of *mowing*—a term he and his friends had used to refer to what happened with the homosexual teacher.

In the next hour Bob related more details about the trip with the teacher. He admitted that he was curious about homosexuals, and the connection between homosexuality and learning was also connected to our relationship. Very early in the analysis I had entered the office to find Bob reading a book by Freud from the Great Books of the Western World series. He was very embarrassed and quickly returned the book to the shelf. The reason for his overreaction did not become clear until two and one-half years later. Then we were able to determine that Bob had been concerned that I might be trying to seduce him while masquerading as a helper, like the teacher who had used the trip as a ruse for seduction. His embarrassment over being "caught" reading the only "psychiatric book" on the shelf was explained by his unconscious wish to be involved in my suspected seduction. If I were a psychiatrist, why was it that only one of my books was on psychiatry? I, like all teachers, academic or medical, was suspect—likely to seduce him and thus stimulate his homosexual wishes.

A few days later Bob's intense curiosity about the seduction and the desire to be in his friend's place were analyzed. This interpretation helped him accept his unconscious wish to be the one being seduced and the intrusion of these thoughts and feelings into the learning experience with all teachers. When Bob felt he was slipping again in school, he related the drop in grades to our work on homosexuality, particularly the incident with the teacher. Bob struggled to recall what his friend had told him about what the teacher had done to him.

> BOB: Anyway, I was asleep and in a different room.
>
> DR. C.: In a different room? That's not what you reported before. You said that the cot and the double bed were in the same room.

Bob was shocked at first and denied he had said that. He was sure that the beds were in different rooms and recalled that he wanted to sleep in the double bed because "it was the thing to do," but he could not have said they were in the same room. I interpreted the distortion of memory and his matter-of-fact statement that sleeping in the same bed was "the thing to do" as ways of not seeing that (1) he was likely in the same room and very curious about what was going on in the double bed, and (2) he wanted to be in the double bed and was jealous because his friend was chosen instead of him.

Once the idea of Bob's involvement in the homosexual experience had been analyzed and it was clearly established that he had unconsciously identified with his friend, he was able to understand that his readiness to fight with teachers was a way of defending against his wishes to submit to them. Learning would be proof that he wanted to submit and was homosexual. From the time it occurred until its analysis, that incident colored all his relationships with teachers. Learning was equated unconsciously with giving in, submitting to seduction, something secretly desired but unacceptable. On a behavioral level, the entire conflict was handled reactively by quarreling, fighting, being a "wise guy" at every turn. Activity and hostile feelings were used to ward off passivity and homosexual feelings.

Bob was now beginning his senior year in high school. For the first time in his life he was able to concentrate and spend long hours studying. He stopped being belligerent and began to be thought of as a good student. By the end of the fall term, he had achieved a solid B average and made the honor roll for the first time in his life.

Avoidance of Learning. As Bob's grades continued to improve during his senior year, the question of applying to college arose. For the first time he felt that he could "make it" in college, but his record was so bad that getting into a "good" college was doubtful without his father's influence. The following hour depicts his struggle to get accepted at a college on his own, the manner in which being taken care of by his father undercut his self-confidence and sexual capacity, and the analysis of his passive identification with his father.

College admission tests were coming up. Bob wanted to do well and thought he could, but he was worried about the effect of his poor record. He had been telling a friend about his dilemma and of the "pull" his father had. The friend remarked that she would have to get into college on her own and that she would not feel right if she used "pull." Bob was upset by her statement. He was able to assess his dilemma realistically.

> Bob: I know now that I can make it studywise in college, but my grades are so lousy I may need pull to get in.
>
> Dr. C.: I think the key question is, what does using pull mean to you?
>
> Bob: Like being a little chick, like being a baby, not a man.
>
> Dr. C.: It sounds like the feelings are ones of being passive, taken care of. This is a good example of what I was trying to convey the other day, that you see your dad as blocking your ability to be successful sexually and intellectually. Here you are saying that he makes you feel like a baby, passive, like a little boy, that you have feelings of being weak, of not being a man.
>
> Bob: I just had a funny thought. Last year at the end of the year one of the seniors wrote in my yearbook, "To Ted D's son." Why didn't he write "To Bob D"?

We went on to conclude that the other student was insulting him, saying he was not his own person but someone who lived in his father's shadow. Bob had had this impression before, that many other students resented him. He knew some of the teachers did.

> Dr. C.: Could this guy have been saying that he felt you used your relationship with your father, his power and position, as a way of controlling him instead of treating him like an equal? Maybe that's what some of the teachers sensed too. They knew that you were in a position to hurt them if you went home and told

your father stories about them. Earlier in the hour you sounded just like the senior when you talked about your anger at your father for controlling your life. Maybe, without realizing it, you were doing the same thing in school, using his big stick, his power, as a club against others.

Bob was sad and dismayed after the interpretation. He commented that it probably was true, but he was not doing it so much anymore. Then he told of an incident in an earlier grade when he had been acting up in class and the teacher slapped him on the head. He had mentioned it at home and the next year the teacher was not rehired. Although Bob did not know if he was the cause of the dismissal, he felt responsible.

In the middle of his senior year, Bob desperately wanted to make the honor roll, a goal he had not approached before. When he succeeded, he was elated. He finally believed that he was not defective and that he could aspire to college and graduate school. Bob's neurosis and consistent academic failure had made it impossible for him to deal with this major psychological task of adolescence, choosing a career (which usually begins earlier in the healthy adolescent); but now he attacked it with a vengeance. After announcing his good news at the beginning of the hour, Bob launched into a series of questions about medicine, psychiatry, and law. How many years did each take? How many hours did you have to study? What courses did you need to get into medical school?

DR. C.: Bob, I think we've spent the time today on questions about college and graduate school because making the honor roll has finally made you realize that you are not defective, that you do have the capacity to make it. It's like saying, now I can really plan my future.

Bob: (*smiling in agreement*) Even though father wants me to work for him after graduation from college, I don't want to. I don't know what I will do, but it will be something on my own.

Dr. C.: You're saying you no longer have to rely on your father's power; you can make it on your own.

Failure to Learn as a Means of Punishing the Parents. The night after he made the honor roll, Bob had a dream. The next day, while talking to his mother, he thought, "I've cleared up what you sent me to analysis for [poor grades], why do I have to continue?" Bob speculated that his dream of the previous night might have had something to do with this thought. In the dream, Bob and Ted, a casual friend and classmate, were in a courtyard doing a puzzle. Ted was ready to leave and Bob asked him to stay and help with the puzzle but Ted refused. Associations were as follows:

Bob: There was a Truman Capote special on TV last night. He was interviewing some guys in prison. One of them was named Ted Something; I think he was involved in the murder of Sharon Tate. I didn't like him at all. I was sort of scared. The other two guys had both murdered their mothers. Sharon Tate was pregnant when she was murdered, so Ted Something had also murdered a mother. One guy blamed his mother for making him a homosexual. She had been a prostitute and one of his sisters was a lesbian. I think there was a courtyard there. I think that's where Capote interviewed those prison guys.

Dr. C.: You've spoken in the past of courtyards at your old house and at the place where you were patterned.

Bob: Yeah, I did. That seems to fit.

Dr. C.: I think a central idea in the dream is rage at your mother. Two of the guys killed their mothers and the third killed a pregnant woman. Because your dream occurred on the night that you found out that you made the honor roll, and considering your remarks about wondering why you should come to analysis anymore, I suspect your rage is directed at your mother because you see her as responsible for eleven years of frustration in school. You see her as the cause of your problems.

Bob: She did say one time that she had done it.

In his dream, Bob chose his classmate Ted, who was only a casual friend, because he had the same first name as Bob's father, and the murderer in the television program. The anger at father for not helping him, as the classmate in the dream had not, was thus neatly disguised. The dream also contained the punishment for the wish. The prison courtyard where the men were being punished for their crimes represented the patterning institute where Bob had been sent because he failed to learn. In all likelihood, this dream could not have occurred earlier in the analysis. Bob was only able to express conscious rage toward his mother and father after proving to himself that retaliation was not possible, that he could not be made defective.

In subsequent hours, Bob was able to put his feelings toward his parents in better perspective. The idea of learning for his parents, or failing academically to spite them, was gradually replaced with the desire to learn for himself, for his own benefit.

Discussion

The severity and chronicity of Bob's borderline performance throughout eleven years of school, and his mother's need to see him as defective and thus perpetuate a clinging, dependent relationship similar to the one she had with her brother, pointed toward a pervasive learning disorder. However, a close, retrospective study of the mother–child relationship during Bob's first three years of life revealed that a warm, supportive interaction existed in all areas except those related to learning. He had mastered the tasks of the oral and anal stages such as weaning and toilet training.

Because learning was so important in the family, it became the focus for the Oedipal relationship between Bob and his parents. Through the interactions surrounding learning, it was possible for Bob to engage and maintain his mother in a close, seductive relationship and to exclude his father and render him relatively impotent by refusing to learn.

At the beginning of the analysis, Bob felt hopeless and defeated; he had given up academically. Aggression had been severely restricted and inhibited, and a strong sense of defectiveness had become a dominant feature of his developing character. By analyzing this sense of defectiveness as identification with his defective uncle, Bob was able to express some competitiveness and aggression, initially displaced toward peers and eventually directed toward the original objects, his father and mother.

But before academic achievement could occur, extensive analytic work had to occur on the passive stance which Bob had adopted. Passivity had become a major component of his personality, and, without analysis, it would have become the most prominent aspect of his character structure.

The unconscious equation of learning with the wish for passive homosexual experience was the most superficial layer of his passive longings. Bob's response to the attempted seduction by the teacher was vivid confirmation of the unconscious connection between learning and passivity and femininity that had been established during the early years of his development.

In the course of normal Oedipal development, a boy is an ardent but fearful admirer of his father's power. This passive admiration is normally transformed through identification to a masculine identity for himself. Bob did not take the second step in the process of masculine identification, which usually occurs during the Oedipal and latency periods, until his analysis. He had remained the ardent but fearful admirer of his father's power and sexuality. Bob unconsciously used his father's position for sadistic control and manipulation of students and teachers. That was one of the few avenues open to him for the expression of aggression. If his conflicts had been unresolved, particularly through adolescence when sexual identification is determined in a more definitive way, Bob might have established a pattern in adulthood of living through another man's position or power.

Underachievers characteristically attack their parents and society indirectly through their failure to achieve. For Bob, whose parents were conspicuously involved in the affairs of his school, it was a particularly effective vehicle. Through the courtyard dream, symbolic of the incestuous ties to mother and murderous rage toward both mother and father, it became possible to analyze Bob's anger at his parents and to help him abandon the infantile position in relation to them. Now he was free to use his considerable intellect to grow and achieve, to speed down the path to adult fulfillment.

5

It All Begins with the Body

The Body in Childhood

"What a beautiful baby!" "Oohs" and "Ahs" from family and friends (even when they don't mean it) warm the cockles of parents' hearts and increase their love for this new physical extension of themselves, and for their own bodies as well, which have produced this amazing new life. By the time the elementary school years roll around, physical beauty and capability have become major means of boosting self-esteem and social standing in the increasingly critical peer group. Then in adolescence, as the body transforms itself almost overnight, self-esteem is puffed up or ravaged by broad shoulders, big breasts, an unexpected pimple on the tip of the nose, or Ichabod Crane gangliness.

Attitudes about the body in childhood and adolescence are dominated by the wish to be bigger, stronger, and better. The future contains deeply desired rewards. The ten-year-old ballerina hopes to dance with greater grace and ease.

The ninth-grade junior varsity quarterback dreams of throwing a fifty-yard touchdown pass. Adolescents long to "make it" with the homecoming queen or varsity letterman, performing on cue to perfection.

Then comes young adulthood—ah, there's the rub. Although there is no interval between the end of growth and the beginning of aging, the two forces overlap during young adulthood. Gradually the aging process replaces the growth process as the dominant biological influence as the twenties fade into the thirties. Slightly sagging skin, a retreating hair line, a bit of cellulite, and the loss of a step on the tennis court are the unwelcome heralds of aging. Women have the added reminder of the incessant ticking of the biological clock. By the end of the fourth decade the tight taken-for-granted body of youth is nothing but a dim memory, searched for expectantly in every mirror.

Accepting and Enjoying the Adult Body

Accepting—and enjoying—the midlife body may appear to be a ridiculous idea, particularly since turning forty is sometimes equated with crossing the River Styx. Such gloomy thoughts are not without a basis in reality since the signs of aging are obvious in the forties and fifties. So where's the enjoyment? As always, it is the end product of facing the developmental tasks of life squarely and honestly.

Part of the searing appraisal of all aspects of life which is at the center of fulfillment in adulthood is the ability to acknowledge and accept the realities of the aging body.

As Marcia Goin expressed it in *New Dimensions in Adult Development*:

> The appearance of one's body in midlife takes on a different significance. Efforts to remain thin and fit are not made to

> develop a sense of identity or to separate and individuate, but to maintain health and youthfulness and to deter the effects of aging. The struggle is to retain body integrity in the face of anxieties about aging, the vulnerabilities of failing health, and the potential loss of independence.(1)

Both males and females must engage the developmental task of mourning for the lost body of youth, continually idealized in *Playboy,* on the cover of *Vogue,* and in movies and MTV. This occurs through a continuous, often unconscious, process of body monitoring in which the midlife body is compared with the body of adolescence and young adulthood. Absentmindedly skipping to the next hole on the belt buckle, agreeing with the salesperson that "You're about a size 10, right?", buying jeans with a "scotch" more room in the seam, or avoiding the bathroom mirror and scale all produce painful pinpricks, drops of cold rain hitting the warm, slightly wrinkled skin.

This struggle between wishes to deny the aging process or accept the loss of a youthful body drive some in their thirties and forties to clamor for sex with younger bodies and others to push themselves beyond their physical limits. Soon after a hysterectomy Mrs. L left her husband and teenaged children in search of "gorgeous young men in their twenties." As long as they want me, she deluded herself, "I'll know I'm still attractive." Mr. B became depressed after dropping out of a 6K race for which he had not trained, with a knee injury. "Hell," he moaned, "I used to be able to run that far in my sleep." Others acquire possessions, art, automobiles, and artifacts, which become narcissistically gratifying substitutes for the body. "See, old is good," said a collector, admiring his miniature Roman bronze.

Healthy individuals accept the aging process in the body and care for it though regular checkups, exercise, and a balanced diet. Their fulfillment is greatly enhanced by the enjoyment of a body that is full of vigor, vitality, and stamina—a source of ongoing pride and pleasure for a lot less money that a tummy tuck or a painting by Tomayo.

Menopausal Release

The response to the dramatic biological changes of middle age varies enormously from individual to individual, as evidenced by the myriad "symptoms" which are supposedly related to the menopause. "I'm a nervous wreck, I'm going through the change of life." "Stay away from me, this is the time of the month when I would have had my period." "I've had so many upset stomachs since I started menopause." "John, open the window, I'm having a hot flash." As surprising as it may seem, only the hot flash and cessation of menstruation are directly related to the decreased production of hormones which cause the menopause. Further, such symptoms may actually *decrease* with age. After conducting a survey of the literature, Carl Eisdorfer and Robert Raskind noted:

> Surprisingly, the common "menopausal" symptoms such as irritability, nervousness, depression, insomnia, and crying spells were reported with a frequency *equal to or lower* by the menopausal group than by the other group examined. The postmenopausal group (age 55 to 64), presumably with the lowest estrogen production levels, reported the lowest incidence of tired feelings, headaches, dizzy spells, irritability and nervousness, depression, crying spells, and difficulty concentrating.(2)

More important for our focus on fulfillment in adulthood, most women respond to this biological revolution with feelings of relief and rejuvenated sexual interest—"pleasure without pregnancy," as one woman put it, not depression and somatic preoccupation. Freed from the demands of reproduction, women are able to reclaim their bodies for themselves and enjoy the considerable pleasures the midlife body can provide.

Men do not experience a dramatic drop in hormone production in midlife and do not lose the ability to procreate. Those with sexual problems may develop menopausal-like symptoms to cloud the real causes of their dysfunction. However, all men do experience a gradual decrease in hormone production as they age. The resulting changes in the strength and frequency of erections can result in a menopausal-like preoccupation with performance which bruises the male ego far out of proportion to actual biological change.

You Mean Mom? And Grandma, Too?

Sex? not *my* mother, and certainly not after menopause. In the minds of many younger individuals, postmenopausal women should be asexual; it's the only dignified thing to do. Yet when the facts are known, mid- and late adulthood can be years of great sexual fulfillment.

First the physiology: Diminished estrogen production leads to thinning of the vaginal wall; decreased length, width, and elasticity; and less lubrication. The result may be pain during intercourse. Fortunately all of these changes can be minimized or reversed with the use of lubricants and estrogen replacement.

Attitudes are harder to change. When Mom and Grandma *allow* themselves to be sexual, often in the face of downright righteous indignation from their children, the fifties and beyond can be years of worry-free sexual enjoyment—*if* they are fortunate enough to have, or find, a sexual partner.

To quote Masters and Johnson:

> Thus the simple fact remains that if opportunity for regularity of coital exposure is created or maintained, the elderly woman suffering from all of the vaginal stigmas of sex-steroid starvation still will retain a far higher capacity for sexual performance than her female counterpart who does not have similar coital opportunities. Thus, in addition to its psychological benefits regular intercourse also counteracts and retards the "vaginal stigma of sex-steroid starvation."(3)

Coping with the "Big I"

Women worry about losing their beauty, men about losing their erections, impotence, the "Big I" as one forty-five-year-old called it. As with many other debilitating myths about the middle years, this one can be assigned to the junk pile. Consider these reassuring words of Masters and Johnson about the functioning of the middle-aged penis.

> These fears were expressed, under interrogation, by every male subject beyond forty years of age, irrespective of reported levels of formal education. Regardless of whether the individual male study subject had ever experienced an instance of erectile difficulty, the probability that . . . impotence was associated directly with the aging process was vocalized constantly. The fallacy that . . . impotence is to be expected as the male ages is probably more firmly entrenched in our culture than any other misapprehension.(4)

So sexual fulfillment in midlife is to be expected—if one understands, and accepts, the aging process in the body. Like everything else there is a time and a place for the explosive sexuality of youth and the more moderate sexual intensity of middle age. Both are there for the taking. Developmental understanding enhances the enjoyment of both.

The Other "Big I"—Intelligence—More Good News!

Many people are under the impression that it's not just the body that loses capability in adulthood. So does the brain. Fulfillment in adulthood—hardly, if you're over the hill sexually *and* intellectually by thirty! For years this was the prevailing idea; you peak early, then lose it. Wechsler, the man who devised the most widely used intelligence test, received two ears and a tail for killing the bull of midlife vitality with a single thrust.

> The data show that intellectual ability after reaching a maximum at 20 to 25 does not continue unaltered for any length of time but starts trailing off immediately thereafter. *Beginning at age 30, the rate of decline maintains almost a constant slope. Intellectual decline follows the same general decline as does physical ability.*(5)

Fortunately, Wechsler was wrong! Longitudinal studies of intelligence conducted over the span of a half-century have replaced this pessimistic portrait of intellectual capability in midlife with another of simple elegance. "If illness does not intervene, cognitive stability is the rule and can be maintained into the ninth decade."(6) In fact, the total IQ may actually increase with age if the following prescription for adult intellectual fulfillment is followed. Maintain good physical health and sustain a high level of mental activity. Take on the challenges of the present and the future with curiosity and determination. You really are smart enough for computers, camcorders, cellular phones, and the as-of-yet-unanticipated wonders of the twenty-first century. In short, use it or lose it.

6

Creating New Life

Becoming a Parent

Picture two nine-year-old girls twirling a jump rope together. A third girl deftly leaps into the space vacated by the revolving cord and dodges it effortlessly as it skips by. The harmonious synchronization of bodies is amplified by the repetition of a simple, rap-like verse: "First comes love, then comes marriage, then comes Jean with a baby carriage." Although the girls pay little attention to the meaning of their words, they are internalizing a culturally dictated plan for their futures. Love. Marriage. Parenthood. Create the next generation and nurture it within the loving confines of the family. In the process provide not only for the propagation of the species and the continuation of your particular culture, but for yourself, the parent, in the most unimaginable ways. Here we will explore adult fulfillment through the experience of parenthood.

The Third Individuation

> The continuous elaboration of the self and differentiation from others which occurs in young and middle adulthood. At its core are children, spouse, and parents; the family, the same psychological constellation which shaped the First and Second Individuations.
>
> CALVIN COLARUSSO, 1990(1)

The first individuation, the gradual psychological separation from parents in infancy, was a rather exclusive affair between infant and parent. The second individuation, which resulted in psychological separation from the parents, occurred as the adolescent burst out of the confines of the nuclear family to love and be loved by others. The transition between the second and third individuation is both exciting and anxiety-ridden. No longer uncertain of the boundaries between self and other, no longer emotionally dependent on parents, the emerging young adult is alone, sheared of childhood attachments to parents but not yet involved with the same degree of intensity or depth with adult replacements. As first this sense of freedom is joyous, liberating, each experience brimming over with the potential for novelty, adventure and pleasure. Consider the mind set of a twenty-one-year-old college student. Having just completed final exams, he and a friend are about to set out, like Lewis and Clark, to explore virgin territory. "I don't know where we're going. I don't know when we'll be back and I don't really care. It's all new to me and I've never met the girls who live out there." Enjoy the moment young man (or woman), the exhilaration, the freedom, the new you. For it is but a moment, a blink of the eye, before inexplicably adventures lose their novelty. They even become tinged with loneliness and an inexplicable desire for sustained closeness. As the twenties tick away, this growing *loneliness of young adulthood* drives most individuals to fill the intrapsychic void with relationships that plumb the depths of their being and reconnect them with the sense of total belonging they had experienced in the past.

And so the stage is set for the third individuation. "I'm ready," said twenty-eight-year-old Carol. "First I had to find out if I could take care of myself. I can and I still enjoy looking at the hunks. That's fun, but I want more—a husband, a home, kids, permanence. Oh, my God, I must be getting old. I sound just like my parents."

Parenthood and the Third Individuation

Father's seed and mother's egg incubate inside the womb to produce the new life which is their genetic extension. A decade or more in the future the preprogrammed experience of puberty will make it possible for the adolescent to repeat the cycle. Then, during young adulthood, men and women will use their prime-of-life bodies to create new life, assume the parental role, and nurture the next generation.

Parenthood leads to fulfillment in adulthood, not only by confirming one's sexuality and creating a new person to love, but also by providing a relationship within which the parent's infantile past and adult present can be related and merged into a highly pleasurable sense of integrity. For example, by becoming involved parents, adults attempt to replicate the extremely gratifying childhood experience of nurturance, just as their parents had nurtured them. As they succeed, the god-like power to create new life is more fully realized and appreciated, both in regard to their own child, and, in retrospect, to their parents who were responsible for creating and raising them. The fusion of these two experiences provides a deep, fulfilling understanding of one of the most basic and gratifying aspects of the human condition—interdependence.

Further, as newly crowned king and queen, benevolent rulers over a populace of one, young parents revel in the taste of total power over another human. Becoming royalty after a childhood of serfdom is a heady experience which facilitates the reworking of infantile feelings of passivity and submission. Then, just as the monarchs begin to settle in for a long reign, the active, increasingly presumptuous toddler begins to rebel, chipping away at parental power and prerogative.

For the parent, feelings of vulnerability are also experienced at the same time, because of the growing adult awareness of the inevitability of one's death. The jarring realization that death will become the ultimate separation—an insight which was totally absent during early childhood and adolescence—illustrates how adult experience adds new dimensions to personality development and strongly influences relationships in the present.

Really Becoming a Parent

The sequence of real and intrapsychic events leading to parenthood can be clearly seen from the lofty vantage point of adulthood. Studying the developmental line of sexuality through childhood and adolescence (Chapters 3 and 4), we noted the emergence of an ingrained sense of masculinity or femininity in infancy (the core gender identity) and later the discovery of the genital differences between the sexes. After exploring sexuality within relationships during the Oedipal phase, we considered the impact of family and culture on sexual development during latency. Following puberty, the body became a physically mature sexual instrument, capable of procreation (biological parenthood). Then in young adulthood the capacity for intimacy and acceptance of responsibility set the stage for the wondrous experience of psychological parenthood.

Childhood play often centers around the fantasy of becoming a parent. In adulthood that wish is turned into reality as couples become parents and confirm the integrity of the body as a procreative instrument. This is not a simple or conflict-free process. Indeed, it creates tension within the blossoming intimacy of the prospective parents.

The psychoanalyst Judith Kestenberg suggests that young men and women want to experience intimacy with their partner before becoming parents.(2) In part they long to recreate the loving relationship that they had with their own parents in childhood. Once the partners have become accustomed to the fact that they cannot be mother and father to each other, they continue the search for ideal closeness through parenthood. Together they take the next developmental step. By consenting to have a child, the man psychologically assumes the role of a masculine protector and sublimates his own infantile wish to emulate his mother and have a child. For him, the seed that perpetuates his father and himself is no longer wasted. For the prospective mother, her inner genitalia receive a confirmation and an enlargement of scope. The conception-coitus allows for a reworking of the adult superego by sanctioning the previously forbidden actions that led to pregnancy.

For both parents-to-be pregnancy adds a new, extremely gratifying dimension to sexual identity by confirming the integrity of their bodies. Both can reproduce, replicate themselves, continue for another generation the genetic link with near and distant ancestors. After birth each adoring glance at this new version of themselves enhances the sense of sexual completeness and stimulates the desire to nurture, together, this fragile new being who so quickly becomes an indispensable part of their lives.

Born Again! The Effect of Reliving Childhood through Parental Eyes: Pregnancy and Birth

"The plumbing's in good shape," said a young father-to-be upon learning that his wife was pregnant. His pride and satisfaction were expressions of the realization of sexual potential, the culmination of his manhood. The amazing ability to create life is gratifying in the extreme, for the mother-to-be as well. As the pregnancy proceeds and she begins to revel in the thumping of life inside her, she too experiences a transformation. Increasingly her thoughts and feelings are directed inward, toward the other, toward the self, toward the duality she has become. As father stands by, participating as best he can, he is flooded with a multitude of feelings—pride in his wife and himself, awe in the presence of the creation of life, and envy of the shadowy competitor for his wife's affections whose most threatening act is the occasional thrusting of arms and legs from behind an impenetrable abdominal shield. Slowly he comes to realize the limitations of his sex, and his power; and for the first time he truly values the potential of the female body.

When the new being breaks through the confines of the uterine world, bursting upon the scene, this product of the parents' union becomes tangible, palpable, and powerful, instantly shattering their dyadic existence forever. As friends and family admire their work a dramatic intrapsychic shift occurs. The new parent changes from sexually immature child to sexually mature adult, from independent adolescent and carefree adult to responsible parent. "You can have fun with a son but you gotta be a father to a girl," said Billy Bigelow in *Carousel* as he recognized his new role.

When a married couple become parents, a family is created whose structure is identical to that of the family of origin. The circle is complete, the infantile role reversed. The former children, now glorying in the roles of parenthood, minister to their creation. Meanwhile, their own parents, just outside the circle, watch, admire, and begin to revel in a most extraordinary, new form of love.

N., aged thirty-five, waited until her career was well established before having children. During "the B.C. years—before Carol"—professional travails and ambitions consumed her waking hours. During the course of our therapeutic relationship I watched in awe as her daughter became the dominant force in her real and intrapsychic worlds. "I can't believe how much I need her," N. said. "I go to work reluctantly and I miss her desperately by midmorning. My mother is worse than me. She calls every day and is talking about moving to California to be near Carol, not me, you understand. I'd like that, but I'm afraid I'll have to battle Mom to get my hands on the baby."

Parental Power

Parenthood is power!—domination and control over another who initially is relatively helpless, passive, and dependent, but who sometimes does not comply with parental needs and expectations. Stimulated by an intense sense of involvement with the child, the progenitors experience both loving and aggressive feelings. In healthy individuals the aggression is sublimated into consistent, tempered limits; in pathological circumstances the result is child abuse. In a similar fashion, loving feelings are expressed through nurturing care, or in unbridled form in sexual overstimulation or pedophilic behavior.

The magnetic pull of the child reactivates polarities in the parents from their own childhood: gratifying fusion and painful separation; raw power and controlled response. As these polarities are repeatedly thrust upon Mom and Dad by their increasingly independent offspring, they are reexperienced, reworked, even mastered by mental mechanisms infinitely more complex than those that existed when they were young. The recognition, understanding, and enjoyment of this mutual process of developmental stimulation and enhancement, parent to child, child to parent, is one of adult life's most intriguing, fulfilling experiences, a proven pathway to emotional health and maturity.

The Revolutionaries

Healthy toddlers are revolutionaries who attack their progenitors' power and prerogatives with impunity. For instance, the toddler's constant challenge to parental authority eventually erodes the control over the toddler's mind and body. The process, which continues throughout the offspring's childhood and adolescence, is concurrent with the parents' young and middle adult years. It serves to diminish feelings of omnipotence and domination and tempers grandiosity. This inescapable decline in authority and power prepares the parents for the painful adult developmental task of accepting the finiteness of life and the inevitability of personal death. The realization that all living things age and are replaced by the young, the essential core concept of adult maturity and wisdom, is, in part, an outgrowth of parental experience with the child's inevitable drive toward autonomy and competence which gradually reduces the need for parenting and eventually makes it entirely superfluous.

Parent to Parent—Parity at Last!

Parenthood transforms the real and intrapsychic relationships with one's own parents. The act of procreation not only confers parental authority but also entitles the new parent to the power which was once the exclusive province of the progenitor. Parity at last!

Further individuation occurs as constant comparisons are made between the way the new parents bring up their child and the manner in which they were raised. In my clinical experience I have been impressed by both the feelings of confidence and self-criticism which arise from such comparisons. "I'll never get divorced like they did," said a young father, still attempting to master the experience of growing up in a shattered family. "My mother did a much better job than I am," said a young professional woman. "She never lost her temper. I do all the time." On the other hand, such comparisons may reinforce the sense of connectedness and continuity between the generations as both define themselves in their new roles as parent and grandparent, particularly if the grandparents are actively involved in the lives of the younger generations.

Last, but not least, the new parents derive a sense of satisfaction from reciprocation for all their parents gave them. They give them the priceless gift of grandchildren. As the source of so great a treasure, the young adults gain status and prestige due to the realization that they have provided their parents with a genetic continuity which is vital to their late life development. This reversal of generational roles foreshadows the day in the future when the older generation may depend in part or completely on their children for sustenance.

Husband and Wife, Mother and Father—Increasingly Indivisible

They began as lovers, soulmates, best friends, husband, and wife. Now they have become parents, mother and father, caretakers of the young—the link between generations. As they work together, gradually over the years, their identities shift from lover to parent, their relationship cemented in this interlocking role in an increasingly indivisible way.

Thirty-one-year-old Mr. A entered therapy for work-related problems but it soon became apparent that he had significant difficulty with intimacy. He constantly belittled his wife and resisted her desire to have children because he wasn't sure he would remain in the marriage. As he worked on his conflicting feelings about his mother, his attitude toward his wife began to soften. Soon she was pregnant. As the pregnancy proceeded, Mr. A was amazed at the powerful feelings of protective tenderness toward his wife that repeatedly washed over him. When his daughter was born he was once again surprised by his admiration for his wife's ability to mother. "She's wonderful with the baby. These two are my whole life now. What would I do without them? Remember when I used to talk about leaving her? We're bound together forever now by that baby—and I love it." Would that this was the response of all fathers.

The Oedipus Revisited: The Sublimated Joys of Seduction

Long buried childhood wishes for access to and control of another's body, particularly the genitals, are reactivated in parents of small children by the necessary parental functions of diapering and bathing. More obvious infantile sexual wishes are gratified by the inappropriate actions of *repeatedly* taking Oedipal-aged children into bed, showering with them, exposing them to parental sexual interactions, or responding to their transparent attempts at sexual seduction.

A healthy new dimension is added to the parents' sexuality when these feelings are engaged and mastered. By graciously tolerating the seductiveness of an immature being who is a biological extension of themselves, and by refusing to respond in kind, parents facilitate their child's sexual development and gain additional mastery of their own similar infantile sexual wishes. The benign sense of pleasure which accompanies such awareness and control is reflective of the growing inner sense of integrity which results from the comfortable fusion of enhanced understanding of both infantile and adult sexual fantasies, wishes, and experiences.

As described in Chapter 3 on the Oedipal Complex, sex is only half of the picture. When Suzie banishes Mother to Siberia or Johnny hurls a Tonka toy at Dad's crotch, bemused contemplation is not the usual response. Parental anger is stimulated by the relentless onslaught of Oedipal competition. But most of the time the threat is empty, the aggressor a paper tiger who is all too easily reduced to tears by an insensitive parental response. Repeated competitive experiences with this beloved extension of one's maleness or femaleness diminish the life or death seriousness attached to

Mom and Dad's childhood memories from similar experiences with their parents and allow aggressive energies to be directed toward the present and the future rather than the past.

Sharing Ownership

The relationship to the spouse is also rattled a bit by involvement in this new version of the Oedipal triangle. Prior to the advent of children, the spouse was viewed somewhat narcissistically, acquired for the exclusive gratification of one's wants and desires. That illusion is partially shattered by the unmistakable love of the spouse for the infant and toddler. But at least he or she was *all* yours in bed. Wrong! During the child's Oedipal years exclusive sexual possession of the spouse, an Oedipal victory in itself which was just recently won, must be relinquished, shared with a rival of the same sex who cannot be sent packing, at least not any further than his or her own bedroom. The intensity of love for *both* spouse and child, and their involvement with each other to the exclusion of the self, precipitates a further reworking of feelings of abandonment and tempers the wish to be the primary recipient of love from significant others.

As Sharon and Bill discussed their five-year-old daughter with me, Sharon complained bitterly about Bill's behavior. "He comes home in the evening and makes a bee line for Jennifer. I don't get a glance, let alone a kiss. He acts like I'm invisible at the dinner table. She's no better. It was 'Mommy, Mommy' all day, but once he's home I'm about as important as her brother." Bill sheepishly rationalized that he got home late and only had an hour or two to spend with Jennifer before she went to bed. He would have time later in the evening for Sharon. "That's what you think," said the twice-rejected outsider.

Victory—At Last!

By unconsciously equating Wife and Mother or Husband with Father, Oedipal victory, only delayed by a mere twenty years or so, is possible. The thrill of victory is even sweeter when a child is produced, the ultimate proof of this "incestuous" union. Evidence of resolution or of continuing conflict with the original Oedipal competitors, one's parents, is often indicated by the attitude toward their role as grandparents. Unresolved Oedipal rivalries may be expressed through conflicts between the parents and grandparents over access to the child, so necessary to both.

Parents may limit the time that grandparents may spend with their grandchild. On the other hand, grandparents may attempt to assume control of childrearing, insensitively shunting the parents aside. For the young parent, facilitation of his or her parent's role as grandparent redefines their real relationship and insures that in this adult version of the Oedipal conflict neither must suffer the agony of defeat. Simultaneously meeting the needs of one's children and parents, with empathy and understanding, produces adult fulfillment of the richest kind.

Latency: Marching Away

Children light up their parent's lives during their babyhood and toddler years. Then, like a wave quietly receding after spectacularly smashing on the shore, children in the latency period begin to march away, out of the home, into a world full of new relationships, ideas, and excitement. As they do, parents experience the bittersweet loss of physical and psychological intimacy which they relished during the first five or six years of their child's life. No longer needed to regulate eating, dressing, or bowel and bladder control, they lose domination of and access to their child's body. Walled in by an increasingly powerful conscience, his or her mind no longer an open book, latency-aged Johnny and Suzie share fewer and fewer thoughts and feelings. Adding insult to injury this caricature of a self-sufficient adult prefers to spend increasing amounts of time away from home—at school, with peers, even with their friends' parents.

As these changes force the parents to separate from their little one psychologically, to accept the child's growing demand for control over his or her thoughts, actions, relationships, and time, parents mourn for the gratifications they had relished earlier in this intensely intimate relationship. Gradually the *parent* is shaped and molded, transformed by the coalescence of the two intense biopsychological fusions—with their parents as child in the past, and with their child as a parent in the present.

As this individuation proceeds, parents, particularly with a child of the same sex, continue to rework aspects of their own latency past. Victor reveled in his son's all-star status on his Little League team. Every cheer soothed his painful memories of an unsuccessful athletic past and allowed him to master aspects of this childhood trauma. The ability to separate the adult present from the childhood past and to prevent past experience from skewing the manner in which the present is perceived and lived is a critical component of the mature mind and a necessary ingredient of adult fulfillment. "I've finally come to terms with who I was as a kid," said Sally. "It wasn't all pretty and I wish a lot of it had been different. But my life is great now. I think about the differences between the past and the present every day." Obviously this process is more difficult—but even more necessary—when childhood was particularly painful and unhappy. Unless the dysfunctional childhood past is psychologically disconnected from the adult present, it will profoundly distort relationships and recreate that which is ardently trying to be avoided.

A disquieting young adult realization is that one is becoming *like* one's parent—"Did I really say that? My mom used to say that to me all the time!" This is heightened by the realization that both are now parents who have been loved—and left—by a young child. As they grow older together and ponder their diminishing future, the two older generations turn toward their offspring for solace, continuity, and hope.

Adolescence: Bursting Out of the Cocoon

Bursting out in all directions, physically mature adolescents demand increasing power and control over their lives. This sometimes rude awakening forces parents to mourn for the lost, malleable child and accept the presence of this physically and sexually mature "stranger" who is planning to replace them with another better able to gratify their mature sexual and emotional needs.

If this were not enough to contend with, now in their middle years, Mom and Dad are likely to be encountering signs of aging or decline in their own parents. Squeezed in the vice of adolescent maturation and parental aging or even death, the parent/child in midlife is transformed into a mature, autonomous adult, more separate and individuated from memories of young, middle-aged, and elderly parents, immature children, and their own youthful past.

Family Transformations

The inevitable march of their children through childhood and adolescence into young adulthood affects every aspect of parents' lives. The manner in which the once all powerful progenitors let go, work to achieve a new relationship with their children which is based on equality and mutuality, and eventually accept in-laws and grandchildren into their lives will make the difference between decades of fulfillment or of rancor and emptiness. The wise parents recognize their profound need for continued connectedness with their progeny and thus quietly, with dignity, work to achieve the following goals.

Letting Go

Youthful vigor and the unchallenged control over young children go hand in hand, but so do the middle-aged awareness of time limitation and physical decline and the inevitable loss of control over adolescent and young adult offspring. For many parents and children the gradual shift in the balance of power between them is symbolized by a single event, seared in memory, undoubtedly embellished over time. Robert Nemiroff and I have described it as "the moment of truth," that climactic instant in a bull fight when the matador kills the bull by plunging his sword between the bull's shoulder blades.(3) For parent and child the moment may be physical or psychological. Although neither acknowledges it in words, Father John and Son Tom both know when Tom "playfully" pins his father against the wall—and holds him there—that the moment has come. Sarah's parents know when she decides to live with her boyfriend despite their strong disapproval of premarital sex.

Each developmental transition brings with it the prospect of significant intrapsychic change, sometimes of seismic proportions, and a reordering of relationships. The cultural anthropologist David Guttman eloquently described the effect of the end of the "chronic emergency of parenthood" on fathers and mothers.(4)

Guttman's studies of older men and women in various cultures led him to conclude that masculine and feminine roles tend to blur as the last child is launched, usually in the parents' middle years. Then postparental men appropriate qualities of nurturance and tenderness that were once relatively alien within themselves, and only tolerable in their dependents. By the same token, postparental women adopt some of the ascendant, competitive qualities that their husbands relinquish. As each becomes as the other used to be, the couple moves toward the normal androgyny of later life. This so-called contrasexual transition is, like paternity and maternity themselves, a quasiuniversal event. As such, it usually precedes a developmental advance. Indeed, after some period of psychic dislocation, most men and women do accommodate to the changes in themselves and in their spouses and gradually direct the energies liberated by the postparental reversal into new activities. They do not at the same time lose their gender identities as men or women. The result, for most men and women, is an expanded sense of self.

Achieving Equality

As sons and daughters traverse their twenties and thirties, the tight skinned, Kourous-like perfection of youth begins to fade, gradually replaced by signs of physical aging. In addition, he or she is likely living independently, involved sexually and emotionally with others, and relating to Mom and Dad primarily through birthday cards and weekly phone calls. The presence of these circumstances pushes the healthy parent–child relationship toward equality but is not in and of itself evidence that the acceptance of equality has been achieved by either parent or child.

Twenty-five-year-old Ron complained bitterly in his therapy that his mother, almost sixty, continued to treat him like a child. Indeed she did. On a recent visit home to attend a family wedding, Ron proudly modeled the new slacks and sport jacket he had bought for the occasion. With a grimace his mother dismissed them as "inappropriate" for the occasion. As the verbal fireworks that followed grew louder, Ron's father stepped between the combatants, as he always did, and encouraged his son's compliance, which was always forthcoming. Ron easily recognized his parents' inappropriate need to control and infantalize him but was unaware of his own ambivalent wish to remain dependent. During two years of psychotherapy he recognized and accepted the fact that his parents had no control over him which he did not give them. At first his refusal to argue or agree produced furious maternal responses but these were eventually replaced by a begrudging acceptance of a more equal relationship.

Wiser parents not only passively accept their child's wishes for independence and autonomy but also facilitate moves in that direction whenever possible. The motivation for such behavior is not entirely altruistic. Losing the battle but winning the war results in the attainment of an important position in the new family constellation which is rising in the midlife sky.

Integrating New Members into the Family

Mother-in-law jokes are not merely the wicked expression of sick humor; they are also reflections of a universal developmental conflict. As *both* generations struggle to separate and individuate from each other, the daunting task for the parents can be stated simply: gracefully give up the primary position of importance to your child to another. Then accept the interloper (unless he or she is severely deranged or criminal) and work to cultivate his or her friendship. Do this because it is the best way to continue to occupy a central, albeit less important, position in your child's life and to form a new relationship with a hopefully interesting and enriching young adult who will control the doors of access to those miraculous extensions of self—grandchildren!

Because the spouse and the parent of the same sex love the same person, a triangle, similar to the infantile Oedipal configuration, is created. This provides an opportunity for all three to rework their childhood experience in this adult context, the outcome determined by the emotional maturity of the participants.

As she sank deeper and deeper into the mist of senility, eighty-six-year-old Lana ranted about her mother-in-law, dead over thirty years. Forced by tradition and economic necessity, she had begun married life in her mother-in-law's home. With an incredible degree of vituperitiveness, Lana never forgot—or forgave—the real and imagined slights and criticisms which she had endured over sixty years ago.

For other more fortunate individuals the outcome of this new triangulated relationship is joyous, lives enriched by multigenerational love and caring, a meshing of roles which results in fulfillment for all three adults who are involved. But even under the best of circumstances the meshing of the new roles may produce tensions. For instance, the failure of young parents to recognize that their parents have other interests than themselves and their children can be a source of conflict between the generations.

Psychoanalysts Bertram Cohler and Robert Galatzer-Levy note that some young adult daughters assume caregiving is an essential ingredient of family ties.(5) However, many studies demonstrate that grandparents rapidly become resentful of demands by their adult offspring for assistance with babysitting. The daughter's disappointed reaction is sometimes a source of tension for the middle-aged parent, who prefers intimacy at a distance.

For those who married relatively young and succeeded in launching their children without serious impediments, the later midlife years can be a time of freedom, pleasure, and intimacy. For those who marry later or begin second families, the middle years are swept away by the challenging but fulfilling task of childrearing. For them Guttman's "chronic emergency of parenthood" stretches out into the forseeable future, skewing the timetables for change suggested in this chapter but answering the question of what do I do in my golden years. As one fifty-five-year-old new father put it, "I know what I'm going to be doing at seventy. I'll be driving car pools, worrying about my daughter's virginity, and saving for a college tuition. Can you believe it?" Yes, I can. It beats a rocking chair any day.

In their midfifties, Jean and Joel, still mourning the death of her mother, the last of their parents to die, were enjoying their bittersweet freedom as they planned for a much needed vacation. With their children all married and their parents dead they were free, for the first time in their adult lives, of significant responsibility for others.

CASE REPORT: A Struggle for Acceptance and Completeness as Son and Parent

Despite sincere efforts and loving intentions, the relationships between parents and children are not always smooth and joyous. The following case report describes the tortuous journey of a well-intentioned young man from bitterness and isolation to emotional closeness and fulfillment.

History

John L. entered therapy with me at age thirty-eight. He presented himself as a trim, well-dressed man with streaks of gray in his hair. Mr. L. came for therapy because, despite a happy marriage and a successful law practice, he was increasingly anxious to the point of panic and had been experiencing fleeting thoughts of running away. He had little idea about what was upsetting him but knew it was "time to talk to somebody."

Mr. L. had married for the second time five years earlier to a woman who had two sons, currently aged twelve and fourteen. He had a fifteen-year-old son of his own from his first marriage. The boy lived with his mother in a nearby city. Mr. L.'s own mother was dead but his father was alive and well, living in the South.

Initially Mr. L. attributed his symptoms primarily to work. His solo practice, in a city overflowing with lawyers, was very successful but demanded eighty plus hours per week of his time. Good help was difficult to find and keep, and it seemed as though his entire existence revolved around his work. His wife thought he worked entirely too hard but demanded little of his time or energy until recently, when her fourteen-year-old began to manifest behavioral problems at home and in school. Mr. L. did what he could to help but felt increasingly guilty as he spent more and more time with his stepson and even less with his natural son, whom he saw only sporadically at best.

The mention of his natural son was accompanied by a striking increase in free-floating anxiety and an unrecognized revelation of important conflictual material. Mr. L.'s girlfriend had become pregnant with his son when they were college students. Both had been virgins prior to dating each other and had only engaged in intercourse three or four times when the pregnancy occurred. His parents were dismayed by the pregnancy since they did not like his girlfriend and wanted him to complete his education before marrying.

When his father announced that he would no longer pay for Mr. L.'s college education, John said one word, "Oh?" and left. The two men never discussed the matter again. Mr. L. did marry his girlfriend and was cut off financially. He, in turn, withdrew emotionally. In the past twenty years, contact with his parents had consisted of four or five frosty phone conversations initiated by his mother and a false display of family togetherness at her funeral five years ago.

The marriage was difficult from the start, beginning as it did with a pregnancy and an absence of family blessing or financial resources. Mr. L. did manage to stay in college—his wife dropped out to care for the baby—but within a short period of time he knew that the marriage was a mistake. He loved his young son desperately but was increasingly distant from his wife, who seemed "superficial and boring." After graduation and a brief trial of marriage counseling, he took off for a distant city, feeling "exhilarated and free—I finally had all of it off my back."

After working for a while, Mr. L. put himself through law school. His former wife followed him hoping for a reconciliation, but to no avail. She eventually married a man who made little money but was a decent stepfather. Mr. L. was painfully aware of the difference between the very comfortable lifestyle he provided for his two stepsons and the rather meager circumstances under which his natural son lived.

When John met his second wife he felt exhilarated and

happy for the first time in many years. She was outgoing, uninhibited sexually, and "made me the center of her life." They were married within six months. Mr. L.'s new stepsons, quiet and unassuming latency-aged boys, "seemed like nice kids, I didn't give them much thought."

Developmental History. Mr. L. did not remember much about his early years but gradually a picture emerged of a quiet, somewhat shy child who was physically healthy and did not manifest any obvious psychological problems or developmental delays or deviations. His mother was at home full-time and seemed to enjoy raising her son.

John's memories of elementary school were clear and not particularly happy. Although an excellent student, he was small in stature and frequently teased. He had a few friends but felt "on the outside looking in." His dad pushed him into sports where he did not excel, and seemed disappointed in him.

Puberty occurred late, in tenth grade. "I remember erections, wet dreams, and thoughts about girls." When I commented on the absence of masturbation from his list, Mr. L. blushed and said, "That was so good, I knew it must be terrible in some way."

College was a time of greater acceptance socially, a sense of "liberation" from his father, and the beginning of dating and a sexual life. Unfortunately, this heady sense of exhilaration and freedom was short-lived, quickly replaced by premature work, marriage, and parenthood.

The Therapy

Initially, Mr. L. had great concern about my reaction to his sexual fantasies and his aggressiveness. Gradually he tested my ability to accept his rage at his father, eventually spewing forth blast after blast at his dad for his coldness and insensitivity, particularly in regard to the pregnancy. Signs of softening and wishes for reconciliation eventually followed, stimulated by our work, to be sure, but also propelled by the patient's position on the threshold of midlife. As he approached forty and his father seventy, he became increasingly aware that if a reconciliation were to take place, it better occur *soon*. It did. Mr. L. called his father, who was mildly receptive, and eventually went, along with his son, to visit him. John was surprised at the pleasure and degree of inner comfort he experienced during the visit but was totally unprepared for—and consciously jealous of—the warmth of the rapport that developed almost instantly between grandfather and grandson; they, too, were strangers just getting to know each other. Son and father have continued to develop their relationship, which is beginning to take the form of a reversal of generations as Mr. L. increasingly cares for his aging father—not without a sense of superiority for being there for his father in his time of need.

In the months following the rapprochement between son and father, Mr. L.'s thoughts increasingly turned to his relationship with his own son. Following the acceptance of the painful interpretation that he had abandoned his son just as his father had abandoned him, John increased their contact and eventually invited his son to come to live with him "during the few years that are left before he becomes a man." The transition took place after several months of slow negotiations with both wives.

Watching Mr. L.'s guilt diminish and self-esteem grow as he incorporated the role of full-time father was a rewarding experience for patient and therapist alike. Although personally satisfying, detailed contact with his son also led to the realization that the teenager was struggling, primarily with social relationships. In a bittersweet burst of newfound similarity, Mr. L. recognized that, "he looks like me, is beginning to talk like me—and seems to have the same problems I did. At least he'll get help when he's fifteen, not forty."His wife's kindness to his son surprised Mr. L. and precipitated more guilt since he had accepted her children but not the role of their stepfather. Gradually he came to accept the realization that he had *three* teenage sons to raise and support.

The development of his relationship with the three boys and his own father, as well as the more intimate, less inhibited relationship with his wife, filled John with a sense of integrity and competence that he had never experienced before. "For the first time in life, I'm doing what I ought to be doing—I'm being a good husband, father, and son. I wish my mom were alive to see this. I think she'd be very proud of me."

But the joy and pleasure in these relationships, the shift from a life almost devoid of closeness to one overflowing with intensity, led to the realization that Mr. L. was *responsible* for his loved ones. Increasingly he began to recognize and accept that as an involved midlife husband, father, and son he had assumed the "burden" of caring for his father as he aged and eventually died; of raising his sons, including probability of putting all three of them through college; and of remaining emotionally and sexually intimate with his wife in a sustained relationship. "It's tough," he said, "but it's great. Life does begin at forty!"

Theoretical Discussion

Mr. L.'s Third Individuation. The ability to separate from parents is one of the major tasks of young adulthood. For most individuals, the emotional detachment from their parents that takes place in adolescence and young adulthood is followed by a new inner definition of themselves as comfortably alone and competent, able to care for themselves in the real and intrapsychic worlds. Sheared of childhood closeness to parents and not yet involved to the same degree with their adult replacements, young adults in transition experience a normally intense loneliness. Sooner or later this psychic state drives most to fill the real and intrapsychic voids left by separation from the parents of childhood by establishing a family of procreation.

Mr. L. was separating from his parents, as evidenced by the growing sense of emotional self sufficiency at college, academic success, and the beginning of an adult sexual pattern, until the unexpected pregnancy and his parents' reaction to it arrested the process. Although Mr. L. *appeared* to have individuated—he married, became a father, had a successful career, and moved to another state—in reality he avoided his sexuality and aggression and ran away from his wife, son, and parents. This state of affairs continued until the death of his mother, the approaching of old age of his father, and the adolescence of his son upset the tenuous emotional equilibrium which had existed through much of young adulthood and resulted in the outbreak of anxiety. The unconscious command was, Do something about these relationships before time runs out!

Problems with Intimacy. John married his first wife out of need and spite. As their relationship was compromised by pregnancy, parenthood, and near poverty, he emotionally withdrew from her. It took more than ten years before he allowed himself to become emotionally involved with another woman. For the second time, he began to fuse sexual and loving feelings, this time in an environment far removed from parental influence and with a woman much more advanced than he along the developmental line of the capacity for intimacy. In fact, some of the anxiety which precipitated the search for treatment was related to a growing conscious awareness that he could not match his wife's level of sexual freedom and comfort or her desire for emotional closeness. The removal of many of his sexual inhibitions through therapy made it possible for him to sustain a fulfilling, intimate relationship with a woman for the first time in his life. For him, life did indeed begin at forty.

Becoming a Father. Biological parenthood begins the process of psychological parenthood, that mental state in which young adults become increasingly attached to and involved with their offspring. After birth, each interaction with the infant enhances a new sense of completeness and stimulates the desire to engage the baby, who is so strongly identified with the self.

John became a biological father in his early twenties but avoided a psychological commitment to his son for over ten years because of the struggles with his wife and family. He attempted to master the devastating psychological abandonment by his parents when his girlfriend became pregnant by doing to his son what was done to him. Because there was a strong positive aspect to the relationship with his parents which facilitated his masculine development during childhood and became part of him, he could not rid himself of the *internalized* parent, or the internalized son. Eventually, without conscious awareness, he had to seek help to rid himself of his guilt by analyzing his conflicts about these relationships and then reestablish the ties with the two most important men in his life while there was still time to affect their adolescent and late life development.

Striving for Equality with Dad. Once a young adult has assumed and internalized the adult roles of spouse-parent, the stage is set for the establishment of an inner sense of equality and mutuality with parents. As adult experiences—marriage, sex, parenthood, work, buying a home, developing adult relationships—become the substance of everyday life, they transform the intrapsychic relationship of children with parents from one of dependency and need to one of mutuality and equality.

As this change occurs, it affects the real relationship with the parents and provides a powerful rationale for remaining invested in them. Only parents and children place one in the center of a genetic continuity that spans three generations. As middle age approaches, with its growing preoccupation with time limitation and personal death, the intrapsychic importance of these relationships grows significantly.

As Mr. L. neared forty, he was deeply engaged in this process with his father. Unfortunately, it was too late to do so with his mother, who had died earlier. His reward was a deep inner sense of integrity and for the first time in many years, the absence of guilt—a true expression of adult fulfillment.

7

The Quest for Sexual Intimacy after Forty

Many misinformed skeptics believe that the search for sexual intimacy in midlife is an exercise in futility. A forty-year-old man lamented, "My body has changed so much since I was twenty. What do I have to look forward to?" The answer to that question can be, "plenty, maybe even the best sex you've ever had"—if the biology and psychology of the middle years are understood.

Intimacy may be defined as the ability to care for the partner at least as much as the self, some of the time. No impossible or unrealistic expectation there. Sex may occur without intimacy and intimacy without sex. In this chapter our focus is on the frequent fusion of the two, in the face of what may appear to be daunting midlife obstacles.

Developmental Considerations

The capacity for intimacy emerges out of adolescent and young adult sexual experience. Although adolescents sometimes care about their partners, the pressing developmental need is to gain sexual experience, to learn how to use the body as a sexual instrument with others. One fourteen-year-old girl, determined to begin experimenting sexually, set her sights on a handsome high school senior. Unrestrained by badly needed parental prohibitions, she proceeded to seduce the young man but quickly dumped him when she discovered that she knew more than he. She had no trouble finding more experienced upperclassmen to take his place. Driven by the relentless demon of youthful biology, conquests rather than caring can continue to be the prime directive well into the twenties. "My dick's got a life of its own," said a twenty-three-year-old. "It takes no prisoners. Line em up, knock em down, and on to the next."

Although the capacity for adult intimacy is apparent in some high-functioning individuals in the late teens and early thirties, it does not become a sustainable capacity until well into the twenties. Then the shift from casual sex to the need for emotional involvement during relations is experienced as a growing sense of emptiness. "If I let myself go to bed with one more man who doesn't really care about me, I'll scream," said twenty-four-year-old Karen. "I feel so alone inside. I want someone to love me."

> It is a truth universally acknowledged, that a single man in possession of a good fortune, must be in want of a wife.
>
> JANE AUSTEN, *Pride and Prejudice*

Slowly but surely the emptiness of one more "my place or yours" and the desire to be anchored in relationships as enriched as those which existed within the family of childhood drive most young adults toward commitment. Not to get anxious, it's actually good for you. As the result of a rare fifty plus-year longitudinal study of development,

Harvard psychiatrist George Vaillant commented that there is "probably no single longitudinal variable that predicted mental health as clearly as a man's capacity to remain happily married over time."(1) Erik Erikson read the palms of those who would not actualize a lasting, intimate relationship in young adulthood and saw a midlife future reeking with the smell of the curdled cream of self-absorption and isolation.

Marriage, that often reviled and frivolously regarded institution, is the best decision to promote development that most young adults can make. Within its supercharged confines, slowly but surely, like the day-long simmering of a homemade pasta sauce, the rawness of youth is transformed into the savory smoothness of adulthood. Profound intrapsychic changes occur. As the partners dare to share and experience together their innermost sexual desires, their fantasies expand to incorporate the sensuousness of the other. Thirty-year-old Jane had only had sex in the missionary position before she married Brad. He was less inhibited than she and introduced masturbation on the freeway and quickies on the living room floor. As she became more comfortable with her own fantasies and gradually shed her inhibitions, she began to take the lead. Plain Jane no more, she surprised Brad with a suggestive call from a motel room known for its vibrating beds and X-rated films. As the years go by, each partner is increasingly identified with the other. Together they look back on the wake of an ever-lengthening shared past and work for and anticipate an enmeshed future. As they playfully possess each other's bodies and produce children the deeply ingrained infantile ignorance about the opposite sex is slowly replaced by the awesome adult acceptance of the equal and complementary nature of the male and female genitalia.

Crossing the Rubicon: Maintaining Intimacy in Midlife

As forty approaches a whole new set of developmental challenges, full of potential and promise, as well as apprehension and anxiety, begin to dominate the landscape. Whereas the young adult is preoccupied with developing the capacity for sustaining *intimacy,* those on the fringe of forty struggle to maintain it in the face of powerful physical, psychological, and environmental distractors. In a long-standing relationship inhibitors include changes in attitudes about sex and sexual functioning due to aging and psychological unavailability because of preoccupation with the realistic demands of work, children, and elderly parents.

"You ought to lose some weight" said he. "I will if you will," said she. "It takes you so long to get turned on," said he. "I wouldn't talk if I were you," said she. "Let's go away for the weekend," said she. "I've got to work," said he. "You're always working," said she. "Janet goes to college next year," said he. "Come to bed now," said he. "I have to call my mother," said she. "You always call your mother," said he. "She's old and alone," said she.

In newer relationships issues unique to second beginnings which interfere with closeness abound. They include the absence of a history together, an absence of old friends in common, age and generational differences between the partners, and the problems of constituting a stepfamily. "Your friends don't like me," said she. "How could they, you hardly talk to them," said he. "I want a baby," said she. "I've already done that," said he. "But not with me," said she. "Your son is knocking at the door again," said he. "He seems to know when we're having sex," said she. "He doesn't like us doing it," said he.

"I thought you said these were the best years of life?"

said the reader. "I did," says the author. "Doesn't sound so good to me," says the reader. "It will when you read on," says the author.

The key to maintaining sexual and psychological intimacy in midlife is knowledge of the normal changes in sexual functioning which occur after forty, the ability to communicate needs and desires, and a sense of humor. After all it's only sex.

Sex and Aging: Good News

"The loss of sexuality is not an inevitable aspect of aging," says researcher Helen Singer Kaplan.(2) In fact, the majority of healthy people remain sexually active on a regular basis until advanced old age. But the subject must be approached a bit differently than at twenty because the aging process does bring with it certain changes in the physiology of the male and female sexual response.

Consider the following. We age from the outside in. In utero the outer, or ectodermal, layer of the embryo develops into skin, the sensory organs, and nervous system. Since these organs age first, plastic surgeons and opthalmologists have a field day in our forties as we rush to smooth out the wrinkles and correct farsightedness. In our fifties, it's muscles, bones, and connective tissue—products of the middle or mesodermal layer—which begin to give out, resulting in sore backs and heart attacks. But still cooking with gas, even if the packaging is a bit frayed, are the inner or endodermal functions of eating and sex, two of life's greatest pleasures. In regard to sexual functioning, researchers across the decades from Kinsey to Masters and Johnson to Kaplan have arrived at the same conclusion: In the presence of good health, the majority of people remain sexually functional and active on a regular basis until virtually the end of life. Or, to put it more succinctly, when they have partners, 70 percent of healthy seventy-year-olds remain sexually active and have sex at least once a week.

THE HUMAN SEXUAL RESPONSE CCYCLE
Desire
Excitement
Orgasm

Age- and Gender-Related Variables

"Vive la différence," say the French. A good idea if the differences in sexual functioning bring pleasure, not pain. The best way to ensure that "la différence" continues to add spice to sex in midlife is to understand the changes in sexual functioning that normally occur with age and accept them in one's self and one's partner. This developmental task is easier said than done because it involves accepting the partial loss of functions which are enormously important to self-esteem in adolescence and young adulthood.

All aspects of fulfillment in adulthood, particularly sexual fulfillment, begin with accepting a constantly changing reality and end with actions that are consistent with that reality. There are certain inevitable age-related changes in sexual physiology which affect men and women differently. According to Kaplan, "Male sexuality peaks sharply at around seventeen and then gradually declines, whereas women do not reach their full sexual potential until their late thirties or early forties, and then they slow down to a lesser degree than men."(3) As disquieting as such a statement may be to the male ego, all is not lost. There's more to mature sexual intimacy than the hormonally driven, bunny rabbit readiness of adolescence.

The human sexual response cycle has three phases, desire, excitement, and orgasm, each of which is affected by age and gender differences.

Desire

The effect of age on sexual desire is highly variable in both sexes. In some individuals there is little change with the passage of time, while others appear to lose their sex drive altogether. Production of testosterone in both sexes is a major biological factor in the maintenance of sexual desire. Most women produce enough adrenal sexual hormones (the adrenal glands produce male and female hormones in both sexes) after menopause to retain their interest in sex. Before menopause that function is performed by the ovaries. In males there is no abrupt drop in testosterone levels in midlife similar to the estrogen loss females experience at menopause. The hormonal basis for male sexual desire remains intact, but psychological factors can produce a loss of desire which resembles aspects of the female climacteric.

Excitement

In middle-aged females, vaginal lubrication and swelling are dependent on estrogen. Diminished ovarian estrogen production results in gradual and progressive vaginal thinning and dryness, first noticed in the forties by the beginning occurrence of raspy, sandpaper-like intercourse. Estrogen replacement therapy and/or vaginal lubrication can diminish or eliminate these effects.

In middle-aged males, the male excitement phase, erection, is affected by aging, but not as severely as changes in vaginal functioning. Middle-aged men may require concomitant physical and psychic stimulation in order to attain and maintain an erection. In the teens and twenties a mere look or a fantasy is enough to spontaneously snap the penis to attention. This ever-ready sexual response gradually diminishes until, by sixty, most men "will seldom, if ever, erect spontaneously" as they approach a partner. Nor can they count on remaining erect without "continuous physical penile stimulation."(4)

Orgasm

Orgasm is produced by the rhythmic contractions located at the base of the penis and around the vaginal entrance. In males the refractory period—the interval after orgasm when a second orgasm cannot occur—increases from just a few minutes at age seventeen to as much as forty-eight hours by age seventy. Women, likely because they do not ejaculate, do not have a significant refractory period at any age. They remain capable of experiencing multiple orgasms throughout life.

Healthy Adaptations

Loving couples who do not have significant sexual problems intuitively adapt to these physical changes. The woman provides more active and intense manual and oral penile stimulation without being asked. She does not expect her partner to maintain his erection as long as he did in the past, minimizes occasional impotence, and encourages pleasurable encounters which do not end in ejaculation.

The man encourages the use of lubrication without criticism or recrimination, penetrates more gently, and responds to his partner's desire for sex more often than his lengthened refractory period allows by participating in intercourse without the expectation of ejaculation.

Problematic Adaptations

Individuals and couples with significant sexual inhibitions ride the sexual crest of the hormonal wave of young adulthood and perform adequately, but run aground on the androgynous shoals of midlife. They usually have sex in the missionary position; avoid oral and manual stimulation; mate in silence, fantasizing, if at all, in a vacuum; and feel guilty about sexual pleasure, particularly from masturbation. Spurred on by their biologically generated excitement, they perform for each other with restricted adequacy until the skill required to play the game increases.

Then, since they cannot use fantasy and direct genital stimulation to adapt to the age-related sexual changes which intrude on their fragile equilibrium, the sexual house of cards they built together begins to collapse. Men with such conflicts avoid intercourse because of their diminished ability to erect spontaneously and their partner's disgust with oral and manual stimulation. "I asked my wife to help me get ready," said one forty-five-year-old male. "After thinking about it for too long she agreed, but she couldn't even look at me while she was doing it. She turned her head away. Some turn on." Women avoid intercourse out of embarrassment over the appearance of their bodies, doubts about continuing to be sexually attractive to their partners and concerns over decreased lubrication. Without adequate physical and mental stimulation and the introduction of lubricants, the quasipleasure of intercourse becomes a painful experience to be avoided. As intercourse becomes less and less frequent, both physical and emotional intimacy wither as the partners retreat into masturbation or the void of sexual abstinence.

This Is as Good as It Gets

Healthy individuals and couples, as we've noted, have largely accepted the age-induced changes in sexual functioning in themselves and their partners and intuitively adapt their sexual practices to compensate. The result is one of the richest experiences of fulfillment which human existence has to offer—touching and caressing, the union of bodies, the crescendo of orgasm, and the melting of minds, all within the comforting security of the acceptance of each other's physical and mental imperfections and a shared history which binds adulthood's most important experiences into a rich, meaningful whole. I'll stack it up against the wanton sex of youth any day. Fortunately there's no need to choose since the one leads to the other.

CASE REPORT: The Development of Intimacy at Age Fifty

The following case history, an abbreviated, altered version of a report by psychoanalyst Eli Miller, M.D., in *The Race against Time*, edited by Robert Nemiroff and myself,[5] indicates that it is never too late to strive for sexual and emotional intimacy, even when the problems are severe and the patient is well into middle age.

Identifying Information and Chief Complaints

When referred for analysis, Mr. Z. was a forty-eight-year-old, unmarried, white male. Casually dressed and a touch overweight, he spoke in a slightly pressured, organized manner. I [the "I" refers to Dr. Miller] found myself responding positively to his wry sense of humor, intelligence, and tight-lipped grin. In a somewhat cautious but serious manner Mr. Z. began to explain his reasons for wanting therapy. "I've been on an emotional treadmill. I've tried to solve it for myself but never got much better over the last twenty years. My old attitude was: 'If I'm not sick, I should solve my own problems; I'm a big boy.' I'm getting older with aches and pains and approaching fifty. My father died at seventy-three and I can afford therapy now. I want to cope and get on with a more pleasant life."

Several sessions later, he was able to verbalize his deeper concern more specifically. "I've never had sex with someone I cared about, just bar girls in the service. I never told anyone before. I've had all the right opportunities [for sex]. I feel like an incomplete person, the Lone Ranger type. I feel that [women] expect sex, but I block and get afraid of failure. The 'Pee Shy' problem [his fear of urination in public places] still bothers me. You know some people have almost begged me to go to bed with them, but I feared failure. I played moralistic. If it was someone I cared for, I'd feel embarrassed."

Although Mr. Z. did not specifically say so, he also seemed troubled by his recent retirement from over twenty years of active military duty and the state of his mother's health—she was dying from a chronic illness.

Developmental History

Infancy. Mr. Z. was a second son, born to thirty-year-old parents. Following an uneventful full-term pregnancy and birth, he was raised by his mother and a full-time governess. According to his mother, Mr. Z. was a healthy, happy, bottle-fed infant. Before and after Mr. Z.'s birth, his mother frequently accompanied his father on business trips, leaving her son in the care of the governess.

During the evaluation, Mr. Z. described his toilet training, which was probably carried out by both mother and governess. "I remember a small pot and being told that I would have soap stuck up my rear as a suppository if I didn't go to the bathroom. Enemas were popular then, and the rule was for me to have a bowel movement in the morning."

Apparently he responded to such pressure by training easily. There were no lapses of bowel or bladder control after age three. When, as a young child (post-toilet training), he lived in Europe with his family, he was horrified to see children defecate on the street and have well-dressed women take out toilet paper and wipe them. Mr. Z. was told that he was a happy, compliant toddler who developed a large vocabulary and was even-tempered. He was very attached to his mother and missed her when she went on his father's frequent business trips.

The Oedipal Phase and Latency. Mr. Z.'s loving attachment to his mother and governess continued throughout the Oedipal years. He recalled with great warmth the considerable amount of time spent alone with either or both of them. By contrast, he remembered his fear of his father, who was very strict and usually preoccupied with business matters or his own health. "I remember once, I must have been five or six,

I lit a match and put it near a thermometer to see the temperature. It shot through the top. I worried all day about what my father would say but he didn't say anything."

Mr. Z. was very frightened of the dark and would only sleep with a nightlight. He was frightened of robbers and ghosts and needed frequent assurance. "My earliest memory is of going to see a Walt Disney movie about the three little pigs. The wolf scared the hell out of me for a long time after. . . . I think I was overprotected as a kid from both disease and danger." When Mr. Z. was six, his parents did "the unthinkable" and sent his governess away. Strong feelings of resentment remain to this day.

During latency Mr. Z. attended a private boys' school, where he was a model student and was well mannered and cooperative. "I tried hard; I worried if I didn't do well." In addition to playing sports such as soccer and baseball, Mr. Z. developed a love for music that continued through his adult years. He had friends and was accepted by his peers but never as a leader or as one of the most popular students.

Mr. Z. enjoyed adolescence. He had many friends and excelled academically. In addition to meticulously editing school publications and participating in sports, he continued a serious study of music. "I stopped taking lessons when I realized my talent only went so far. I would have liked to be *world class* in music because it's a field where you can please yourself and others; it frustrates me when I cannot measure up to the excelling people. [There were some girlfriends but] I didn't have any sex with girls in high school because it was a highly puritanical area and sex was just not done. People didn't even talk about it."

Masturbation occurred regularly after puberty, particularly before a date to prevent arousal. Mr. Z. was troubled by the intensity of his sexual feelings and the details of sexual fantasies. These were heterosexual in nature and centered upon foreplay and intercourse. At age fourteen, he attributed pain in his lower abdomen and testicles to masturbation and a strong sex drive. With trepidation he approached a trusted family doctor who attributed the pain to "walking around in a wet bathing suit."

Young Adulthood (Ages 20–40). After such an easy time academically in high school, Mr. Z. was shaken by the demands of college. "My brother flunked out, and I didn't want to follow in his footsteps." Mr. Z. completed four years of college and went on to graduate school. A minicrisis and significant turning point in his life occurred upon completion of graduate work, when it was time to make a career choice. "My father suggested that I get a job, but I got chicken pox instead." Soon after, Mr. Z. joined the military and remained on active duty for the next twenty years.

Concerns about sexual performance continued throughout young adulthood. He dated occasionally but avoided emotional involvement with the several women who expressed a serious interest. Intimacy was never achieved with anyone. "I didn't think I could afford to get married. I tried hard not to hurt anyone's feelings." Actual sexual involvement, "which was never very satisfactory," was rare and confined to one-night stands and prostitutes. Afterward, he feared disease and sometimes developed pains, "probably psychosomatic," for which he sought treatment.

Middle Adulthood (Ages 40–Present). As he approached forty, Mr. Z. had settled into a lifestyle that was centered around his career, friendships, and travel. He was keenly aware of the absence of intimacy from his life but was unable to do anything about it. Frequent visits to his parents were uncomfortable because he felt dominated and childlike in their presence.

His father's death when Mr. Z. was forty-three was easily adapted to and accompanied by a conscious sense of relief. Then, as the decade progressed, the patient became more involved with his mother due to her failing health and incipient senility.

Mr. Z. experienced a significant adult trauma when he unexpectedly failed (likely due to performance anxiety) a military recertification examination and was not promoted. Soon after, he left the service and returned home to care for his increasingly incapacitated mother.

Course of the Analysis

For me, as the analysis began, the central question was, is analysis a strong enough therapeutic instrument to help this man undo a major inhibition against sexuality and heterosexual intimacy that had dominated his life for nearly fifty years?

At intervals during the opening phase, Mr. Z. talked about the important women in his past. He particularly remembered T., who had died of cancer several years before. Mr. Z. expressed his sadness that she had not left him anything as a memento of the feeling that existed between them. His search for sustenance from past relationships was due in part to the void experienced in his present life. While mourning a lifestyle that had sustained him for twenty years, he had little else to do but care for his mother and her affairs.

During the thirty-eighth session, the patient bemoaned his lack of sexual experimentation as a teenager, feeling that he was too obedient, "too good for my own good." Two sessions later he reported the following dream: "In San

Francisco Bay was a large old-fashioned sailboat with broad decks. It was sitting in the mud, permanently, like a wreck. A work boat; it suddenly had tall masts. A lot of people start hauling up the sails. I'm not doing my share. It got under way and began moving around narrow streets. I saw a high school girlfriend, B. She looked pretty. I went to ask her out, but her schedule was very busy. I wondered whether to ask her out for lunch or dinner. I gave her a choice. Lunch would be rejection. If it was dinner, it would be more like she was interested and would stay the night. She said that the evening was fine."

Mr. Z. responded to the dream. "I was reasonably content in high school. I felt more rejection in college. In my sophomore year, I invited B. to a dance. She got ill and couldn't come; this was a real blow to me! My friends had dates and I was without one."

I thought of the boat as representing Mr. Z. floundering in the mud, needing my help to get moving (sailing) and to get his mast (penis) up.

Dr. M.: The wrecked work boat becomes impressive with the sail up.

Mr. Z.: Yet stuck in mud and silt.

Dr. M.: A very positive dream—you may be the boat getting out of the mud and going after the girl, who says yes!

Mr. Z.: I hope!

Soon, his mother's illness intensified, and her decompensation appeared to unearth several hypochondriacal and childhood separation fears. Childhood phobias, particularly including fears of the dark and of being alone, reappeared. Mr. Z. was also troubled by a recurrent fantasy in which he was swimming alone in shark-infested waters. He was muted in his response to his mother's deterioration, and he cried openly when a beloved cat died. "I loved that cat more than anything in the world." It was interesting that the pet cemetery was located on the same road where the patient's father was buried.

In this same period, Mr. Z. also communicated that he perceived the loss of the governess as "negative for my emotional development. I resented that my parents did not realize that fact!" He described the governess as an interesting and capable woman who was later hired by a rich man with several children. He knew she had subsequently died of cancer.

During this period of time, when Mr. Z. was increasingly preoccupied with his age and health, he began to diet and exercise. His fears of being alone in the house at night were repeatedly surfacing, and he began to notice his style of holding grudges and in general of having trouble "letting go."

As Mr. Z. approached his forty-ninth birthday, he mentioned that he did not like the feeling of being forced or obligated to come to analysis. He began to express concerns about how I felt about him and wished that I would say that he was an "OK guy." "I really want to change! Where there's a will there's a way."

Concern about his appearance and baldness followed.

Mr. Z.: People wouldn't say, "You're a fat blob; take off 100 pounds," or "You are wrinkled." A woman said to Don Rickles: "Don, why do you comb your hair up that way?" It's OK if I know the person likes me a lot. It's a problem with new relationships. I hate to force myself on people.

Dr. M.: I don't really buy that!

Mr. Z.: Yeah, if they come on to me, I feel something is wrong with them, because they want me.

Dr. M.: Groucho Marx once joked that he refused to be a member of any club that would take him.

When I pointed out that, despite what he felt were mild imperfections in his appearance, he was often approached by women whom *he* rebuffed, he replied: "Yes, if they come on to me I feel something is wrong with them because they want me. The unobtainable is more desirable." Mr. Z. recalled the fraternities at college; the ones that wanted him were "second best" and therefore he refused to join any of them.

During those first hundred hours of the analysis, Mr. Z. struggled with a growing recognition of his position in relationship to the developmental tasks of midlife. "I feel mine is a midlife crisis but a little different. Most of the men I heard about have situations involving children and a wife. My fear is a fear of life passing me by and my becoming old and lonely. Every problem I have is associated with the feeling that I'm not of a normal range of sexuality. We could talk for ten years, and all these other things would be just beating around the bush. I've only had sexual relationships a few times in my life, and I'm afraid to start with someone else; it's that abnormal. People lose interest after marriage, or some men give up. I feel I'm missing something vital." His specific fears about sexual performance included concern about partial erections and premature ejaculations. Enjoyable sex might bring back the pains he experienced in his testicles as a teenager. Mr. Z. emphasized that "satisfactory sex gives one an exuberance, vitality, and a desire to get things done."

Mr. Z.'s wish for more meaningful human contact and the desire to complete his masculine identity by producing offspring became more urgent as he considered his age. "At the core of the problem I can get along with people quite well or explain why I'm not married or dating. But I don't seek new friends; I'm not in the mainstream. I'm aloof toward other people and I have a fear of being in the house by myself. I could invite girls over if I wanted, but I can't make myself take the first step. . . . It all gets down to sex! I don't even know if I'm sterile or not at forty-nine years of age."

Mr. Z.'s Mother's Death. In hour 125, Mr. Z. reported with very little affect that his mother had finally died of her long illness. "Now I'm at a *turning point*. I do feel very relieved." During the session he repeatedly strayed from the subject in an attempt to deny intense feelings about his mother's loss. Mr. Z. rationalized his lack of feeling by suggesting that he had done his mourning during the long course of her illness. Sympathy notes from family and friends produced momentary feelings of love and sadness that were quickly dissipated. Mr. Z. began to plan frequent vacations as another means of avoiding his feelings, his fear of staying alone, and the analysis.

In the sessions following his mother's death, Mr. Z. considered a wide range of topics. He wondered why his closest friends were two to three decades older than he. Surprisingly, he felt closer to his brother and sister-in-law and decided to invite them to dinner. Warm memories of his cherished governess flowed more easily into consciousness. "Like she could control the world and make things pleasant. All things were good with her. It was like a sense of order; *like at one time I had it!*"

The Urge to Travel. As Mr. Z. began to discuss plans for additional vacations and travel, some of the dynamics behind this new interest began to emerge. Although he was phobic and frightened at home alone, particularly at night, he was very comfortable alone in public places or when on trips. At those times he experienced a sense of control, largely because he did not have to deal with familiar people. He hated intrusions beyond his control. I interpreted that to mean that Mr. Z. might be feeling intruded upon by his feelings for me and my comments in the analysis. "True! If I care I open up and I might get hurt." He then expressed the fantasy of being a king who could command people to be there only when he wanted them. Mr. Z. was aware that he was reneging on the analytic contract, but he saw positive reasons for his behavior. "I feel so strongly I want to do it [travel]. It would be counterproductive not to. I shouldn't deny myself at forty-nine years of age what I want to do! Yet, I know that I should concentrate on the analysis more."

I understood the analytic work to this point in the following manner: Mr. Z. felt that as a young child he had been trapped in relationships that had hurt him and left him vulnerable to the wishes of others. He feared a repetition of this pattern in other significant relationships. This conflict was being recreated in the analysis as he felt emotionally involved with me and began to react against these feelings. He appeared to be attempting to master his feelings of being "left" by his mother and governess by continually leaving me. Outside of the analysis, he was able to titrate emotional involvements by avoiding women his own age and by spending most of his time with friends in their seventies and eighties. Because Mr. Z. saw these elderly friends as asexual, he was more comfortable with them, a common bias that strengthened the defense.

In hour 155, Mr. Z. spoke of recent contact with a woman he had known many years ago. This woman, P., aged forty-seven, was in the process of obtaining a separation and possible divorce from her husband. Mr. Z. was attracted to her and enjoyed her company. He mentioned casually that she had had an unsuccessful pregnancy at age forty-four.

Soon after, Mr. Z. was invited by P. to spend Christmas with her. To his surprise, he wanted to accept the invitation. "Before you ask, I'll tell you, there's been no sex! I wonder if sex with P. would have helped. I think she is as screwed up as I am in terms of relationships. A relationship with her would be a disaster! She's *so* into her problems, she couldn't possibly understand my problems!" He began to ruminate about being fifty and wondered if any woman would be suitable for him.

After the December holiday break with P., Mr. Z. returned with increased self-esteem and an open desire to date. As he began to consider an active sex life, he decided to have a sperm count done. "Before it was beyond my realm of reality to do something like that. Even making the appointment would have been hard to do!" The normal result from the sperm count greatly increased his feelings of potency and masculinity. Mr. Z. lamented his thirty adult years of sexual inhibition. "What a terrible waste," he said.

Soon he spoke of another woman, G., a divorcee he had known for many years. "I've seen her off and on over the years. I held off or backed off with the sex. . . . This year I called her at New Year's. She knew my voice immediately. She cares. I told her to come down. . . . This time, if she wants sex, she'll get it! Maybe the sperm count helped! I'm less inhibited. . . . She could be my surrogate. . . . The fact I can say this, this is considerable progress!"

Significant Life Changes. Mr. Z. began to change his life. He planned to move out of his parents' home into one of his own. Over the years he had collected piles of records and knick knacks. They had to go! A friend had suggested a blind date with a lawyer. Would she find him unattractive, too heavy? When Mr. Z. actually began to clean out the clothes from his parents' home in anticipation of a move, he found himself unable to give away a number of his father's old hats. He initiated a ritual burning of them instead. "Throwing them out would be like putting pieces of father in the garbage. It's like a tattered flag. . . . How hard it is to get rid of things!"

Shortly thereafter, he bought a home of his own. As Mr. Z. began to take more interest in his real estate purchase and dating activity, he experienced an upsurge in hypochondriacal concerns and increased negative feelings. These continued to center on money, time away from the analysis, and missed analytic visits. Mr. Z. made a plea to cut the analysis to two days a week. "I dislike being preoccupied with the analytic appointments. This thing permeates my whole day. It's becoming my whole life. In some ways it's ruining my life."

Despite our work, Mr. Z. went off on another vacation. Upon returning, he reported being thrown into a semidating situation with a middle-aged German woman. He was dismayed with the interaction, describing her as a "single, dumpy, cheapskate." She reminded him of his great aunts in their late sixties. Following associations to his father's "standards" and lectures on meeting one's obligations, I interpreted [again] Mr. Z.'s belief that his father—and I—would strongly disapprove of his having an active, satisfying sexual life. He responded:

> Mr. Z.: It's true. You know, I yearn for the old days. When we lived in the country when I was a kid, life was simpler. You could leave your keys in the ignition without fear of burglary.
>
> Dr. M.: And you didn't have to worry about a sex life when you were a kid.

Mr. Z. reported a "key breakthrough" in hour 215. After a comfortable evening with another old girlfriend, he had finally taken the initiative, with some help from alcohol, and slept with her, although they did not actually have intercourse. The girlfriend, B., was described as a personable, uninhibited, divorced, forty-four-year-old career woman who had known the patient since he was ten years old. For years he had thought of her as a sister.

The possibility of an ongoing sexual relationship brought back fears of performance anxiety and sexual inadequacy. Mr. Z. was pleased that B. was not "uptight about sex," because this made the sexual relationship easier for him. But he became notably more anxious as the sexual relationship progressed. In hour 218, he had a preoccupation with his pulse and various pains. I helped Mr. Z. see that his sexual experience in addition to producing much pleasure was causing him concerns about his health and a sense of guilt expressed through a fear of impending doom. He acknowledged this, but he felt positive that this girlfriend, who was very attracted to him, liked him "as I am."

Mr. Z. continued to get more involved with his new girlfriend. He wanted to take time off from the analysis to spend a long weekend with her: "Having to keep the schedule makes it difficult. I want no schedule with anybody! I want to do exactly as I want to do." Despite continuing [though lessened] hypochondriacal concerns and feelings of guilt, Mr. Z. was exhilarated by his new relationships.

A New Chapter at Middle Age. "I want her to know I care for her; that it's not just therapy for me. It's a new lease on life. At fifty, sex is routine to a lot of people, or they don't do it anymore. A new lease on life at fifty! A new chapter at middle age! Not routine, that's good." Mr. Z. continued to view B. as nearly the ideal woman, and at this point he told her that he loved her. "Two years ago I couldn't imagine talking to anyone about erections or what went on with a woman overnight. Never in my wildest imagination!"

In hour 230, Mr. Z. began making comparisons between his old girlfriend, P., who was very rejecting, with his new, very accepting girlfriend, B.; he compared his warm German governess of childhood with his less demonstrative mother.

As his relationship with B. deepened, Mr. Z. reported that he was now looking forward to his upcoming fiftieth birthday. "I was fortunate I found B., she's uninhibited. I'm more inhibited in the way I act. . . . It's not just a short passing thing with her. . . . I feel fortunate. I had never looked forward to being fifty before. It's nice to have something fresh and new at fifty. I'm still searching; yet now I'm a little bit more optimistic."

Mr. Z. became more responsive to B. and others as well. He was more open, warm, physical, and communicative with friends and family. For the first time in his life, Mr. Z. kissed relatives and female friends on the cheeks. He began to entertain more often and expressed a desire to have a closer, "regular" group of friends.

Now that he felt fairly secure about his relationship with B., Mr. Z. began to explore his traveling and past gravitation toward elderly people as a means of isolating himself from women his age. He also began to communicate with a male friend about sexuality. "I told him B. was uninhibited, and it was good for me. I can talk to another man about sex without being embarrassed. It opens new dimensions for me. You know, I had it in my head that women were more prim and proper than they are! . . . When I first told B. I loved her it seemed to bother her. Now she said: 'I do love you?' "

Mr. Z. initiated another vacation and did not return to the analysis. He called, saying he had married B., was happy and "free," and had gotten what he wanted from treatment. He wished to stop without any further exploration of his actions or feelings. Mr. Z. seemed to fear further analysis would ruin his dream come true. There had been signs during the previous several months, particularly in regard to the travel issue, that Mr. Z. might bolt from the analysis. He had expressed the magical fear that analyzing his new relationship would cause him to lose it. On the positive side, he was expressing feelings and opening himself to friends, both old and new. The fear of aging, the loss of his mother, a responsive new woman, and the analysis appeared to combine to allow a partial developmental reworking and a subsequent freeing of developmental progression. Mr. Z. had now moved past a lifelong fixation toward more fulfilling intimate relationships—for the first time, at age fifty!

8

Friendships in Adulthood

> There can be no friendship where there is no freedom. Friendship loves a free air, and will not be fenced up in straight and narrow enclosures.
>
> William Penn

Friendships in childhood and adolescence are complex relationships shaped by a powerful mix of sexual and aggressive feelings and developmental pressures. From the latency phase onward, friendships are an integral part of human experience. Throughout the remainder of childhood and adulthood, including old age, the character and substance of healthy friendships are determined by the mutual need to engage and resolve major developmental tasks and themes that are specific to each phase.

As our young Tom Sawyers and Nancy Drews are transformed by puberty into uncertain adolescents, they lean on each other for moral support and companionship during their determined march out of childhood. Then young adulthood brings new challenges and pressures which continue to shape the nature of friendships during the twenties and thirties.

In the late teens and early twenties, before marriage and parenthood, friendships become the primary source of emotional sustenance. Sheared of the infantile attachments to Mom and Dad, not yet committed to spouse and child, alone and independent, young men and women experience the loneliness of young adulthood. With little opportunity for nurturing within committed relationships, college students and coworkers, entrepreneurs and adventurers turn to each other for sustenance and support. "Roomies" and apartment mates, sorority "sisters," fraternity "brothers," as indicated by the names we give them, are substitutes for family—temporary stand-ins until more permanent replacements are found and created. The emotional needs for companionship, acceptance, and confidentiality are satisfied within friendships.

Whenever they weren't dating anyone, Jane and Roslyn "hung out" together. They watched TV, did laundry, drank coffee, and complained about the scarcity of decent guys. Doris and Bill were roommates, friends who worked at the same place. Uncommitted to others and struggling to pay the rent and their expensive credit card balances, they spent hours berating the boss and dreaming up schemes to get rich quick.

For those who are gay or divorced, friendships may be the most significant emotional relationships throughout adulthood. For those who marry, the plot thickens.

Make New Friends but Keep the Old

One of the central developmental tasks of young adulthood is finding a spouse, a loved one to replace parents and siblings and provide a new center of gravity for the adult years. Once this new, more permanent relationship is in place, friendships assume different and less central roles in the developmental process. Increasingly the significant other replaces the friend as confidant, providing comfort against the pains and pressures of daily life. "Those wedding bells are breaking up that old gang of mine," says a popular song from the fifties. Many friendships do become casualties of this developmental progression since the spouse may not accept the friend, recognizing at some level that they are competitors.

"I don't want you to invite them over, he's an airhead," said Mary about one of her husband's oldest friends. "Invite Joe and Kathy instead." And so begins the shifting and sorting out that eventually leads to the emergence of a new form of friendship—couples friendships—which reflect the committed status of the newly married but are more difficult to form and maintain because four individuals must be compatible, not just two.

Sometimes a compromise is struck which reflects the wisdom of the old camp song "Make new friends, but keep the old. One is silver and the other gold." Refusing to be steamrolled by her mate's pressure, Rob stood his ground. "Matt's one of my oldest friends. If you don't want to see him, I'll meet him myself. And, by the way, he's not an airhead!" After a pregnant pause which told her that he would accept her extension of an olive branch, Mary responded softly. "That's fine, honey. I didn't mean you had to stop being friends with him." The absence of a scowl allowed her to go on. "Shall I ask Joe and Kathy to come over?" "Yes," came back the formal, over-the-shoulder reply.

As children grow and begin to move into the community, parents are swept along by the momentum. At dance classes and Little League games they meet other young parents doing the same thing and become acquaintances and friends. The mutual task of child rearing provides the fertile soil from which friendships grow, organized around powerful adult developmental tasks and themes which cement relationships within the family and without for the next decade or two. When children and spouse are lost through divorce, friendships once again assume a role of increased importance, providing refuge, a calm harbor of protection from matrimonial storms.

Midlife Friendships

> There is a friend that sticketh closer than a brother.
>
> The Bible

Unlike friendships in latency and adolescence, and to some extent in young adulthood as well, midlife friendships are not characterized by intense longing or a sense of urgency. Enjoying the fulfillment which comes from having mastered the developmental tasks of earlier phases, mature individuals have neither the pressured need to grow up (as do the latency-age child or adolescent) nor the pressing desire to find and create persons to love. Healthy midlife individuals have created a nourishing network of family, friends, colleagues, and acquaintances which sustains them. They *belong*, enriched and fulfilled by loving relationships, familiar places, and comfortable routines which make day-to-day living an extraordinary experience.

Because of their unique position in the lifecycle, midlifers can easily initiate and sustain friendships with those who are younger and older as well as their chronological peers. Considerable understanding of human nature and their own needs allows them to conduct friendly relationships at an adult level with relative ease. A friendship with an adolescent may be motivated by an envious craving for his or her youth and abundant future, a sharp contrast to the consistency of midlife concerns about staid sexuality and aging. However, the same set of feelings may cause these pubertal pariahs to be avoided like the plague.

Friendships with young adults are soothing and enriching because they allow one to reexperience vicariously the luxurious richness of youth in full bloom, full of matter-of-fact, automatic sexual functioning, abundant career potential, and the wonders of early parenthood—all recently lost and not fully appreciated in their time of abundance. Relationships with older individuals may be motivated by unconscious longings to be a carefree child again, free of the crushing responsibilities of midlife, able to lean on someone else for a change rather than continuing to serve as the Rock of Gibraltar at home and at work. Of course, the specter of old age may also produce avoidance of the elderly.

Another characteristic of mature, midlife friendships is the ease with which they can be maintained. Because they occur after the establishment of regular sexual relationships and intimacy, pressures to sexualize the relationship, so prominent in adolescence and young adulthood, are diminished, if not absent. Despite concern about the real and imagined threat of an affair, this is also true of opposite sex friendships. However, as at all other points in the lifecycle, Freud's recognition that friends can rapidly be transformed into lovers or enemies remains completely valid. Midlifers are not immune from the uncertainties of life which can rapidly destabilize relationships and inner tranquility.

Thus midlife friendships are both the result of, and a stimulus to, further maturity and fulfillment because of their stability and lack of urgency and vulnerability. The true midlife friend is at ease, able to enjoy the enriching warmth and intimacy which radiates from this most ubiquitous form of human intercourse.

Friendships and Parenthood: Smoothing the Way to Separation

When seventeen-year-old Glen returned home from a date at 2 A.M., two hours after curfew, his furious father was storming about in the kitchen, waiting. "I'll be damned if I'm going to let you disobey me like that!" he thundered. "I'll see you at 5 A.M. as planned." The "plan" was for father and son to bale hay until the harvest was gathered.

Glen was in lust. As his stay in lover's lane stretched on and on he knew that his father would attempt to extract a heavy price for his pleasure. "Screw him," he thought. "I'm not a kid anymore." Clearly father did not agree and was determined to teach his disrespectful son a lesson.

The enemies met at the stroke of five and drove out to the fields without communicating. Father was surprised to see that his son looked so fresh. He was determined to hide the fact that he was reeling from a near total lack of sleep because his precious few hours between the sheets were repeatedly disturbed by a cacophony of rock and roll, whistling tea pots, and clattering pots and pans. It seemed that Glen, bent on a confrontation and revenge, was showing the old man what he was made of.

At first they worked rapidly in the cool, early morning light. As the sun, temperature, and humidity rose in unison, father's pace began to slacken. By noon Dad had had it and attempted to save face by mumbling incoherently something about "teaching you a lesson." Glen, flush with youthful triumph, said nothing but flashed "a shit-eating grin" which said "your day is over, old man. Get off my back."

That night father poured out his righteous indignation to his best friend, Harry, condemning his son with four-letter invectives and threats of retaliation. Fully expecting complete support, he was shocked by Harry's mocking laughter and admiration of Glen's spunk, determination, physical stamina, and imagined sexual exploits of the night before. "Remember the Dobson twins?" he laughed. "We were about seventeen that night, weren't we?" Father's smile of recognition of the similarities between his own adolescent experience and that of his son's brought with it relaxing feelings of resolution and relief. His friend had performed a most valuable service. By listening and then juxtaposing father and son's adolescent experience he had helped father—as perhaps no one else could have—to let go, mourn for the loss of power over his offspring, and begin to enjoy the emergence of a very special new man—father's ticket to an enriched later life and genetic immortality, maybe sooner than planned.

At all points in the lifecycle friends provide acceptance, support, and perspective—most valuable functions, indeed. And sometimes, friendships can serve as a comfortable cushion, a replacement for vanishing gratification as children turn into adults.

As their first-born sons turned their attention and affection to football and girls, two professional women in their late thirties became fast friends. In addition to running their careers and families, they ran roughshod over a totally outclassed coach, raised money for the team, and determined its use. At the games they shouted unashamedly for their sons—"Stick 'em defense!"—and kept a wary eye on advancing cheerleaders. Afterward they spent hours talking about the boys' successes, girlfriends, and college plans. Their husbands, thrown together by their wives' friendship, watched from the sidelines, literally and figuratively, taken back a bit by the power of maternal love and determination. After their sons left for college the intensity of the relationship diminished some, peaking again during vacations, and in subsequent years when forgetful sons and insensitive daughters-in-law carelessly wounded maternal sensitivities.

This was a friendship created by the need of both women to master the midlife experience of separating from their firstborns. Over the years as they struggled together to let go of long established patterns of mothering they helped each other channel energies into new directions and formed an emotional bond which outlived its original purpose and continued to enrich their lives, as a true friendship should! Adult fulfillment includes the ability to give up sources of gratification which are no longer developmentally appropriate and to replace them with new ones.

Maintaining Intimacy: There's No Fool Like an Old Fool—Unless He's Got a Good Friend

Midlife couples struggle with the difficult task of maintaining intimacy in the face of major physical, psychological, and environmental changes. If intimacy is to deepen in texture, enriched by the lengthening trail of intertwined memories and the sharing of new pains and pleasures, both partners must make a determined effort to weather the winds of change which continually threaten their closeness. Like Teyva's wife in *Fiddler on the Roof,* their midlife maturity and wisdom teaches them that the answer to the question "Do you love me?" is not a simple one.

Friends may play important, sometimes critical, roles in the redefinition of midlife intimate relationships. Comfortable closeness and nondemanding loyalty provide an ideal framework within which to ventilate sexual and aggressive issues which cannot be easily contained or managed alone, as demonstrated by the following examples.

As her husband passed forty, Jane found him less and less attractive. Eventually she began an affair with a younger coworker, thrilled by the intrigue and his youthful sexual energy. Unable to contain her excitement and anxiety, one day she blurted out the news to her best friend who was titillated, encouraging, and envious. As weeks turned into months and Jane revealed more details, her friend felt less envy for Jane. It seemed to her that the man was cancelling at the last minute more and more rendezvous and was more interested in the expensive gifts Jane lavished on him than Jane herself. The friend's concern changed to downright dismay when Jane announced her intention to ask Romeo to marry her (he had made no such suggestion).

My concurrent therapeutic efforts to get Jane, who came into therapy to deal with feelings about her mother, to consider the potential consequences of this "plan" for her future fell on deaf ears, drowned out by the excitement of the affair and the irrational internal clamor to shed fifteen or twenty years. Sometimes serendipity can be more effective than the best therapeutic intervention. I listened with relief and appreciation as Jane told me about her friend's most recent psychiatric intervention. "She told me that I was being stupid and irrational. Jeff didn't really love me and was only taking me for my money. Sleeping with him was one thing, but throwing my life away was another. I don't think I'll ever speak to her again."

But Jane did speak to her friend again, and increasingly to me as well, particularly after Jeff "tried not to laugh out loud when I suggested living together. I guess I really am nothing more than an old fool. Thank God June talked some sense into me before it was too late."

When Ben's wife of twenty-one years left him and their

three children, he was devastated. As we reconstructed the collapse of the marriage in therapy it was clear that there were plenty of warning signs, but Ben had ignored them out of fear. At the lowest point in his life, feeling alone and almost desperate, he turned to his friends, new and old. When his situation became known he was amazed at the number of casual friends and coworkers who told him similar stories. Several became frequent companions, talking and comforting as they jogged and went to movies and dinners. But Ben was knocked off his feet by the response of three old friends from his college and Air Force days. They called constantly, listened patiently to the seemingly endless flow of sadness and rage and invited Ben to their homes, Ben's kids included. Their loving concern created a holding environment which no therapist alone could provide and laid the groundwork for Ben to mourn, accept himself as a single person, and eventually begin to look for a new relationship.

Growing Old—Together?

The inevitable march of time stomps on youthful appearance and ideas and eventually forces the middle-aged individual to swallow the bitter pill of awareness of personal mortality and time limitation. The power of this realization can now become a driving developmental force, redefining the body image, clarifying and reordering goals and priorities, and increasing the importance of family and friends. Because of their unique nature, friendships can become a critically important vehicle for the expression, engagement, and resolution of these monumental midlife themes.

When Illness Intervenes

When serious illness intervenes, the mutuality and equality at the basis of friendships can be affected. The well friend experiences a surge of caring feelings. The sick friend may be at a loss to reciprocate but longs to provide some emotional support. As they commiserate and care for each other, they worry about the loss of their companionship and the shivering prospect of death.

But aggressive feelings may also be stimulated by a friend's illness because of his or her unavailability and the recognition of an impotence and inability to erase illness and death. The eruption of such aggressive impulses from the unconscious forces the healthy friend to deal with disturbing feelings of hostility and even competition and envy. Mature individuals can accept their dark side, recognizing and containing their aggressive thoughts—as this patient did—and continue to *act* in a loving way.

Because he was a shy man struggling against significant neurotic anxieties and fears, Joel did not make friends easily. However, in his forty-two years he had made a number of lasting friendships. When a close friend had a severe heart attack the underbelly of Joel's neurosis was exposed, releasing a torrent of very uncomfortable thoughts and emotions which I would suggest lurk in the shadows within each of us.

After the initial shock wore off, Joel was upset to discover that his concerns about himself superseded those for his friend. "It could have been me! . . . I didn't want this to happen to Ed, but better him than me." These thoughts made visits to the hospital difficult but also propelled him to go. "Maybe, somehow, my being there will make him get better."

Frequent contacts with Ed's wife, Ellen, began to stimulate blatantly sexual fantasies. Guilt overwhelmed him as he told me the following thoughts. Surely his friend's sexual prowess was compromised. He might even die. In either event Ellen would be "horny" and desperate for a good man, "and you know who that would be." His guilt was intensified by the recognition that his own wife and Ellen were good friends.

The continued analysis of these feelings did not prevent Joel from caring for his friend and his wife in a sincere, loving way. As Ed recovered the friendship deepened, strengthened by Joel's genuine concern at a time of need and by *his* greater understanding. "I have the potential to be a rotten human being, that's obvious; but I guess I'm not such a bad guy, am I?"

Friends and Family

As old age approaches friends may again assume positions of paramount importance, similar to those they occupied in late adolescence and early young adulthood. When the children have gone off to distant places to seek their fortune and raise their own little ones, Sunday morning phone calls and occasional visits do not fill the void created by their chronic failure to return home. The periodic pulsating awareness of abandonment is intensified by the additional losses of parents, aunts, and uncles.

One is left with friends—other widows or widowers, other aging couples, other retirees, others toward whom to direct loving feelings and still abundant energies, others to cushion the task of growing old.

Mature midlifers prepare for their later years by conducting a searingly honest appraisal of the presence or absence of the support system of family and friends. Those lucky individuals, as illustrated by the three couples in the following example, who anticipate the future and nurture friendships as they raise their families, reap later rewards.

The friendships of three couples had formed in their early thirties, forged by shared religious interests and child-rearing, despite the fact that they lived separated by five to ten big-city miles. Over the years the intensity of involvement had waxed and waned with the uneven demands of work and parenthood. By the time the last of their children had left home they had shared cookouts, car pooling, chicken pox, and a thousand and one other experiences which molded them into a quasifamily. One night, over dinner, they wondered where the last twenty-five years had gone and began to consider where the next twenty-five would go.

As they crowed about their childrens' successes—and lamented their unavailability—a collective sense of loneliness pushed them into a discussion of whether or not they would end up in old-age homes. Their particular solution arose spontaneously out of the discussion, at first as a joke, then as a frivolous idea, and then as a subject for serious consideration. We'll buy three condos in a downtown high rise near restaurants, theaters, and each other. We'll continue to live full lives, visit our grandchildren, and know that in times of need, when they do finally come, we'll have each other, for as long as we can.

Could we ask more of friendship at any age? Not really.

9

Play in Adulthood

> A mode of coping with conflicts, developmental demands, deprivation, loss, and yearnings throughout the life cycle.
>
> ALBERT SOLNIT(1)

Playing peek-a-boo, hopscotch or baseball; listening to rock and roll, Sondheim, or Sebelius; reading romance novels or watching a Shakespearian play—what do they all have in common? All are expressions of one of the most ubiquitous and intriguing human activities—play. Play is not random, carefree action, free from the psychic restraints of more mundane human pursuits. Like all other thought and behavior it is molded by the forces of the mind and the environment into nearly endless forms which fascinate us from shortly after birth until the end of life.

Do Adults Play?

Do adults play? The lifestyle of some adults might, at first glance, suggest a negative response. So would the writings of that good Victorian, Sigmund Freud, and his daughter Anna. Adults worked, Freud suggested, whereas chil-

This chapter originally appeared as *Play in Adulthood: A Developmental Consideration,* Psychoanalytic Study of the Child, vol. 48 (1993), pp. 225–245.

dren played. Based on her observations of children Anna Freud suggested a gradual shift from play to work beginning in the latency years. "Direct or displaced satisfaction from the play activity itself gives way increasingly to the pleasure in the finished product of the activity, a pleasure which has been described in academic psychology as pleasure in task completion, in problem solving, etc." But, alas, by the time we arrive at the demanding doors of adulthood, the "ability to play changes into the ability to work."(2)

But if this was the case, how would we explain such activities as football, chess, cards, and the enormous involvement in spectator sports? More recent thinkers have contested Freud's belief and present a very different conceptualization. The psychoanalyst Eric Plaut, in particular, attributes Freud's view that play was "inappropriate" in adulthood to the turn-of-the-century Victorian culture's "highly ambivalent attitude toward pleasure and an elevation of work to a dominant position in its value system." The same nose-to-the-grindstone attitude is sanctioned in Freud's definition of health as the freedom to love and work, but not to play. Plaut (and I) would elevate play to the same exalted level as love and work. Plaut contends, "From a psychological point of view, love, work, and play are the three ideal types of action."(3) Ideal because they produce fulfillment.

In order to understand play in adulthood we must consider the motivations which prompt this universal form of human expression and discuss its characteristics in both childhood and adulthood.

What Motivates Play?

In a brilliant study of children's play, one of Freud's first disciples suggested that children played so incessantly because they had to, not because they wanted to, because their minds were not fully developed and could not easily understand or integrate the multitude of new ideas and situations which they encountered every day.(4) Thus children live in a state of "traumatic stimulation." In their play they attempt to master those experiences which are too overwhelming to be integrated in one fell swoop. Two decades later the psychoanalyst Lilli Peller expanded Waelder's ideas, relating the particular forms of children's play to phase-specific developmental challenges.(5) In other words, play will be different at different ages because of gradually increasing levels of mental sophistication and the need to address new challenges that arise as the developmental stages of childhood are traversed.

But what of adults? Better able to meet the challenges of everyday living, they have less need to play. However, adult existence is certainly not free from stress or traumatic overstimulation; hence, the same basic human needs motivate play throughout the lifecycle.

People play because it provides a mechanism for disengaging from frustration and disappointment in the real world and temporarily cloaks the mind in a soothing balm of illusory gratification which reduces tension and distress. But most important of all, particularly for adults, the psychoanalyst Mortimer Ostow suggests that "play seems to provide, not for the unrestrained pursuit of pleasure, but rather for an exposure to realistic or realistic-like challenges, the overcoming of which relaxes tension and replaces it with pleasure."(6) Play is a simulated, attenuated, and controllable reality. When the pain becomes too great or the threat too formidable, it can be terminated.

By providing a mechanism for the reduction of stress and the mastery of traumatic experience, play becomes a means of pushing the individual toward new levels of mental and physical competence. The eminent child psychoanalyst, Albert Solnit, notes that as the capacities of the mind grow and the demands of daily life multiply, play becomes "an indirect approach to seeking an adaptive, defensive, skill-acquiring, and creative expression. *It is a mode of coping with conflicts, developmental demands, deprivation, loss, and yearnings throughout the life cycle*" (my italics).(7)

The Nature of Play

Thought and action
Pretending without consequence
Free of expectable consequences

Thought and Action

Childhood play is made up of two interlocking components: conscious and unconscious wishes and fantasies, and physical actions which magically create observable enactments. The adult-usurping bravado of the five-year-old—"Let's play house. I'll be the Mommy. You be the baby"—or the rhythmic hum of the jump rope to the accompaniment of "Rover, Rover, come over" are examples.

However, action may be greatly minimized or entirely absent in some forms of play in both childhood and adulthood, although much more so in adulthood. Sometimes we lazily prefer to let others do the physical work for us—let Steffi Graf race back and forth across the baseline or Nolan Ryan ram the third strike through the batter's futile swing: we'll lounge on the couch and munch junk food. In these situations the person at play *identifies* with the athlete's actions, adding his or her own fantasies to what is being seen and heard. This form of passive, nonmotoric participation in play activity through identification with others is the key component in all forms of spectator play, if not great for the cardiovascular system.

Some games such as checkers and Monopoly require little in the way of physical exertion. In others such as bridge or chess the enormous mental machinations going on barely spill over into the physical realm.

Special note should be taken of those eighty-year-old golfers who shoot their age and those senior athletes of all sorts who prove that, although strenuous physical activity is a less frequent component of play in middle and late adulthood, it remains a joyous mechanism for transforming mind into matter throughout life. The rush of adrenalin at the approach of a tennis ball and the sensation of physical competence during a smooth golf swing are joyous reminders that the body is still subject to command, still capable of fulfilling performance.

Pretending without Consequence

Play ceases to be play when the capacity to pretend is lost. Because of their relative mental immaturity, children are less able to sustain the capacity to pretend than adults. Theirs is a world of perpetual transitions from play to reality and back again. Adults play less but sustain the ability to pretend for longer periods, sometimes to exquisite (or excruciating) degrees—be it the mental gymnastics required to complete a Wagnerian ring or the physical stamina and mental toughness needed to complete a marathon.

Free of Expectable Consequences

Play must be free of expectable consequences. It is an activity, says Mortimer Ostow, "that is enjoyed for the moment; after it is over, nothing that has happened is carried over into the real world."(8) Well, not quite; sometimes there is some carryover. Consider the value attached to a coveted Little League trophy, or to being "Number One" in an after-work softball league or the Big Ten. Although none of these play results matter much in the grand scheme of things (a statement which would be disputed by any rabid fan), all are after-effects carried over into the real world.

As Ostow suggests, this spillover into reality adds spice to play. A game becomes more exciting if there is even a small reward or a prize for the winner of a contest. A novel becomes more engrossing if the reader recognizes him- or herself in a character's fictional experiences. The historical novel, the roman à clef, and the drama that portrays the human situation are all more compelling than the fantasy in which no aspect of life can be recognized. Indeed, there are a number of human activities in which it is difficult to sort out the play from the serious elements, for example, social activities, sports, sexual relations, and humor.

In some instances when adults lose the capacity to pretend, the consequences can be very real indeed. Fights among fans before, during, or after a European soccer match or the big-city burnings that follow winning "world" championships in professional football or basketball demonstrate that, as does the following example. In the midst of an "important" Little League baseball game, the two opposing coaches confronted each other over a disputed call. While their eight-year-old players and some disbelieving parents watched, the coaches began throwing punches. In "real" life one was a doctor, the other a judge.

Levels of Play

Understanding the evolution of play from childhood through adulthood is central to our understanding of maturity and adult fulfillment because it is a basic universal mechanism for *becoming* mature and because it is a major activity for achieving fulfillment in adulthood, along with the two other mainstays of adult life—love and work.

I have conceptualized play according to levels of complexity.

Level I Play

Through "peek-a-boo" and other playful interactions with their parents, infants and toddlers in Level I play learn the rudiments of play. In the process they expand their experience with actions and feelings and develop new awareness of the body. This seemingly innocuous activity has far-reaching consequences. "On the basis of play is built the whole of man's experiential existence" said David Winnicott.(9) The British analyst, George Moran, related play in infancy to the dawning awareness of body boundaries, the filling and emptying of body cavities and containers, information-processing, cognitive schemes, and the discharge of instinctual tensions.(10) In addition, Solnit suggests that play is a major source for "initially trying on, practicing, and imaginatively elaborating the capacity for wit, humor, pathos, and a whole host of affective experiences (tolerating the feelings) and their expressive communication to others."(11)

Level II Play

Level II play, occurring primarily between ages three and seven or eight (the Oedipal phase with some spillover into latency), is characterized by an endless variety of fantasy enacted through resourceful and sometimes highly original characterizations. Because the ability to pretend is more fully developed and the conscience (which becomes a potent force in early latency, ages six to eight) has not yet smothered that eye-popping early childhood openness and naïveté, Level II play is unabashedly exhibitionistic and unembarrassed, and highly intriguing to adults. In therapy with young children, play is the royal road not only to the unconscious, to paraphrase Freud, but also a broad freeway providing easy access into all avenues of the child's life, provided that the therapist, or parent in nontherapeutic settings, has the knowledge to understand this form of communication and the tolerance to accept it.

Five-year-old Sarah was a magnificent ham, easily as talented as the actress Bernhardt who shared her first name. She was also determined to displace her mother from her position of prominence. Her Oedipal struggles were unashamedly spread across her play canvas for all to see. Alone in a corner of the family room she was overheard in the midst of animated conversation with her dolls by her somewhat bemused parents "Hello, Jane" (mother), said Tom (father). "Sarah and I are going shopping to buy dresses." "Yes, Mommy," said Sarah, you stay home with David (brother) and clean the house."

Later. "Mommy, it's time for you to go to bed now. Daddy and I are going out to eat."

Still later. "Mommy, you've been a bad girl. You cannot live in this house ever again." Father doll, with conviction. "Good."

A reassuring pat on the head from real Dad kept real Mom from attacking her brazen challenger.

Level III Play

As the forces of development turn Oedipal competitors into admirers and industrious elementary school-aged students, so do they transform the character of play. Because the latency aged child (six to eleven) is increasingly capable of a variety of complicated motor skills, has the ability to read and write, has independent peer relationships, and has the capacity consistently to adhere to rules and tolerate frustrations, play changes dramatically. The impressionistic fantasies of playing house are replaced by the resolute rules of kickball, the grandiosity of dressing up in mother's blouse and high heels is muted by the torn pants and bruised knees of Capture the Flag, and the omnipotent command of a fantasized space ship is decimated by the ignominious wail of "strike three!"

Once the capacity for Level III play emerges in latency, it continues to be used throughout life. Board games and ballet, baseball and billiards are enjoyed by eight- and eighty-year-olds (as player or spectator). However, although the form remains the same, the underlying developmental themes and conflicts that energize the play change dramatically from developmental phase to developmental phase.

In adolescence and young adulthood, when physical prowess is at its zenith and peer relationships are a major form of social interaction, organized games are the most characteristic form of play. This is reflected in the importance placed in nearly every culture on games played by individuals in this age group, be it participation in a high school basketball game in Indiana, a Ping-Pong tournament in China, or, heaven help us, the frenzy of an English or Italian soccer match. Nor is the psychological impact of the games limited to the participants. The few hundred watching the high school basketball game and the billion or so who are glued to their television sets during the quatroannual orgy of the World Cup are also at play.

Level IV Play

Level IV play is *mental* play. Although it reaches its most mature form of expression in the second half of life, it is also very common in childhood. In Level IV play, thoughts and words are substituted for actions. Even when play material such as cards are involved, they are of secondary importance, providing the springboard for transformations, abstractions, and the formation of symbolic networks. Much of this play is originated and controlled by the individual fantasizer, but the motoric component (games), original fantasy (plays, novels, and books), or auditory and visual stimuli (music or dance) may be provided by others. This is known as *spectator play*.

Watching and Listening: Spectator Play

When Grandpa takes his grandson to a ballgame, as they eat hot dogs and cheer for each home run, both are also hard at work resolving developmental conflicts. Through identification with the players on the field, freckle-faced, glove-in-hand grandson is dealing with latency-aged, phase-specific issues such as competitiveness, exhibitionism, and sexual identity. At the same time, sixty-year-old Grandpa, also through identification, is mourning for his lost body of youth and coming to terms with success or failure in his chosen fields of endeavor, now that he no longer has the abundant future still available to the younger man on the baseball diamond. Nurtured by their play and each other, when the game is over, the score soon forgotten, both child and adult return to the "real" world.

Listening to music is another extremely common form of play. Highly evocative and capable of stimulating a wide variety of sexual and aggressive fantasies, its ethereal, non-tangible nature is consistent with the abstract nature of Level IV play. From hard rock to Haydn, the endless variety of musical expression enhances its developmental usefulness to individuals of all ages.

Music with words, song, is particularly effective in this regard. "It was an itsy-bitsy, teeny-weeny, yellow polka dot bikini," "I've got a brand new pair of roller skates, you've got a brand new key," and "Baby, I want to make love to you" have helped successive generations of teenagers "play" safely with the serious, anxiety-provoking business of adolescent sexuality by enveloping themselves in the suggestive rhythms, words, and appearance of the most audacious music and popular groups. Psychological separation from parents is also facilitated since their musical tastes are usually quite different from their children. The parents, in turn, nostalgically rework their own adolescent and young adult experiences by listening to the music of their own generation often with an air of superiority which stems from the conviction that they listened to "good" music and their children are obsessed with trash. It is not surprising that older adults are often attracted to the highly abstract aspects of classical music which often deal with the more philosophical and serious preoccupations of the second half of life such as Mozart's "Requiem" or Strauss' "Four Last Songs."

> The play's the thing to catch the conscience of the king.
>
> *Hamlet*

Creativity and Play

Freud suggested that creative writing, like a daydream, is a continuation of and substitute for the play of childhood.

Both the author and the child at play create a new world by stringing together fantasy and experience in novel ways. Unlike children, adults usually hide their fantasies because their childlike quality and sexual and aggressive nature meet with internal and external derision unless they are couched in terms which make them suitable for the light of day, as in the novel. Unlike the child who is not primarily interested in communication, the author of any sort must take into consideration the effect of his or her creation on the audience, filtering fantasies through the organizing and critical influences of the ego and superego. By so doing, play blends with work, a blurring of boundaries which occurs frequently in adulthood. On the other hand, the playgoers or readers, who have no responsibility for the creative work, are closer to pure play as they sit in their seats, keep their mental and emotional responses to themselves, and experience a brief respite from the relentless pressures of work and reality.

In a similar fashion, reading diminishes mental tension by allowing the reader to play along with the author's fantasies, nimbly deflecting criticisms of the conscience from the self to the author who, after all, created the stimulating and potentially offensive ideas. Further, the reader is protected from the danger and hardships endured by the characters in the novel by the simple act of closing the book, ending the play, and returning to a momentarily less threatening reality.

The Organizers of Adult Play

Rumbling beneath the surface of most Level III and IV play in adulthood are powerful developmental forces, unique to the sixth, seventh, and eighth phases of life which transform the *meanings* behind the conventional forms and levels of play. Among these are the aging process in the body, the growing awareness of time limitation and mortality, conflicts over significant relationships, sex, and work.

The Body

Thoughts and feelings about the body are a major conscious and unconscious dynamic theme underlying play throughout the adult years. In *young adulthood* this somatic influence is expressed through two contradictory and dissonant themes: the enjoyment of the body at its peak of competence, and, toward the second half of this phase, the painful awareness of physical decline and mourning for the fading body of youth. Pleasure and pain, joyful competence, and the realization of loss push healthy young adult players to choose play-tasks which challenge them to the utmost, produce real exhilaration and achievement, and at the same time perpetuate the youthful illusion of personal invincibility and invulnerability. This internal tug-of-war causes the healthy young adult gradually to abandon those sports such as football or basketball which tax the body beyond its slightly shrunken limits and seek fulfillment through less arduous challenges.

In addition to mourning for the lost body of youth, those approaching midlife must also relinquish their unrealized fantasies of athletic fame and fortune. As athletic heroes become first chronological contemporaries and then the age of sons and daughters, they become unsuitable subjects for identification who no longer bolster fantasies of future success. But the desire for eternal youth and perpetual glory die hard in some. These individuals continue to bask in the now pale glow of a faded past or are reincarnated in the bodies of sons and daughters or grandchildren who provide them with the perpetual gifts of youth and physical ability.

Bruce began psychoanalysis at age thirty-five because of sexual inhibitions and an inability to bring himself to marry. The victim of an abusive father who belittled his considerable academic achievement and ignored his outstanding athletic success, Bruce turned to sports as a source of gratification and an acceptable outlet for his displaced rage. He was both admired and feared by his competitors, who endured a losing streak which lasted nearly two decades. But, now, for the first time, in his midthirties Bruce began to lose to the relentless assaults of a seemingly endless procession of younger men. His reports of boasting, verbal assaults, and temper tantrums while at "play" became a major vehicle for the analysis of his unresolved conflicts from childhood, particularly about his father; the abhorred young adult task of mourning for his youth; and the inappropriate, but no longer successful, use of sports as a substitute for sexual intimacy and marriage.

In *middle adulthood*, physical play is abandoned by many because of diminished ability and the pain of poor performance. Others continue to use athletics as a method of dealing with the aging process, compensating for the anxiety connected with the idea that "my body is not as competent as it used to be" with the compensatory fantasy "my body is as capable as it was when I was young." The illusion is enhanced by the occasional great golf shot or the tennis backhand that zings down the line, momentarily conquering age and time. However, healthy midlife players do continue to get great pleasure and fulfillment (to say nothing of exercise) from their play, tempering its intensity in harmony with their bodies' changing capabilities—more doubles, shorter jogs, no more sandlot football—while continuing to experience the thrill of victory and the agony of defeat.

Those in *late adulthood* use physical play for all of the same psychological reasons as those who are younger, but in addition they are focused on the developmental task of maintaining body integrity in the face of the onslaught of age and ill health. While athletic forms of play continue to provide a mechanism for experiencing the fulfilling feeling of physical intactness, they also facilitate the acceptance of aging because repeated imperfect attempts at accomplishing complicated actions such as hitting a baseball thrown by a grandson or sinking a three-foot putt are constant reminders of the body's limitations.

Temporal Attitudes

As young adulthood shifts into midlife, the monumental developmental task of the acceptance of time limitation and one's own mortality comes into focus. As the realization of aging and eventually dying permeates every aspect of mental and physical life, play becomes a fanciful mechanism for mastering such a serious subject.

Physical games such as tennis and golf are like magic carpets, obliterating time. Unlike life, which has only one beginning, midpoint, and ending, these games are a grab bag of starts and finishes which provide the soothing, symbolic luxury of the mastery of time and imperfection—again and again, alone or with partners or teammates. Demanding games such as football and basketball, in which time runs out, are usually played by the young, reveling in their abundant futures. Older individuals participate in these sports as spectators, narcissistically shielded from the sting of time limitation by the young stalwarts with whom they identify and by the realization that even though time ended this particular contest in the make-believe world of play, another may begin.

All forms of mental games are enjoyed for the same conscious and unconscious reasons. Played without physical exertion, they eliminate the unreliable, aging body almost entirely and instead rely on the rock solid Zen-like currency of intelligence! Chess and checkers, rummy and bridge provide the arena in which midlifers may shine, nimbly conquering, for the moment, youthful competitors and Father Time.

So do various forms of gambling. The wish to get rich quick, to get something for nothing, to rely on Lady Luck implies that one is special, singled out for favors by the all-powerful forces which govern the universe and control human life and death. The mundane is sucked out of the fairy lands of Las Vegas and Atlantic City by play money, free liquor, perpetual participation, and the absence of clocks. Despite these real and intrapsychic efforts to blot out awareness of impermanence and the possibility of sudden death, unwanted reality intrudes, symbolized by the silent slot machine, craps, and a bust in blackjack.

Fulfillment comes to those in late adulthood who, having accepted the idea that they will die, are more concerned with how death will come—with dignity surrounded by family and friends or painfully and alone. Young adult and midlife themes do not disappear, but they are muted. Playfulness in the later works of geniuses such as Picasso and Verdi may be a reflection of the acceptance of time limitation and mortality. Freed of this midlife preoccupation, they and healthy older individuals from all walks of life are able to reflect joyfully on the wonders of human existence and calmly to accept their limited place in the cosmic order.

Relationships

In adulthood, fulfillment is based in part on the ability to recognize and accept the central position of change in life.

This is particularly true for significant emotional relationships which are in a constant state of flux. Robert Nemiroff and I have observed that in midlife, in particular, healthy marriages deepen in significance while others break up on the shoals of middle-age developmental issues: Parents become dependent and die and children individuate and leave. As opposed to childhood and in some respects to old age as well, the task is to sort out, categorize, and set priorities among relationships in an effort to balance internal pressures and external demands.

Because it is a form of activity familiar to all, from the youngest child to the oldest adult, play provides a crucible in which relationships can be forged and maintained. When young children want to engage another person, be it a friend or a stranger, they ask, "Do you want to play with me?" Adults are not so forthright in their approach, but they too use play to form and sustain relationships.

Play is an important activity for cementing the relationship between parents and children. As Grampa John played catch with his son and grandson, he heard his son shout some familiar words: "Great catch, Billy. You did that like a pro!" Turning to his father, he beamed, "Remember when you used to say that to me, Dad?" But when the parents' needs are pathological and excessive, the result is not so positive. For example, one of my adolescent patients had to contend with an overpowering father who pushed him into football and wrestling, sports in which the boy had limited interest and ability. In addition to loudly condemning his son's every move from the stands, the father challenged the boy to head-to-head competition. Even a recommendation for psychotherapy for the father was turned into a contest. "Sure," he said, "I accept your challenge—and I'll finish before he does!"

Grownups also attempt to master current adult themes, as well as childhood experience, through "play" with their children. As noted earlier, using the analogy of the corrida and the "Moment of Truth," the point in the bull fight when the matador dramatically pauses before plunging his blade through the bull's aorta, Nemiroff and I described the moment in which both parents and child recognize, if not acknowledge, that the child is stronger or more physically capable than the parent. Often the realization occurs during a play situation.

When pumped up, fourteen-year-old Billy tauntingly challenged his father, Phil, to a tennis match in which he boasted he would defeat "the old man" 6–0, 6–0 for $20, his father readily accepted. Although he had occasionally lost a set to this "cocky young upstart," Phil had never come close to losing a match, and certainly not 6–0, 6–0. As he described it to me, Phil planned to "let the kid win a few games, pocket the $20, and teach him a lesson." Instead of recklessly pounding the ball on each stroke as he usually did, Billy methodically returned every ball, every time, running his father from side to side, until my exhausted patient quit at 4–0 in the second set, leaving behind a trail of invectives and four-letter words. Phil refused to pay the debt, claiming that Billy had competed unfairly (his language was actually a bit more colorful than that). The analysis of this episode eventually led father to the realization of the depth of his envy of his son's youthful vigor and to a beginning understanding of his rage at "anyone under twenty." Discussions of the episode surfaced again and again as Phil worked through feelings about physical aging, loss of power over a no longer dependent child, and pride and envy over his son's emerging manhood.

The sense of genetic immortality which galvanizes grandparents to their grandchildren is heightened through play. The conscious and unconscious fusion of memories from childhood and play activities in the present with the grandchild produces a profoundly gratifying sense of *connectedness* with the beginning of life rather than the end. But as those same memories tumble into consciousness in a seemingly unending flow, they are reminders of childhood friends, parents and grandparents, and playmates who have died. Beginnings and endings, childhood and old age fuse, heightening the significance of loved ones, past and present, and the preciousness of time.

Sex

Sexual play is an integral part of adult fulfillment, enhancing enjoyment, heightening connectedness, and stimulating the engagement and mastery of infantile and adolescent themes. When a sexual relationship between two adults is mature and secure, it provides them with a framework in which to expose and act out their own childhood, adolescent, and adult sexual fantasies and to become part of the fantasy play of another. Permission is mutually granted to use the two bodies as playthings, not so far removed from the play invitation extended many years before, "Let's play house, I'll be the Mommy, you be the Daddy."

Sexual playfulness does not begin in adulthood. The toddler's joyful touching of exposed genitals during diapering, the excitement of playing doctor, the pleasures of adolescent masturbation, and the overwhelming rush which accompanies early sexual encounters are all examples of children and young adults at play, waystations on the path to healthy adult sexuality.

The failure to integrate sexual playfulness into the sexual repertoire in adolescence and young adulthood may be a significant factor in midlife dissatisfaction. Fifty-year-old Bernie left his "wonderful" wife of thirty years because of an incomprehensible sense of anger at her and the nagging feeling that he had missed out on youthful sexual adventure by marrying too young. He entered therapy after leaving her in order to decide about his future. The early months of treatment were spent in his embarrassing elaboration of sexual wishes and fantasies which he had been unable to experience with his wife despite her openness. Eventually Bernie began dating a much younger woman and acted on his fantasies, at first experiencing a sense of exhilaration and playfulness that was highly gratifying. But in time the realization that he had little in common with "somebody as young as my daughter who's dating me for what I can give her, and I don't mean sexually," led to the end of the relationship. After nearly two years of "playing around" with other "young things" and considerable work on his sexual inhibitions and fears of aging, the patient returned home to an uncertain future with a woman who reluctantly agreed to give him "one last chance."

Work and Responsibility

For most healthy individuals midlife is a time of immense responsibility—for growing and grown children, aging parents, and grandchildren; for the demands of work; and for partner and self in the present and the future (retirement). Play provides a safety valve from the pressure cooker of responsibility, furnishing an outlet for the powerful emotions generated therein. For example, in games played by individuals, the player is only responsible for himself or herself, not a dying mother or a troubled teenager. In group games teammates bear equal responsibility for victory or defeat; the load is shared. Then, too, as with all play, the consequences are miniscule, unlike the obligations of everyday life. Television, plays, and movies appeal to adults for similar reasons. By climbing into the shoes of characters in make-believe situations, pressures and responsibilities can be confronted—and mastered—without risk or consequence.

Most people reach their highest level of work achievement and power in midlife and will advance no further. This sometimes painful reality can be compensated for through play. In the world of play and make-believe, continued achievement and maintenance of power are possible without concern for aging, obsolescence, or the driving ambition of younger colleagues.

10

Work

Midlife is the time when those who have been successful exercise position and power in the workplace. Capable and in charge, they experience the financial and emotional gratification of achievement and guide the next generation through their role as mentors. Obviously, this picture does not describe many workers who experience their jobs as drudgery and spend their time dreaming of retirement. Here I plan to focus on the former group, exploring the developmental impacts on attitudes toward work and relationships with colleagues, and describing the fulfillment that work can bring. For it is my belief that work is truly one of the paths, no, one of the broad freeways, which can lead to fulfillment in adulthood.

Developmental Antecedents

Childhood

The capacity for work begins to develop in the second and third years of life, as parents introduce toilet training and other limit-setting experiences. As the parents regularly say "No," frustrates the toddler's wish for total freedom, replace chaos with order, and impose routines and restrictions, they help the child to begin to tolerate frustration, delay gratification, and establish the capacity to control mind and body—essential components of a mature capacity to work.

Toilet training adds a major new dimension to the personality. As they interact with their child around his or her "jobbies" (stools) and gently insist on adherence to societal demands for bowel and bladder control and cleanliness, parents facilitate the emergence of a core of strength which forms the basis on which the ability to work is built.

As described in Chapter 3, as a result of love and limits, particularly in regard to control of the body and its products, *character* emerges. The tough, responsible integrity which is found in abundance in every mature adult originates there. Or as Anna Freud put it, "In short, what takes place in this period is the far-reaching modification and transformation of the [personality] which—if kept within normal limits—supply the individual personality with a background of highly desirable, valuable qualities."(1)

During the Oedipal years ambition and initiative, then directed primarily toward parental competitors, are integrated into the future worker's armamentarium. To quote Erikson, "While autonomy concentrates on keeping potential rivals out, and therefore, can lead to jealous rage most often directed against encroachments by younger siblings, initiative brings with it anticipatory rivalry with those who have been there first and may, therefore, occupy with their superior equipment, the field toward which one's initiative is directed."(2) Success in the workplace is predicted on the ability to face potential rivals and challenges, to work with and learn from those with "superior equipment," and to direct one's initiative beyond the limits imposed by current-day procedures and knowledge. The child who successfully traverses the Oedipal stage and its developmental tasks is at the same time internalizing the capacities and characteristics required for success and fulfillment in the workplace.

During these years children begin to think about the idea of work and career choice, building their ideas on knowledge gained from parents and the popular culture. Choices such as mommy or mechanic, president or pilot are given equal consideration, with little understanding of what is actually involved. Family values, socioeconomic status, and cultural stereotypes begin to limit choices, particularly for girls, as parents subtly support or discourage various speculations.

Latency is the first phase of development in which children in Western society are expected to work. Their form of work is contained in the work in homework, which expresses the emphasis placed by the culture on formal learning. In order to be a successful worker–learner, many capabilities must be present to meet the demands of the school-workplace. These capacities also form the nucleus of the skills required by the adult worker including the ability comfortably to control the body and utilize its potential; to modulate gratification and frustration and remain focused on a task for increasingly long intervals; to possess intellectual skills, beginning with the ability to read and write; and to relate to peers and superiors in a manner which facilitates accomplishment and productivity. All of these characteristics emerge in the elementary school classroom.

With the internalization of the conscience in early latency the child begins to possess the moral values, ability to control impulses, and self-generated expectations for achievement which are indispensable attributes of the successful worker. Such an individual is self-motivated, focused, and goal-oriented, continually responding to a powerful inner gyroscope that directs him or her toward higher levels of achievement. These are the qualities which twenty years later produce outstanding academic achievement, new discoveries, and the guts to begin a new business.

Erikson recognized the importance placed on work as a future expectation when he described the developmental dilemma of latency as industry versus inferiority.(3) As they enter the school years, children must develop the mentality needed to be industrious, to work, to achieve. If they do not the result is a growing sense of inferiority perpetuated by the realization that with the failure to master each academic and developmental challenge they fall further and further behind their peers, whose newly acquired skills and capabilities propel them toward a prominent position in the workplace.

Adolescence

Recently during the course of a single day, three adolescent patients spontaneously introduced the subject of work—one begrudgingly, because her parents insisted she get a job, the other two with ambivalence because they wanted money for clothes and gasoline. The desire to partake of the pleasures of adolescent/adult life—and parental insistence—push adolescents into the work force, where there they earn a little money and learn about the demands and expectations connected with work. These experiences are mixed blessings in my opinion. Although they provide valuable experience they often detract from time which could be more profitably (in every sense of that word) spent on studies, preparing for the future when educational credentials literally translate into dollars, a high standard of living, and meaningful, interesting work.

The rush for immediate gratification and inner conflicts stand in the way of academic achievement for many adolescents, limiting adult futures in ways which are incomprehensible, and uninteresting, to them, but all too clear to more experienced adults.

In his senior year, Bill was in the catbird seat. He had a 4.0 average in advanced classes and a 1410 score (1600 is perfect) on his Scholastic Aptitude Test. He was an excellent candidate for acceptance at an Ivy League college. Barely remembered, except by me, were the horrendous times we went through in his sophomore year, when fights with and between his divorced parents, failure to complete homework assignments, and a cheating episode on a test despite his knowing the material cold almost derailed the college express. As we discussed his conflicted feelings about his parents, success in the future through academic achievement, work and financial independence became recognized as the key to autonomy and independence. From then on Bill "put it all together. I finally realized making it in college was the way to take charge of my life."

By contrast, Sarah is an example of a very bright young woman whose emotional immaturity and addiction to immediate gratification are seriously undermining the development of the intellectual tools and academic credentials necessary for success in the adult workplace. In elementary school she did not develop the study skills required of successful students. The situation deteriorated in adolescence when intense involvement with friends, dating, and a refusal to do homework because of a fear of failure produced a C– average and an 810 SAT score. "I wish I could whisk you twenty years into the future so you could see how differently you will feel then about working," I said wistfully. "But you can't," she smiled sadistically. "I guess I'll have to learn it for myself." Yes, indeed, the final word is not in on Sarah. Her attractiveness, high intelligence, and basic emotional intactness may blossom into success in the workplace in adulthood. Only time will tell as she runs the rapids of young adult development.

Young Adulthood

Work becomes a central, often dominant, activity in young adulthood. When the childhood developmental line leading to adult work is relatively conflict free, there is a smooth transition from high school to on-the-job training or college and beyond. The transition from learning and play to work may be gradual or abrupt, but at some point in the late teens or twenties the realization gradually dawns that the pleasure of play and the luxurious life of the student, dripping with freedom and free time, must be subordinated to the temporal and emotional demands of work.

June had adored her five years in college, where she reveled in the swirl of "sorority and Sartre," as she so elegantly phrased it. Only reluctantly did she accept a job with a large real estate firm. Somewhat of a hippie, she had limited interest in her appearance and began work in a borrowed and battered wardrobe. At first she scoffed when her boss insisted on a clothing advance, but soon she began to enjoy the upscale clothing which engendered admiring glances from friends and colleagues alike. She was even more enthralled by her unexpected success. She was *good* at what she did. Rather quickly work became a source of pleasure and enhanced self-esteem rather than "the drudge I thought it would be."

The motivations to work are multiple and for the most part obvious. Young adults work because they must, in order to earn a living. Like young animals in the wild whose mothers will no longer feed them they must survive. Other driving forces behind work are not so basic or negative. Many young adults fall into a line of work and enjoy it. The desire to learn, to achieve, to succeed is driven by healthy curiosity and ambition. Abundant self-esteem is the reward, bolstered as it is by relationships with others who are engaged in the same or similar work. Children play together, young adults work together and in the process become friends.

As they meet, fall in love, and intertwine their lives, young adults begin to work for each other, scrambling to save enough for downpayments, dishwashers, and dining. A powerful stimulus to work occurs when children appear. With their presence mothers and fathers double their efforts to provide a bountiful present and a secure future for their offspring.

While all of this is occurring, slowly but surely, work begins to permeate the deepest recesses of the psyche, becoming an integral part of one's identity, often a source of pleasure, even of security because of the nurturing aspects of its familiar routines. For some lucky ones there are moments, even days, when work becomes a *preferred* activity, replacing play or other activities as a significant source of pleasure. Love, play, and work—as young adulthood progresses, the last becomes elevated to equal status with the first two, completing the triumvirate of activities which produce lasting adult fulfillment.

The Mentor and the Student

Every young adult, regardless of job or career, must assume the role of student or protegé, related to mentors in order to acquire the skills and knowledge needed to forge an adult work identity. Usually less in number then the fingers on one hand, these larger-than-life figures from the past or present have likely already sprung into the reader's mind. Usually much loved, their importance exaggerated by an intrapsychic fusion with parents and other significant figures from the childhood past, they open the doors to new treasure chests of knowledge and serve the developmental function of facilitating the establishment of a work identity.

Like other inevitable developmental sequences, the relationship with the mentor passes through stages. First the teacher is idealized, possessing knowledge and expertise which seem hopelessly beyond reach of the apprentice. But as the mentor's secrets are captured by the student and his or her inevitable limitations recognized and scrutinized, a more realistic appraisal begins to emerge. Sooner or later the teacher–student relationship ends. Then, suitably transformed by the experience, a new sense of self emerges in the student, who now possesses the knowledge required to strike out in new directions, make a unique contribution to human knowledge, and in the process—we hope—surpass the mentor in wisdom and accomplishment. Then the stage is set for the process to begin again, with the former student, now in the teacher's role, struggling with the pains and pleasures of being a mentor.

Midlife

For many midlife adults in Western society, work is an activity of major importance, boosting self-esteem, providing meaning and purpose to daily existence, organizing the use of time, and facilitating friendships and the achievement of financial security. Midlife workers are at the top of the heap. Capable, accomplished, and powerful, they are reaping the rewards of years of effort during which skills were mastered and seniority earned.

The narcissistic gratifications emanating from work may be considerable. Soothing, reliable, and stable, they compensate for the painful realities of life related to aging, parental death, children getting older, and the crush of responsibilities. Sometimes the imbalance is such that work becomes the *main* source of emotional sustenance and stability, a refuge from doubts, debt, and difficult relationships. Such overinvestment in work may block the engagement of a related developmental task, planning for retirement and replacement by the next generation. The awkward juxtaposition of maximum achievement and power in the workplace and the simultaneous realization of approaching loss and displacement is at the core of the midlife worker's intrapsychic and real predicament. Sometimes recognition of the conflict is facilitated as early as the midforties, by the phenomenon of *plateauing*, psychologist Judith Bardwick's term for lateral movement instead of promotion, indicating that the crest has been reached and that higher levels of position and power are not forthcoming.(4)

Position at or near the top of the pyramid includes the exercise of power toward subordinates, particularly younger, potential successors. As one CEO patient put it, "My toughest job is not running the company, it's finding and training someone to succeed me. I know whomever I choose will be grateful and appreciative, but they'll also be anxious to get me the hell out of there."

Ah, there's the rub!, the essence of the conflict of the midlife mentor—to educate the next generation while recognizing that mentor relationships are the means of one's displacement. Awareness of the snapping at the heels of those hungry to displace you is not limited to near-retirees.

It begins in the late thirties and early forties when the harbingers of middle age are beginning to appear.

For those with sufficient self-confidence and sources of fulfillment outside the workplace, the anger at and envy of promising subordinates is not acted on to any significant degree. Instead, the fantasies and feelings are recognized and processed at a mental level, often sublimated into *generativity,* Erik Erikson's term for caring for the next generation. For others whose lives are unsatisfying and fractured along several planes, fear of successors can result in cruel and sadistic verbal attacks and actions intended to destroy the progression of the protegé.

Attitudes toward money are closely related to work, particularly in midlife. For all but the very wealthy the dilemma is the same—not enough money to meet the demands of daily expenses, provide children with the opportunity for higher education and/or transition to independent status, care for aging parents, and last (unfortunately) but not least, enjoy oneself in the present and save for retirement.

Anticipating Retirement

As they grapple with the prospects of plateauing and displacement by younger workers, individuals in their forties begin to anticipate the day when they will no longer work, or will need to change jobs or careers. Thoughts of retirement are frequently blotted out by those at the peak of their prowess, but prospects for fulfillment in later life are greatly enhanced by the ability to take that searing look into the future, to anticipate, to plan. The time to plan for the future is always now, and the mature adult constructs a flexible, life-long plan in all areas, not just work.

Retirement is clearly not for everyone. For others, it is

the closest thing to heaven. Phyllis retired at fifty-nine after thirty years in middle management at a large company. The enormous pressures of the job were taking their toll physically and mentally. "Retirement is almost too good to be true," she said. "Nobody breathing down my neck. I have time to read, exercise, enjoy my family, and play some golf. I may get a part-time job in the future, but I doubt it. I'm content."

By contrast, Peter is an eighty-seven-year-old man who works six days a week at his own business. Mentally sharp, intensely curious about current events, business cycles, and the personal lives of his employees, he feels that work is partly responsible for his enormous fulfillment and longevity. "Retire to what?" he asks with complete sincerity. "I love what I'm doing. It brings me pleasure."

The paths to fulfillment are indeed many and varied. For those wrapped up in the dizzying pace of the midlife workplace, the choice of a future course may be quite peripheral. But sooner or later it will become a central concern, another important choice on the road to fulfillment.

CASE REPORT: A Difficult Transition to Young Adulthood

Despite good looks, intelligence, and a college degree, the young man in this case report was not able to make a smooth transition to young adulthood. His struggle to find a place for himself in the workplace and to achieve independence, intimacy, and self-esteem was difficult indeed.

History

I first met Jim when he was nine years old, when his parents brought him for evaluation because of a general sense of unhappiness, temper tantrums, and difficulty in making friends. We worked together for three years, during which time I came to know a very bright, engaging child with an excellent capacity for introspection and insight. Happy, friendly, and calm, Jim terminated his childhood therapy five days before his twelfth birthday.

Although I thought of him many times in the intervening years, there was no direct contact between us until I greeted him thirteen years later at age twenty-five, in the same office in which the child therapy had occurred.

His mother had called once, when he was in high school, with a question about his brother. When I asked how Jim was doing, the reply was a sparse, "fine."

When Jim called and asked to see me because he was having difficulty deciding on a choice of career, I readily agreed. Now I would have the opportunity to determine the effect of our work on his adolescent and young adult development. Greeting him in the waiting room was somewhat of a shock since I half expected to see the preadolescent boy I had come to know so well. In his stead was a handsome, slim young man over six feet tall. The one clear link between the boy and the man was a distinctive broad smile.

I was struck by the sense of warmth and familiarity which was instantly present. Despite the many intervening years and the changes that had occurred in both of us, the intimacy and positive alliance that were present during the child therapy immediately came to life. Jim commented on this indirectly by warmly remembering various pieces of furniture and pictures which were present during his child therapy. "You haven't changed much either," he quipped with a wry smile. "The same office, the same furniture, the same doctor," I thought. He was comforted and reassured by the familiar and ready to work.

Without my asking, Jim told me of his occupational

doubts. He loved golf and wanted to make a career as a professional golfer but was concerned about the financial uncertainty of such a venture. He had graduated from college two years ago and was living at home, working occasionally—and contending with his parents' dissatisfaction with his life. A second problem of significance emerged as Jim began to tell me about his adolescent and adult development. A summary of that information, which was gathered over the next year-and-one-half, follows.

The junior high school years were good ones. Jim went through puberty easily between thirteen and fourteen, had many friends, and was very active in sports. He easily maintained a B+, A− average throughout high school and college. The sometimes difficult relationship with his father improved considerably during adolescence because of Jim's academic and athletic success and his plans to attend college. Currently they were at loggerheads again because his father was so dissatisfied with Jim's lack of direction. During adolescence he had not been a disciplinary problem at home or in school and had never been involved with the police.

Jim dated fairly regularly throughout high school and college and had intercourse for the first time at the end of tenth grade. As he put it "I was pretty good at getting girls into bed, better than I was at keeping them as girlfriends." In fact, he had only had one steady girlfriend during those years.

He did not currently have a girlfriend and wasn't looking for one since, as he stated with bitterness and conviction, he doubted that he would ever marry. Occasional, casual contacts were easy to come by and met his sexual needs. Here was clear evidence of unresolved sexual conflict, I thought, hoping that we would have the opportunity to explore the subject as time went on.

Toward the middle of our first session, Jim volunteered that he began smoking pot off and on in high school and smoked "a lot" in college. "I still do," he continued, "it makes me happy with the status quo." If he were me, he continued, he would tell him to stop smoking pot, and to give up alcohol, which he also used frequently. The ease with which he told me about his drug use and the suggestion that I should tell him that he should stop were indications that despite an absence of conscious memory of the child therapy experience, he had not lost the capacity to face painful problems or to force himself to change them.

After a few diagnostic sessions, I conveyed my concern about the significance of his drug use and offered various ways to address it, including a return to therapy. Jim decided to try to stop on his own but asked if I would agree to see him two or three times a month. When I suggested that more frequent visits would be necessary because of the severity of his problems, he calmly stood his ground. He did not want to rely on his father for financial support or me. All he needed was the chance to sort out a few things with me and he would be on his way. After expressing doubts about his plan, but in the face of his determination to do it his way, I agreed to see him as often as he wished for a trial period. To my surprise, he did make dramatic changes in his life, including stopping drinking and smoking pot—cold turkey!—and within a month obtaining a job as a clerk at a large discount chain.

Clinical Material

Jim and I met two or three times a month for three years. Then, at his suggestion, we met once every two or three months. My approach throughout this time has been primarily supportive. I conceptualized that the rather remarkable changes which took place with a minimum of therapeutic contact were based on a strong, positive relationship with me, which had continued since the child therapy, and Jim's determination. I was the empathetic, caring parent who supported his development with love and unwavering support. Most of our sessions were focused on three topics: work and career, his relationship with his parents, and dating and sex. Jim introduced the subject matter and directed the sessions. I asked questions to help elaborate the material and made clarifications and an occasional interpretation.

During the first year of our time together, Jim begrudgingly worked regularly at his "very, very boring" job as a clerk and contemplated his future. Gradually he abandoned his plans for a career as a golf pro and began to focus on the prospect of becoming a schoolteacher. When I supported this interest, he found a volunteer position as an aide in an elementary school classroom. Over the course of several months, as his interest in teaching grew, he decided to seek a teaching credential. During this time, he was not drinking or smoking and was living at home, coexisting with his concerned parents. He remained strongly interested in girls but did very little dating.

Once Jim decided to apply for the year of full-time study required to obtain his teaching credential, his self-esteem improved noticeably. His parents were also pleased with his plan. Jim continued working and had saved $3,000 toward his tuition. His father agreed to pay half. Soon after, Jim asked a woman at work for a date. They dated for a brief while and then "she dumped me."

The following material from a session about a year into the therapy illustrates Jim's thinking at that time. He began by discussing his successful efforts not to drink or use pot and proudly reminded me that he had been totally drug free for four months now. With a tinge of sadness, he described how his old using friends were beginning to drop away. They didn't have much in common anymore. Since he worked on Friday and Saturday nights, he didn't get to go out much. He did go to a club with a friend but "it was just a bunch of drunk people."

Jim's eyes lit up as he began to tell me about school. He got an A on one test and a high B on another. He was cutting his work week back to twenty-five hours so that he could have more time to concentrate on his studies. With apprehension, he began to consider the prospects of getting a teaching job after he finished school. The market was tough. Maybe he would have to move to a smaller state. His sales job was much more tolerable now because he had a goal. "It's not a dead end anymore."

Then he began to talk about his father. "We're getting along fantastically now." When I inquired why, he jokingly commented that they rarely saw each other. No, it was because he was doing well in school and his father approved of his goal. Jim compared himself to his brother. Life always seemed easier for him and their father was quite pleased with the brother's college performance. But he was about to graduate and didn't seem to have any clear plans for the future. "I hope he doesn't do what I did," he said.

Easily switching subjects, Jim bemoaned his lack of a social life. He had recently slept with a girl but the sex was only fair. By this, he meant that the girl was basically passive and nonresponsive, "laying there like a sack of potatoes. Building a relationship shouldn't be this much trouble. It seems like honesty is such a tough thing." He went on to explain that he wanted an "honest girl who has it together a little bit." When I inquired about what he meant by honest, he replied, "Someone who lets me know how she feels about me. Who doesn't make excuses. Sometimes I feel like I'm the only person out there my age who tries to be responsible." As I listened, I heard the emergence of the young adult need for a loving, caring relationship with a woman. This was in sharp contrast to Jim's opening comment that he might never marry and his feeling that he had little to offer a woman. I attributed the change to his vastly improved self-esteem, which emanated from his success on his chosen career path and my unambivalent acceptance of his sexual and professional interests.

Near the end of the session, Jim described a recent house-warming party. He had a good time without drinking. He was feeling better physically and had begun to ride his bicycle regularly. "I feel like I'm healing my life," he said. "If I can just keep this on track."

During the second year of therapy, Jim completed his course work and began student teaching. Unfortunately he found himself in an extremely tight job market and was unable to find a permanent job. Fighting off disappointment and depression, he decided to continue working and to place his name on the substitute teaching list. Soon after, he moved into a condo, paid a reasonable rent, and enjoyed his newfound freedom. Dating became more sporadic as his feelings of self-esteem plummeted when he was unable to get a teaching job.

Fortunately Jim did begin to get some substitute teaching days and was pleased by the positive comments that were forthcoming from administrators and teachers. He began subbing on a fairly regular basis and was much more upbeat about his life as evidenced by the following material from a session toward the end of the second year of therapy. In characteristic fashion, Jim began the session without delay. He had just totaled up his teaching days for the year thus far. "Fifty," he announced proudly. But there was still no prospect for a permanent job. Confidence emanated from him as he talked about his experiences in the classroom. Since we were now only meeting at his request—the last time had been three months before—he was anxious to bring me up to date. He proudly described a vacation he had just taken and paid for, his first as a working man, and announced the fact that between his job and substituting he was earning $1600 to $1800 a month. In midsentence, he switched topics. "I've got my eye on this girl," he said. She was down-to-earth and the "perfect" age, twenty-three. For what, I asked, anticipating his answer. He laughed. "Well, great for sex, but I know what you were getting at. For getting married, too." He could see himself married, but not until he had a steady job and a few thousand in the bank. "It'll happen. I don't know when, but it *will* happen."

"My family is very happy with me now." He went on to comment that he and his Dad had a very enjoyable discussion about politics. I said, "It sounds like your attitude toward him is changing." Jim responded, "Yeah, we're more even now." When I commented that Jim seemed to feel more on an equal basis with his father now because both had professions, he shook his head in agreement. I then said that I remembered how much he had felt disapproved of by his father during the child analysis. "During all of my life," he corrected me, "but I wonder how much of that was me." He was nearly independent now and didn't need his father anymore. I commented that even though he might no longer need his father, his thoughts and feelings about his dad might influence his relationship with his wife and children, a subject I wished he and I might explore in more depth. With a distancing twinkle in his eye, he responded, "You're not going anywhere in the next five years, are you? If I need you then, I'll be back."

Changing the subject, he said, "I got car insurance yesterday. I haven't had any for almost two years. I guess that's another sign of growing up, isn't it?" I nodded in agreement.

Toward the end of the session, he described a recent sexual experience with a girl he had met. The sex was OK, but she was kind of weird, indicating that she was distant and unresponsive. He enjoyed himself but still felt unfulfilled. I commented, "You seem to need more than sex these days." Jim replied, "I'm just waiting for the right girl to come along. I've figured out you have to pick a wife when she's young because that's when the good ones go. About twenty-three to twenty-six is the right age." As I listened I thought, this man is telling me that he is attempting to master his conflicts surrounding the young adult developmental tasks of intimacy, marriage, and parenthood in his own way. Developmental progression was clearly related to separating and individuating from his real and psychiatric parents—doing it on his own while leaving the door open for a future relationship with them and me.

In characteristic fashion, he ended the session with a summary statement of his current situation. "I'm as happy as I've ever been," he said. "I'm moving forward."

I didn't hear from Jim again until three months later when he called and asked to meet. Very anxious when he arrived, Jim immediately launched into his current dilemma. He had been substituting fairly regularly at an elementary school. The teacher in the next classroom liked his work and had asked him to begin the school year with her class since she would be on maternity leave. He was set to begin. Then a few days ago, he got a call from another school. He had recently substituted there and had done a good job with a difficult, unruly class. The principal told him that there might be an opening for a regular position in September. Would he like to apply? To make a long story short, he had boned up on the interview procedure, prepared himself to ask and answer questions, and within two hours after the interview was offered the job. Now it all depended on the enrollment figures and whether or not there were enough children to justify another classroom.

Then came the dilemma. He might not get the job, so he didn't want to quit his clerking job until he was sure. But he couldn't hold down two full-time jobs at the same time and he needed all of his energies to do a great job in the classroom. His anxiety was palpable as he described his conflict. What would he live on if the teaching job fell through? When I supported his decision to give up his discount store job and concentrate on his teaching, he visibly relaxed. "Thanks," he said. "I really appreciate that."

Later Jim reported that his brother was doing "nothing." "He's in the same position I was three years ago. He's a pain in the ass to my parents, but I don't want him to suffer the way I did."

I last saw Jim a few months later. He felt we were nearing the end of our work together because his life was going so well. As I listened, I was aware of the longstanding, still unresolved conflicts around autonomy, sexuality, and aggression which I had first observed nearly two decades ago; but I saw, too, the progress he was reveling in and was fascinated by the power of the developmental thrust that was propelling him forward.

Jim began the session with a joyous pronouncement: "This has been the best time of my life." I didn't have to ask why. He had quit his job at the discount store right after our last meeting and had spent the time vacationing and teaching. "I went camping for a week. Then I opened up a classroom for a pregnant teacher for eight days. I think I did a real good job." Then he went to visit a friend, spent a few days with his brother, and visited another friend. But his real enthusiasm was reserved for talking about teaching. He was very excited about beginning his first permanent job—"It's permanent, that is, if the enrollment holds up. If not, I'll substitute. I'm definitely not going back to my old job."

Jim's mood saddened as he spoke of his brother. "Stan is in bad shape. I've never seen him depressed like this. He's home with my parents just like I was and he has no idea what he's going to do."

After a pause he brightened. "All of a sudden, I'm looking like the successful one in the family. It's novel."
"You seem to have mixed feelings about his situation," I clarified.

"Yeah, I do. I'm sad for Stan but a little part of me is enjoying it."

As if to avoid further awareness of his brother's plight and his own mixed feelings, Jim changed the subject to his latest female interest. "It's a real soap opera," he said with glee, and went on to describe the convoluted relationships among himself, the woman, and his friend who "told me to stay away from her, but he's not even dating her. I'm not going to do it." As Jim described the situation, he seemed more interested in standing up to his friend than dating the girl.

Near the end of the session, Jim proudly described his loss of ten pounds and his frequent trips to the weight room. He did, indeed, look neat and trim, in the best shape I had seen him since we had become reacquainted three years before. In fact, that statement is an apt description of his mental state as well.

Although we have no regularly scheduled appointments planned for the future, I'm sure I'll see Jim again, possibly soon. I look forward with anticipation and awe to the rare privilege of observing the unfolding of developmental potential in this very special man as he moves through his young adult years.

Discussion

Jim's third individuation: Adult developmental theory postulates a growing complexity in relationships as the individual moves from infancy through childhood and adolescence. The first individuation is a rather exclusive affair between infant and parent. The base expands during the second individuation in adolescence to include important nonfamilial relationships such as friends, girlfriends, and mentors. They become the recipients of some of the feelings formerly directed toward the parents and thus facilitate the process of psychological separation from them.

The transition from the second to the third individuation is a young adult experience, stimulated by the growing capacity for intrapsychic separation from the parents and engagement of the phase-specific developmental tasks of young adulthood.

This normative process was partially arrested in Jim and he has not yet functioned fully as an *emotionally* self-sufficient adult. Jim's energies remain overly focused on his parents. My interpretive interventions addressed the degree to which Jim sought his parents' approval for his young adult aspirations and actions, indicated by the degree of anger he experienced when that approval was less than total. As evidenced by the clinical material from our last session, Jim was progressing along this developmental line, but not without frustration and difficulty.

Developing the Capacity for Intimacy. Erikson defined the major developmental dichotomy of his Stage VI, *young adulthood*, as *intimacy versus stagnation*. The achievement of intimacy in young adulthood is a difficult task for many men and women, particularly in their twenties. Driven by the power of sexual hormones, healthy young adults are often more focused on sexual pleasure.

The developmental shift toward intimacy is often heralded, as illustrated by Jim, by a growing feeling of loneliness during and after sex. Increasingly, the desire is for emotional connectedness in a sexual context. At an unconscious level the shift is driven by the growing need to reexperience the sustaining closeness of the parent–child bond in this new adult context and the desire to produce a child. Sooner or later the result is a committed relationship, with or without marriage.

Because Jim was still struggling with his feelings about his father, he was ambivalent about—although no longer strongly rejecting—the idea of becoming a lover and a husband. However, he is attempting to psychologically prepare himself for greater intimacy. The question is whether or not this will be possible without further treatment.

Becoming a Father. The experience of impregnating a woman adds a new dimension to a young man's sexual identity by confirming that his penis and testicles are capable of performing the primary function for which they are intended. For Jim and most other males in their teens and early twenties, the goal is avoidance of this state.

When a young man becomes a father he participates in the creation of a *family*, its structure identical to the family of origin except for the reversal of roles. The former son, now the parent, assumes the role for which he was prepared many years before by watching his own father interact with him. Assuming a role that was formerly the exclusive prerogative of his progenitor gradually leads to an internal sense of parity. In the healthy situation, this is an experience which is beneficial to, and enjoyed by, both men.

Jim's most intense criticism of his dad was and is for his performance as a father. Since I knew his father during the child therapy, I know that there is a considerable amount of distortion in Jim's evaluation, even though his dad did have very high standards for himself and his son and was somewhat distant. Regardless of the cause, Jim's current problem is that he sees fatherhood as a burden, a source of pain and conflict, not as one of young adulthood's richest experiences which will fulfill developmental potential along several different lines. I believe he will become a father one day; his strong desire to teach is evidence of the other side of his ambivalence.

The attainment of equality and mutuality with parents may continue throughout the remainder of young and middle adulthood, or it may be short-lived, depending on the mental and physical well being of the parents. At some point, the adult "child" will be confronted with the psychological and possibly physical task of caring for vulnerable, dependent parents who no longer can care for themselves. When this occurs, the internal representations of the dependent, vulnerable childhood self and the aging parent are brought together in the superego/ego ideal and compared. In the normal adult, the superego demands that the "child" reenter the parent–child dyad, now reversed, and assume the role of caretaker.

Simultaneously, throughout the young adult and middle years, living fathers and grandfathers provide examples of how the developmental tasks of these phases may be engaged. As the young adult father and his sons internalize these examples, they lay the foundation for their own interaction in the years to come when their roles will be reversed.

Reaching for Equality. Jim is on the way to establishing a sense of mutuality and equality with his parents. These feelings will undoubtedly intensify as he becomes a teacher, as he achieves financial independence, marries, and has a family; in other words, when he masters the major developmental tasks of young adulthood. I hope for both him and them that he will facilitate their mid- and late life development by providing them with grandchildren, and when the time comes, to be there during their declining years.

When their normal development is not significantly impeded, adolescent males (and females) enter young adulthood, that marvelous time of life when masculinity reaches mature fruition, and in the process become independent adults, loving husbands, and, last but not least, fathers to their children and eventually parents to their parents. That is my wish for Jim.

11

The Power of Time

Birthdays

In childhood *every* birthday is a joyous occasion signifying the urgent wish to be older, more capable, more mature. Then as childhood passes into adolescence, certain birthdays become more significant, but still signify the attainment of privilege and status. Sixteen—"and never been kissed." Eighteen—"I made it. I can vote and go to war" and twenty-one—"No more fake I.D.'s, I can drink legally."

As the twenties—"Twenty-five, my God, that's a quarter of a century!"—pass into the thirties—"Is it true you can't trust people over thirty?"—birthdays are accompanied by mild apprehension because they no longer signify growth and freedom. Instead they demarcate aging and the gradual loss of the endless summer of youth.

And then comes forty, crossing the Rubicon, the unequivocal indicator of middle age. "I never thought I'd be forty, but here I am!"

Freud noted that we show an unmistakable tendency to put death to one side, to eliminate it from life. There is nothing instinctive in us, he said, which accepts the idea of death. In the timelessness of the unconscious we reign, immortal.

The first half of life is characterized by a tendency to ignore the inevitability of death. In childhood and adolescence the denial is bolstered by limited awareness and understanding of the concept of time and absorption in the progressive physical and psychological forces that characterize early development. There is little in the anabolic thrust of growth and maturation to indicate a personal end.

The first crack in the armor appears in late adolescence as the physical and emotional ties to parents and childhood are painfully severed. Past (childhood), present (young adulthood), and future (midlife) are sharply delineated. The painful notion that time is limited begins to creep into awareness but is warded off by exciting new beginnings in work and relationships and by the god-like ability to create new life—and thus new quantities of time.

Then as midlife approaches and grabs the normal adult by the throat, he or she comes face to face with mortality, indicated by the unmistakable signs of physical aging, the death of parents, the maturation of children toward physiological adulthood, and the jarring realization that not all of life's ambitions and goals will be realized. The race against time has truly begun.

The adult at midlife is at a critical juncture on the developmental path to maturity. As at all such junctures there is the potential for emotional growth or regression. Some degree of regression is a normal response to the stress of everyday living, regardless of age or developmental challenge. In midlife that may include excessive exercise or no exertion whatsoever; competitiveness and envy of adolescent and young-adult offspring; neglect of aging parents; or sexual adventurism with younger partners.

Pathological responses to the anticipation of death can take the form of suddenly fractured marriages and careers in a frenzied attempt to reverse the passage of time—the infamous midlife crisis.

For example, Mr. D, a productive, athletic man of forty, developed acute anxiety when a recommendation was made for arthroscopic knee surgery because of an injury sustained while playing tennis. He came for an evaluation, stating that his youth was gone and his life over. Despite my best efforts, he refused to analyze his reaction and in a short period of time moved out of his home, began an affair with a much younger woman, lost interest in his bewildered children, and abandoned a highly successful career.

Death Awareness: The Quintessential Midlife Experience

Despite the obvious pain involved in confronting time limitation and one's own mortality, this developmental task can have far-reaching, growth-promoting consequences, producing the most profound awareness of what it means to be human.

In a series of fascinating books, the eminent psychiatrist Robert Lifton has described the impact of death awareness on the human psyche.(1–5) He describes a shift in perspective from Victorian preoccupations with sex and morality to a current-day preoccupation with absurd death and annihilation. Confronted with death and violence at every turn, on our street corners and television screens, we have lost the ability to recognize the psychological connection between the phenomenon of death and the flow of life.

Lifton contends:

> The broken connection exists in the tissues of our mental life. It has to do with a very new historical—one could also say evolutionary—relationship to death. We are haunted by the image of exterminating ourselves as a species by means of our own technology." In addition man is unique because he knows he will die. This awareness is a major stimulus to the creation of culture, which is a reflection of the symbolizing imagination to explore the idea of death and relate it to the principle of life—continuity. That is the capacity for culture.(6)

The poet Wallace Stevens said it succinctly: "Death is the mother of beauty."

These ideas have particular relevance for development in midlife because of the beginning intrusion of thoughts about death into consciousness during the late thirties and forties, producing what Erikson called "an ego chill," a shutter attending the growing awareness of eventual nonexistence. According to researchers such as psychologist Daniel Levinson, psychiatrist Roger Gould, sociologist Bernice Neugarten, and Robert Nemiroff and me, the engagement of this developmental task is a ubiquitous experience in Western culture, sometimes occurring behind a wall of deceptive, external calm, at other times erupting with extreme intensity. Lifton suggested that the internal drama can take the form of low-key, self questioning, or be filled with pain and suffering. But he saved his most eloquent prose for the growth-promoting, sublimatory results of the successful, midlife engagement of this most unfathomable mystery of human existence:

> There is a special quality of life-power available only to those seasoned by struggles of four or more decades. That seasoning includes extensive cultivation of images and forms having to do with love and caring, with experienced parenthood, with teaching and mentorship, with work combinations and

> professional creativity, with responses to intellectual and artistic images around one, and above all with humor and a sense of the absurd. The seasoned psychic forms are by no means devoid of death imagery. Rather they are characterized by ingenious combinations of death equivalents and immediate affirmations, or melancholic recognition of the fragmentation and threat surrounding all ultimate involvements, along with dogged insistence upon one's own connections beyond the self—one's own relationship to collective modes of symbolic immortality. Like the despair, the life-power of this stage can be especially profound.(7)

Driven by death imagery and mature midlife power, the healthy adult personality reorganizes along positive lines. Increased acceptance of physical aging produces a redefinition of the body image, caring attention to the body and its health, and the development of new physical and nonphysical means of gratification appropriate to a realistic level of physical competence. The recognition of time limitation stimulates a redefinition of goals and channels energies and resources into *obtainable* objectives that enrich the levels of oneself and loved ones. The quest for gratification now, before time runs out, if moderated by mature reason, can breach outmoded superego barriers and stretch the ability to explore inner and outer worlds of love, play, and ambition which were formerly considered taboo.

And what of the narcissistic investment in the self, a self no longer seen as omnipotent and everlasting? According to Erikson the midlife acceptance of the notion of personal death paves the way for a mystic union with the cosmos and wards off despair in old age.

> It is a post-narcissistic love of the human ego—not of the self—as an experience which conveys some world order and spiritual sense . . . the acceptance of one's one and only life cycle as something that has to be . . . it is a comradeship with the ordering ways of distant times and different pursuits.(8)

Death and the Midlife Crisis

The title for this section is taken from an article by British psychiatrist Eliot Jacques, who was one of the first to describe the impact of the midlife preoccupation with time limitation and personal death on normal and pathological development in adulthood.(8) He proposed that death awareness could shatter existing psyche equilibrium and precipitate the now familiar midlife crisis or propel the individual to new heights of understanding and awareness of the human condition. What are the myths and realities surrounding the seemingly sudden, inexplicable behavior of those individuals who are unable to tolerate the stress of midlife development and in a furious frenzy destroy life structures and relationships that took many years to build?

The Gauguin Syndrome

In attempting to understand and describe this phenomenon, my colleague and coauthor Robert Nemiroff coined the term the Gauguin Syndrome.(9) The popular *myth* swirling around the famous painter suggests that suddenly, at midlife, he abandoned his family and career and escaped to the tropics, there to bask in the sun free from responsibility, to sleep with exotic bare-breasted native women, and to thumb his nose at conventional, European society by memorializing it all on canvas.

Deeper investigation suggests a very different scenario, one of lengthy struggle with career ambitions and personal relationships. Gauguin had gradually become bored with the banking business and had slowly gravitated toward the art world, first as a patron of the early Impressionists and then as an amateur painter. Gauguin's marital problems did not occur suddenly either. He and his wife, Mette, had been marching to different drummers for years—he into the bohemian world of art, she into the straightlaced confines of middle class society. Before leaving for Tahiti he had spent years imploring her to accompany him, but she would have none of it.

Gauguin's midlife metamorphosis becomes even more understandable when his family background and childhood are taken into account. His maternal grandmother, Flora Tristan, was a fiery revolutionary who regarded herself as a pariah and a missionary of social change. Gauguin seems to have identified with this aspect of his grandmother's character. Nor was his thirst for foreign soil inexplicable. His father died when the young Gauguin was en route with his family to Peru to join the household of the Peruvian viceroy, Gauguin's maternal uncle. Part of Gauguin's childhood was spent in the materially abundant, sparkling aristocratic environment in which his mother flourished. Apparently he was strongly influenced by her presence in that exotic setting because he later painted her many times as "Eve" in a tropical paradise. When the family was forced abruptly to return to France by political upheaval when Paul was seven, the boy's shimmering, golden world vanished, to be replaced by the gray and pallid environment of Orleans. As if to capture his early Peruvian experience, Gauguin went to sea during his adolescence. While he was away his mother died. The loss of both parents during childhood and the influence of extraordinary experiences within a powerful, iconoclastic family are the likely reasons that Gauguin went to Tahiti, there to attempt to relive and master his early adventures and traumas, while there was still time.

The Gauguin myth has compelling appeal for those individuals who are more oriented toward action than introspection, toward those who would rather change their environment than change themselves. In fact, suggests writer Nathan Mayer, there was nothing noble about Gauguin's life. He was actually a driven, self-destructive man whose flight into fantasy ended in despair. Instead of being reborn in his tropical paradise, he actually spent his last years as an embittered exile who never abandoned his desperate desire to be acclaimed by the society he supposedly despised.

A comparison of the myth and reality of Gauguin's life exposes the tendency to romanticize and oversimplify midlife crisis and transition in an attempt to avoid the painful confrontations with past and present which are the critical test of midlife stability and integrity.

Crisis, Transition, and Change

The term *midlife crisis* has become a cliché, the subject of movies, Oprah and Geraldo television shows, backyard gossip, and dinner-table conversation. But it is also a term used by serious professionals to describe a dramatic, relatively uncommon form of midlife psychopathology probably experienced by less than 10 percent of the population. A true midlife crisis is a revolutionary event which, like a Class V hurricane, utterly destroys everything in its path, leaving behind a trail of broken marriages, shattered careers, distraught children, and bewildered friends.

A person in the midst of a true crisis acts suddenly and impulsively, throwing away relationships and careers which often took many years to build in a frantic attempt to escape what has become unbearable. Reason is abandoned and advice from spouses, relatives, friends, and therapists to stop and think before making major decisions and burning bridges falls on deaf ears—so intense is the urge to escape from the intolerable present.

In the late 1970s, researcher Daniel Levinson and his

leagues described the *midlife transition*—a profound, sometimes agonizing, reappraisal of all aspects of life which affects *everyone* who approaches and traverses the early forties.(10) For a few the searing examination of success, disappointments and failures is not particularly painful, but for many the questioning of assumptions, illusions, and vested interests is difficult in the extreme.

The basic developmental conflict underlying both the midlife transition and crisis is the same—the dawning realization that time is running out and major changes, if they are ever to occur, must be made *now*! Those in the midst of transition conduct their agonizing reappraisal at the level of thought. If they do decide to abandon a marriage or a career they do so carefully, after considerable assessment of the consequences. Those in the midst of a true midlife crisis act—abruptly and precipitously—so as not to think about their past choices, present responsibilities, and narrowing future opportunities. The grim reaper can be cheated, a lost youth recaptured, the brass ring snatched the second time around in a different city with a younger partner and a new career.

"Is That All There Is?"

"Is that all there is?" asked pop vocalist Peggy Lee, "Is that all there is?" Have I squeezed every ounce of pleasure out of life? Seen all there is to see? Had it all? For each of us the answer is the same, a resounding no! But the disappointing realization is tempered by pleasant memories and a valued present. I haven't had it all but I've had my share and there's more to come. I think I'll just keep on dancing. These are not only the thoughts of the sick or selfish, they emanate from responsible, caring people as well, generated by a confluence of universal midlife concerns which fuel the midlife transition. For example:

Bodily changes such as wrinkles, gray hair, cellulite, near-sightedness, and occasional impotence generate anxiety because they symbolize the rush of sand in the hour glass, an increased awareness that time is running out.

This *change in time perception* is experienced as the remaining hours of life being rapidly used up. "Total time left" is another preoccupation, suggests Bernice Neugarten, as thinking shifts from time lived to time left to live.(11) Those in transition react to this awareness with dignified pain, those in crisis with frenzied panic.

The distance between *career* aspirations and achievement is another indicator that time is running out. As they feel the heat from hungry younger rivals eager to replace them, middle-aged workers double their efforts to cover their backsides. This is particularly true, says psychologist Judith Bardwick, for those with limited educations or redundant jobs who have plateaued and been shunted aside or pushed out the door into the sometimes desperate world of middle-aged unemployment.(12) Particularly in poor economic times job insecurity may puncture the complacent illusion that life will remain the same forever and force a serious questioning of all aspects of relationships, values, and goals.

As children leave home and expose *marital relationships* to an intense dose of sometimes unwanted togetherness, commitment to marriage and family are put to the test. Each partner must assess his or her relationship to determine whether it has the necessary ingredients to justify continuing. Have the partners developed similarly? Do they have enough in common? If estranged, can they reestablish their relationship?

The churning concern that time is running out may reignite the youthful quest for the ideal love. The yearning for the thrilling satiation of adolescent infatuation drives many into preoccupation with first loves and others into extramarital affairs or divorce. The realization that one cannot go back in time, cannot magically restore youth or reexperience perfection, drives many to distraction. A fifty-nine-year-old, recently divorced man became incensed when I questioned whether he could, at his age, reexperience "you know, that total feeling of love, when you walk around in a daze all day long and nothing else matters but your lover."

When *children* break through the biological barriers of latency and undergo the Dr. Jekyll and Mr. Hyde metamorphosis from infantile innocence to raucous physical maturity, they shatter the parents' sense of calm and continuity and become the harbingers of uncontrollable change and uncertainty. In her novel *The War Between the Tates,* Allison Lurie captured the parental predicament perfectly.

> They were a happy family once, she thinks. Jeffrey and Matilda were beautiful, healthy babies; charming toddlers; intelligent, lively, affectionate children. . . . Then last year, when Jeffrey turned fourteen and Matilda twelve, they had begun to change; to grow rude, coarse, selfish, insolent, nasty, brutish, and tall. It was as if she were keeping a boarding house in a bad dream and the children she had loved were turning into awful lodgers—lodgers who paid no rent, whose leases could not be terminated. They were awful at home and abroad; in company and alone, in the morning, the afternoon and the evening.(13)

Middle age, in the middle, between two generations, often responsible for both—both serve as constant reminders of the passage of time, one by maturing, the other by aging and dying. Mother and Father Time, those guarantors of an endless future, of immortality, themselves wither and die, exposing their children to a similar fate as they become the oldest generation, the first in line, closest to the grave. Freud described the death of his father as a profound experience which stimulated a profound internal reorganization. The same is true for all of us as parental death forces us to shed some of the last illusions of immortality and accept a limited life span and a lesser position in the cosmos.

A True Midlife Crisis

The same experiences which bring on the midlife transition also precipitate midlife crisis in susceptible individuals. The following description of an actual midlife crisis is presented to give the large majority of adults, who (fortunately) will never have such an experience, a standard against which to compare their own situations.

Dr. R came to therapy "to pick up the pieces of my life and start over." Aged forty-four, he had recently come to San Diego from an East Coast city "to get away from everything and everybody who ever meant anything to me."

"I just got up one morning and said this is it. I took $100,000 out of my pension plan, drove to the airport, and threw a dart at a map of the West Coast. It landed on San Diego, so I bought a ticket and here I am."

After a couple weeks of walking on the beach, Dr. R called his frantic family and told them he wasn't coming back. He told his wife to forget about him and to keep everything. He refused to talk to his children but agreed to contact them later.

Dr. R went on to explain that although he couldn't put it into words, his life had become unbearable. "You're going to laugh like everyone else," he said. "They thought I had it all. A nice wife, big home, three kids, and a great practice. I used to think so too, but it all began to smother me. I couldn't do what I wanted."

What he wanted only became clear to both of us as therapy progressed. Foremost was to actualize the search for his first love. After she rejected him he married his wife on the rebound. "My wife's a great lady," he said. "Don't get me wrong. It's not her. It's me. I want to feel that overwhelming rush in my crotch again. I want to *really* care. She'll never make me feel that way."

And he was sick of his patients. "They claw at me. They never get enough. There's always another one. I want time for myself. If I don't take it now, I'm going to wake up one day and discover I'm sixty-five and haven't done anything."

"My kids weren't any better. They kept needing more and more. I couldn't stand the thought of working for ten more years to put them through college. There's enough left in the pension plan to see them through. They'll be alright."

Although the underlying causes of his midlife crisis were clear to me—a paternal death at age five, a neurotically inhibited sexuality, and the death of his devoted mother on his forty-fifth birthday—Dr. R had little interest in exploring causes and refused to even consider returning home. What he wanted from me was empathy, support, and acceptance of his new life, which consisted of living alone in a rented apartment, daily surfing, and occasional ventures into bars. Despite my best efforts, Dr. R left therapy after a year of stubbornly refusing to examine what had happened to him. "Thanks for your help," he said. "I feel a lot better." "I'm glad you do," I thought, as I pictured his wife and children and visualized his uncertain future.

And Then What?

This book has, hopefully, made the reader more aware of his or her mortality and its effect on development, but hasn't addressed the ultimate question—What happens after death?

At this point science and developmental theory exit and religion enters. Atheist or agnostic, monk or minister—all ponder the same question and arrive at different answers. The true believer who is at one with the notion of a higher being feels a special kind of fulfillment, enriched by an answer to the mystery of death. The nonbeliever at midlife ponders the unponderable and accepts the realization that he or she will never know, but finds fulfillment by reveling in the beauty and wonders that life in the here and now has to offer.

CASE REPORT: Turning Forty in Analysis

In this abbreviated, amended chapter from *The Race Against Time*, physician and psychoanalyst John Hassler studies his patient's reaction to that watershed birthday, forty, and provides us with a rare, detailed insight into the power of time.(14)

Birthdays have a special meaning for everyone. For the American middle-class child, birthdays are occasions for expanding the sense of personal worth through peer acceptance and family love. Gifts, cakes, and other expressions of love are offered and received as proof of worth. For happy children, the present joys and affirmations matter more than reflections on past or future anticipations. However, for adults, birthdays are occasions for introspection. Beyond the celebrations of worth, adults use them to review achievements and frustrations of the past and define hopes for the future.

A fortieth birthday often has very special significance

as one reviews what has happened in life and anticipates all that is to come. The halfway point—thirty-five, half the biblical threescore and ten—was viewed in the same way prior to the extension of longevity by good nutrition and medical care in the last few decades. The lifting of the denial of death is the central and crucial feature of the midlife phase. Both Arthur Schopenhauer and Albert Camus vividly described the awareness that struck them in their late thirties—that they had already lived half their lives and that death was inevitable.

Each of us faces this reality in our own way. Bach accepted his cantorship at Leipzig at thirty-eight and began to compose. Albert Schweitzer chose midlife as the time to retire from his career as a concert organist in Europe and become a physician in Africa. Major shifts in self-image, love relationships, and career directions frequently are provoked or facilitated by the lifting of the denial of aging and the realization that the halfway point of life has been reached. Suddenly, it is clear that life is half over and that the "race against time" cannot be stopped.

In psychoanalysis, birthdays may be used to elaborate a variety of neurotic or developmental conflicts. Beyond the special meaning of specific time events, the passage of time itself is often a major implicit or explicit theme in therapy. Review of past development, the examination of present realities, and the preview of future hopes are a part of many individual sessions. It is as if there were a compression of time, a time warp, allowing the patient to look at his or her whole life course from one vantage point. This compression gradually brings adult aging realities into sharp focus.

Detailed clinical material from the psychoanalysis of Mr. B. highlights the importance of time and the conflicts of aging in midlife.

The Analysis of Mr. B.

Mr. B. entered analysis when he was thirty-six and turned forty twelve months before termination. A review of those hours during the few weeks on either side of his fortieth birthday revealed how time and aging perceptions colored his thoughts and his use of the fortieth birthday to focus on and move beyond the problems confronting him in the analysis. Mr. B.'s adaptation to aging provides another example of an individual, this time at mid-life, who traveled a rocky road on the way to adult fulfillment.

Presenting Symptoms and Background

An intelligent, articulate architect, Mr. B. sought help after a year of depression, self-doubt, and intermittent resentment toward his adolescent daughter. The onset of his depression coincided with her pubescence.

The patient was the oldest of two children. A sister had been born when he was two years old. His mother was loving but hot tempered and would occasionally "knock heads together." His father, a successful builder, was caring and available in early childhood. At three, Mr. B. recalled, he happily helped his father build the house they lived in during his childhood. When he was ten his parents divorced. From that point onward, he viewed both mother and father as angry, aloof, and emotionally unavailable.

Mr. B. was a wanted child, the product of an uncomplicated pregnancy. He was breast-fed and within the norm of all early maturational and developmental guidelines. There were no childhood surgeries or major illnesses. He did not recall weaning or toilet-training experience, or later problems with eating or bowel and bladder control. "My mother ran the place . . . she insisted on dinner manners and clean rooms."

At five, while roughhousing with him in a treehouse, Mr. B.'s three-year-old sister fell and was nearly killed. This event shaped the family destiny ("my mother always said that that's why father left") and was so elaborated by the patient that he forever after felt like "a rotten kid . . . a potential killer." Soon after the accident, the father began working some distance from home. At six his mother also went off to work and during many evenings the patient was left in the care of baby-sitters "who would leave us in the attic to discipline us." Despite these problems, the boy "did O.K. until my parents divorced. . . . I got real depressed . . . all my friends still had fathers." He rarely saw his father after puberty.

The patient always did well in school, although from the second grade on he was in trouble for taunting teachers and provoking fights. After high school he joined the army. "I believed the ads about making a man out of you."

After the service Mr. B. returned home, entered college, married in his sophomore year, and was content for the next three years. "I made the dean's list and felt comfortable with my wife and her family." Marital discord began when a daughter was born and when undesirable job changes occurred. However, basic compatibility persisted until a year or two before the analysis—until his daughter reached puberty.

Mr. B.'s Fortieth Birthday

The following propositions are helpful in conceptualizing the clinical material about the birthday.

Turning forty prompted a significant, although partial and temporary, lifting of denials of the aging process.

After many analytic hours of introspection and psychological reflection, Mr. B. could look more easily at the adaptive choices of a forty-year-old and accept the considerable pleasures available to him at midlife.

Clinical Data

Three Weeks Prior to the Birthday. Twenty days prior to his birthday, Mr. B. presented the following material, which was typical of the preceding few months. He came back from a vacation weekend and began to complain.

> MR. B.: I drove back in a hurry, I wanted to see my wife . . . but I was in a bad mood as soon as I got home . . . all we did was argue, she makes me so mad . . . over trivia.
>
> DR. H.: What feelings are beneath the anger? As you mentioned, you were angry over trivia.
>
> MR. B.: I just don't enjoy being with her . . . I don't know if she even has to say anything . . . it'd almost as if I am not supposed to be in love with anyone . . . I try and talk with my wife but get nowhere, constant arguing . . . I don't seem to be able to change . . . I wonder if I give my daughter enough.

In the second session of this week, Mr. B. started by looking further at his tendency to withdraw and withold. He had been guiltily involved in an extramarital affair for some time; hence the reference in this material to his girlfriend.

> MR. B.: My daughter was out so my wife and I made love . . . but somehow there is much more emotional release with my girlfriend . . . yet rationally, I don't want her . . . it is almost as if I'm not supposed to show satisfaction, pleasure with my wife . . . guess I

> don't trust . . . don't see her as my friend, afraid to share my wish for warmth.

And then in his first reference to aging, he mentioned the following:

> MR. B.: I guess I can't be a kid fooling around with my wife; yet I can be a kid with my girlfriend.
>
> DR. H.: Only kids are allowed to express warmth and passion with women, not men?

One Week Prior to the Birthday. In the first session of the week: "I don't want a divorce, I used to . . . I get a lot of joy out of marriage."

At the beginning of the following session, he started with the following: "Heck of a day yesterday . . . I talked with a new junior associate who began working for me . . . she's only 25 . . . a lot younger than I thought . . . I am feeling older and older, oh well."

In the final session of the week, the last before his birthday, he mentions the following for the first time: "My birthday is coming up . . . I don't want a cake . . . [later in the session he comments] I think I want to take a vacation for a day or two . . . the senior partner has been out all week; I wish there were more sunny days . . . I wish it were September and I could ride a bike around with the sun in my face."

First Week after the Birthday. In the first session of the week: "I don't feel like letting people fawn over me as if I can't take care of myself." He then went on to describe his indifference to a surprise fortieth birthday party attended by six couples that his partner had organized for him.

> MR. B.: Forty candles on a cake are too many . . . but

they were a nice group of people . . . one of the ladies was crying.

Dr. H.: Why do you feel she cried?

Mr. B.: A sad affair, birthdays . . . [after a long silence he added] . . . I kind of think that the thing with my girlfriend is over; it is not a very satisfying relationship . . . [later in the session] I have been irritated with everyone . . . and myself since I have the feeling I don't do the things I want to with my life.

The following day he started by reviewing how sick and weak he felt. This was the only time in the analysis that he complained of a cold, although he had colds at other times. He then went on: "I'm frosted at my parents for putting me in school a year early . . . I was smart enough but I just wasn't ready emotionally . . . [later] . . . my partner has been a real disappointment in life . . . maybe I put him in a role he didn't fit . . . [later still] maybe I have confused my girlfriend in the same way . . . she is a burden . . . I find it difficult to remember that she is only 26 . . . there is quite a disparity between 26 and 40 . . . the needs are different . . . I don't want to start all over again . . . [etc.] . . . I don't seem to be getting anywhere . . . maybe tomorrow I'll feel better . . . [silence] . . . I'm also irritated at turning forty . . . it beats the alternatives, but I'm tired of all the problems; I spend my whole life learning how to grow up.

In the third session of the week following his birthday, after complaining about his cold, Mr. B. presented this dream. (The analysis of dreams often provides considerable insight into an individual's inner world.)

Mr. B. (*dream*): At the stadium, quarterbacking a professional football team, crowded stands . . . I was on the better team but couldn't complete my passes; it was halftime and I was talking with Ed . . . he had a lot of money bet on the point spread, and I was going to try to increase the lead so he could win . . . I wasn't starting in the second half so I was walking over to the other side of the field . . . but then I had to get back to the game, and I threw a touchdown pass even though all the men in front of me were taller.

MR. B. (*thoughts about the dream*): I am putting myself on the winning team . . . not the biggest but the best man . . . I'm about average height . . . even though I am bigger than my father now, of course, I wasn't as a boy . . . used to be self-conscious about being short as a kid . . . in fact, I still have difficulty seeing myself as big . . . inferiority complex, keeps me thinking small.

DR. H.: I wonder if your dream doesn't help us understand your conflict over accepting height, prowess, success.

MR. B.: And I can perform for others too . . . going to make Ed a winner . . . you may have met him, he runs the gas station around the corner . . . in reality, for him I don't need to be successful or a winner . . . just a hell of a nice guy . . . trying to repay a friendship.

DR. H.: Am I involved with this move toward success and friendship?

MR. B.: You do care about my growth.

Although there are other sections of the dream that relate to working through a variety of conflicts, what is crucial for a review of analysis at the fortieth birthday is Mr. B.'s assumption of manly prerogative now that he is at "halftime" and his move toward a more loving image of adult males. In the last session of this first week following his birthday, Mr. B. reported a dream of success.

Mr. B. (*dream*): At work with the partners, around a table at the cafeteria . . . discussing applications for new men . . . I was advocating certain people . . . but the senior partner had only trivial cut downs and then I walked off for lunch with his wife.

Mr. B. (*thoughts about the dream*): Actually, it has occurred to me recently that I'll be senior partner when he retires in three or four years . . . it is the part of me that is still sorting out, manhood . . . (*later in the session*) . . . I don't think I am looking to leave my wife . . . I enjoy life more with her.

Second Week after the Birthday. In the first session, Mr. B. mentioned for the first time that he was now handling the family finances (his wife always had before), and he reported a dream.

Mr. B. (*dream*): I was trying to comfort this old woman . . . I was hugging her, and she was crying on my shoulder . . . I wasn't sure why.

Mr. B. (*thoughts on the dream*): The closer I get to my wife, the happier she is, but the more she cries . . . we have gone through a lot . . . and I guess she really is still mourning over her partner's death . . . I can't change someone else's sorrow . . . but I love my family and home is fun again.

In the second session, Mr. B. mentioned for the first time that he was building an addition on his house. "As a family room . . . it's about time . . . why didn't I do it five years ago?"

In this material, concerns over age, stage of life, loss, and growth were everywhere. The patient accepted his forty years with anguish and ambivalence—"Forty candles are too many." Although the new addition, the joys as husband

and father, and a successful profession were some compensation for aging, his mood was more one of acceptance and resignation than joy.

Assignations, not resignations, are what we much prefer to hope for. Mr. B. was overtly gleeful earlier in the analysis while expressing grandiosity and acting on adolescent wishes. Childhood wishes, no matter how disguised or distorted, still carried the hope of great pleasure.

Objective adult pleasures pale next to childhood wishes in much the same ways that earthly joys pale next to anticipated heavenly delights, which include, of course, the promise of immortality. Nevertheless, with the help of analysis, Mr. B. decided that he might as well enjoy "the nice group of people" that were with him at forty. On balance, the adult condition was more pleasurable than his childhood fantasies and illusionary adult reenactments. References to the aging process largely disappeared over the eight months of further analysis prior to termination. He focused instead on his pride of family, success in career, and how he could do more for those around him than was done for him.

Theoretical Comments on Birthdays

If birthdays hurt so much, why do we celebrate them? Why celebrate aging? Why acknowledge death? Some past cultures and present subcultures have no birthday traditions. Among possible conjectures, this may relate to the relative absence of accurate calendars, a lack of relevance in human life as only the god-king has importance, or from a total belief in immortality or reincarnation. The American Witness Christian sects do not acknowledge birthdays or death partly for these latter reasons.

For Western culture, where all human life is defined as precious and the hereafter is culturally doubted, birthdays may paradoxically mark success. Woody Allen is reputed to have said that to live forever is the only immortality he is interested in. Although birthday celebrations also evoke reflections on aging and death, these are usually by-products and fleeting if adaptive processes are functional. Less consciously, birthdays help focus the developmental challenge of aging.

Mr. B.'s midlife analysis and birthday reflections also prompt a broader look at developmental theory. Erikson, in his eight stages of development, takes a positive view of aging. With considerable psychological effort, we develop the resources for intimacy, generativity, and wisdom. Yet, every expansion of psychological resource is also a posture for undervaluing or justifying the inevitable demise. We learn to give successfully so that some part of ourselves might survive, through the germ plasm, through the culture. Yet, all around us is biological and archaeological evidence that nothing survives forever.

12

Wisdom, Maturity, and Fulfillment

> If a man will begin with certainties, he shall end in doubts; but if he will be content to begin with doubts, he shall end in certainties.
>
> FRANCIS BACON, *Advancement of Learning*

Now that we have completed our journey through the stages of life to the pinnacle of adulthood, what have we learned? Have we found the Holy Grail, the answer to life's mysteries? Ah, that it were that simple. But perhaps we have become a bit wiser, a step or two closer to fulfillment. What is wisdom, you may ask? Can it be defined? And fulfillment; is it really an obtainable goal or a cruel illusion? Despite the impossibility of arriving at precise definitions, or ones which would be agreed to by a majority, I humbly present the following ideas.

Wisdom may be defined, simply, as a mature understanding of life. The wise individual has learned from the past and is fully engaged in life in the present. Just as important, he or she anticipates the future and makes the decisions necessary to enhance prospects for health and happiness. In other words, a philosophy of life has been developed, one which includes an understanding—and acceptance—of the person's place in the order of human existence. That world view, which will vary widely from individual to individual, produces fulfillment when the following aspects of the human condition are accepted and integrated.

1. The body must be cared for—in health through regular checkups, exercise, and a healthy diet, and in sickness through prompt treatment and proper care. Caring for the body is not an end in and of itself but is critically important because sentience, the essence of human experience, springs from a healthy brain and body.

2. Human beings are individuals alone with themselves, separated and individuated from all others. The most basic human experience is to be alone. For the immature this isolation may be a prison, cold and depriving; for the mature, it is a palace, full of the inexhaustible richness of human emotion and thought.

3. Paradoxically, human beings cannot survive or develop on their own. Helpless at birth and relatively dependent throughout childhood, all of us, even the most self-sufficient, require the sustaining presence of others. We exist in a framework of *interdependence,* a basic characteristic of all human relationships, be it the parental view of the child as a confirmation of his or her sexuality, the need of the child for the parents' loving care and protection, or the reversal of these roles between adult child and aging progenitor. The mature adult, unlike the child who takes, uses, controls, and dominates, mutes the grandiose expectations of childhood and propels the self toward interactions characterized by caring and mutuality, thus striking a balance between personal needs and those of others.

4. Change is a constant in life, modifying the landscape

of experience as powerfully as the effect of wind, waves, and tectonic plates on the earth's surface. A basic aspect of that change is the shifting nature of significant relationships. Adult involvement with loved ones such as children, parents, colleagues, and friends is in constant realignment. Healthy marriages deepen in significance while others break up on the shoals of midlife development. Parents die. Children grow, leave, and return with new family members. As opposed to old age and in some respects childhood as well, the task for the mature person is to sort out, categorize, and set priorities among relationships, in the process balancing emotional needs and realistic demands and responsibilities. The shifting nature of relationships stimulates the achievement of greater maturity by forcing a constant redefinition of who one is in relationship to others. Mature individuals mourn for lost relationships but are able to remain focused on current and future ones.

5. All human beings—regardless of wealth, position, power, achievement, appearance, or cultural background—are on the same developmental course. All are born and will die. All have a body with the same functions. All have the same emotional needs for closeness and love and the same vulnerability to loss and deprivation. Recognition of this fact heightens respect for everyone and to a small degree diminishes the impact of social and economic inequities.

6. Further, few individuals have an exaggerated importance. The wish for such grandiose prominence is universal, the result of the untempered narcissism of infancy and childhood. In reality most individuals are important to themselves and a relatively limited number of others who know and love them. The mature individual accepts this fact without despair and uses the knowledge to set realistic goals and priorities which will result in personal happiness and fulfillment.

7. Personal time is limited. Everyone will die. Young children do not have the cognitive capacity to understand the notion of personal death. Spurred on by the thrust of physical growth and a seemingly endless future, adolescents and young adults think and act as though they are immortal. The true acceptance of time limitation and personal death occurs in midlife. Then the mature individual, religious or not, stimulated by an awareness of the aging process in the body, the maturation of children, the death of parents and friends, and the arrival of grandchildren, accepts the inevitability of a personal end. As with the realization of the limited importance of each individual in nature's grand design, this painful recognition, which precipitates panicked midlife crises in some, stimulates the mature individual to seek fulfillment in each moment, to define what is truly important, and to plan the future with the goal of actualizing those priorities.

8. Money and possessions have limited intrinsic value. They are a means to an end, tools for enriching life and improving the human condition in loved ones and the broader community. Further, ownership of tangible objects is temporary. Sooner or later they will be lost, left behind, or given to others.

9. Work occupies a central position in adult life. Considered a drudgery by some, the wise person recognizes its extraordinary value. In addition to the obvious function of earning a living, work is organizing, an activity that provides purpose and direction, a meaningful way to manage time, and an environment in which to form sustaining relationships.

The satisfied midlife worker, at the peak of power and position in the workplace, facilitates the development of the skills and capabilities of younger colleagues while fully realizing that these are the very individuals who will, sooner or later, replace him or her, and assume control of the levers of power. Wishes to hold down and attack younger workers are sublimated into generativity, Erikson's term for enhancing the development of the next generation.

10. The seventh stage is the phase of life in which the experience of being human can be realized—and enjoyed—most fully. It is a time when the combination of physical health and vigor, power and prestige in the work place, accumulation of wealth and possessions, and meaningful relationships from within the midst of three or four generations provide the potential for a life overflowing with richness and complexity. The mature life is one in which the triumvirate of human experiences—love, work, and play—are successfully balanced, bringing true fulfillment.

11. Unfortunately, the joys of midlife do not last forever. Old age lies ahead. Although the hope and statistical expectation is for many years of mental competence and independence, physical and/or mental decline, increased dependence, and eventually death must be anticipated. Late adulthood has its own great pleasure when there is a focus on continued mental and physical activity, a dominant preoccupation with the present and the future, and involvement with and facilitation of the young. Then death can be met with feelings of satisfaction and acceptance, the natural end-point of human existence that follows a lifetime well lived and well loved.

CASE REPORT: New Beginnings at Seventy—A Decade of Psychotherapy in Late Adulthood

This remarkable case report is a fitting way to close this book because it demonstrates that it is truly *never* too late to seek fulfillment, regardless of the shambles that one has made of life. This abridged, amended case history by psychiatrist and psychoanalyst Gary Levinson was originally published in *The Race Against Time.*(1)

History

Mrs. A. presented for treatment at age sixty-three as an obese, twice-divorced woman. The mother of three, she lived alone, supporting herself on Social Security disability payments. The patient described herself as suffering from "neurotic fears" about her health; she was experiencing blurred vision, dizziness, and an unsteadiness in gait, all of which made her feel "nervous" and "in turmoil." The patient assumed these symptoms to be "neurotic" because she had been diagnosed as such at a midwestern clinic some twenty years previously. Mrs. A also believed that her recent heart attack had intensified these concerns.

The immediate reason for referral from the patient's internist, who assured me that the somatic complaints were not organic in nature, was marked obesity. He described her 220-pound weight as life threatening. The weight gain had all occurred during the patient's fifties, probably resulting from her role as caretaker of an increasingly debilitated and senile mother. Until that time, the patient was very interested in her appearance, highly valuing her slimness. At present, however, she saw her weight as of no consequence because she was "old and hopelessly ugly."

Following her mother's death three years prior to beginning treatment, the patient began living with a brother and his wife. He died three months before her own heart attack nine months before the treatment began. Mrs. A. had weathered both of those losses without serious emotional consequence, and only now, as she confronted her own mortality, did she experience recurrent feelings of depression, alienation, and isolation. One of her worst fears was of becoming an invalid, confined to a wheelchair while living in a "sleazy nursing home."

Mrs. A. was also preoccupied with "guilty feelings about the past." Increasingly, she experienced recurrent, intrusive thoughts about how "I screwed up the past," especially in relation to a lack of responsibility toward her children, siblings, and parents. The patient lamented the fact that her son from her first marriage (who was at that time in his fifties) had totally rejected her after she left him with his father at the time of the divorce. She had not seen him for approximately thirty years and was crushed when he emphatically refused a rapprochement at the time of her mother's death. Even more heartbreaking were recurrent memories of two daughters from a second marriage (now in their thirties) who had been spirited off to another country by her foreign-born husband. She had last seen them when they were latency-aged children. Mrs. A. feared that she was remembered by them as an alcoholic uncaring mother who had deserted them in their time of need.

Whereas most of her life had been spent in a free-wheeling, adventuresome manner without a thought about tomorrow, she now found herself confronted by a bleak, limited future and cruel past. Her inner pain was mirrored in the deprivation present in her current life. Until recently, she had been financially secure, provided for by trust funds from her parents. Because she had spent freely, these monies had run out. Although Mrs. A. longed to resume her life of travel and pleasure, she could not because of her financial circumstance and physical limitations. "I'm trapped, my own worse enemy."

Whenever the patient had been confronted with limitations and restrictions in the past, she had merely left the situation, moved to another locality, and begun life anew.

The inability to run made Mrs. A. more aware of the importance of others. Fear of alienating her few friends prompted her to monitor actions and limit opinions. This resulted in uncharacteristic attitudes of compliance and dependence. She asked if therapy could help her feel less "blocked and nervous."

Family History

The patient was the first of four children born to a stable western couple. The family moved to the East when Mrs. A. was five and returned to the West when she was fifteen. This move followed a severe business reversal. Of three male siblings, two became professional men, and the third was chronically ill. The oldest brother, her favorite, had died a year before treatment began. The patient described him as a man constantly searching for his place in life but never finding it. In his later years, he abused alcohol and was prone to depression. The middle brother, her mother's favorite, raised a family and developed a successful professional practice. The patient always resented him, feeling that he was spoiled and constantly trying to embarrass her. They had little contact over the years; their last meeting was at their mother's funeral when he accused her of treating their mother poorly. The patient's youngest brother had been the least favored of the children. In his early twenties, after dropping out of college, he joined the service and became floridly psychotic. He has been hospitalized or institutionalized consistently since that time. The patient recently found him in a board-and-care home in another community and was taking steps to have him moved to a facility near her apartment when she entered therapy.

The mother was described as a domineering woman who always had Mrs. A's best interests in mind. At best, their relationship was an ambivalent one: the patient alternated between attitudes of deep attachment and rejection. During the patient's preschool years, her mother worked and was seen as a respectable, outgoing, capable woman. She came from a well-to-do aristocratic family who felt she had "married down" and "lived beneath herself."

The patient's father, whom she described as a "wonderful tyrant," was the principal person with whom she felt allied during her latency and preadolescent years. Although he was short-tempered and difficult, he favored the patient. After the severe financial reversal when Mrs. A. was fifteen, he became severely depressed. Thereafter, she remembered him as prone to recurring periods of depression and alcohol abuse. When the patient was in her midthirties, he died.

Developmental History

Mrs. A. remembers being told that she was a planned and wanted child. Her mother's pregnancy and delivery were described as uneventful. She was breast-fed and reportedly accomplished her developmental milestones of crawling, walking, and talking within the usual expected framework. She does not know when she was weaned or toilet trained but believes it was done in a "strict fashion," which was her mother's style.

Mrs. A. did not recall nightmares or other symptoms during childhood. She described a very close relationship with her father that began "before I started school" and intensified during the elementary school years. Her teasing, bantering antics with her father were both exciting and pleasant until he would "get to be too much." Teasing would turn into needling, "Can't you do it better than that?" Then she would feel criticized and angry. Mrs. A. was an excellent student who was outgoing and popular. Many of her friends were boys. Her relationships with girls and, later, women were always fraught with conflict, because she felt that they might be jealous, turn on her, and be untrustworthy. Menarche was a difficult time. Mrs. A. remembers herself as quite irritable and withdrawn prior to the onset of her menses at age fourteen. Afterward she began to date and was more outgoing and comfortable. At age seventeen, she impulsively ran away with a boyfriend.

Adult Developmental History

Mrs. A.'s first husband, whom she married soon after leaving home, was an itinerant musician who traveled the country during the big band era. The patient enjoyed accompanying him, spending days and nights in different places, seeing and doing "different things." Soon, she was episodically drinking to excess. When her parents began having serious marital problems, Mrs. A. invited her mother to travel with her, her husband, and infant son, a pattern that continued for almost seven years.

By the time Mrs. A. was in her late twenties, the excitement had gone out of the marriage. She wanted to continue living an adventuresome life, but without the constant nagging and constraints of her mother and husband. Therefore, she divorced her husband, who took custody of their son, initially in conjunction with the patient's mother. This produced a major rift between mother and daughter, after which Mrs. A. impulsively left and went to a foreign country.

A new era began in the patient's life as she traveled back and forth between continents. She felt free, unrestricted by family or responsibility, able to be carefree and to give "free rein" to her feelings. At that time, Mrs. A. described herself as attractive and outgoing, a woman who easily made friends and attracted interesting men. She was slim, well-built, and the center of attention.

At age thirty-three she married her second husband, a foreign businessman. After several years and two children, Mrs. A. began to experience him as overbearing and dominating. Further, she was torn between her husband and children and her mother, who by that time was having recurrent periods of depression and asked the patient to come home and take care of her. Mrs. A. began to make frequent trips to her mother's side. On one such occasion, after a stay of three months without her daughters, her husband initiated divorce proceedings. A long legal battle resulted in a divorce and paternal custody of the children. Mrs. A.'s first serious bout of depression, during which she took an overdose of pills, followed.

When Mrs. A. was in her early forties she developed hypochondriacal symptoms of dizziness, nausea, and unsteady gait. Menopause occurred at age forty-six. Her mother insisted that she go to a midwestern clinic where she herself had been treated on numerous occasions. There Mrs. A. saw a psychiatrist who told her that she suffered from a neurosis for which psychotherapy was indicated. After refusing his advice, Mrs. A. returned to the maternal home, dismissed her symptoms as unimportant, and began to work for the first time as a salesperson in a store. This was interspersed with occasional trips out of the country to escape the feeling of being cornered and being dominated by her mother, whose health gradually deteriorated to the point of dementia.

Through the remaining years until her mother died when the patient was fifty-eight, Mrs. A. occasionally used alcohol and barbituates. Her involvement with men, which had been one of recurrent "flings," became less frequent. With advancing age and rapid weight gain, the patient no longer saw herself as an attractive, seductive woman, and she increasingly denied the significance of this change. She found herself "not caring" about her appearance because "it didn't matter anymore." Her body was now experienced as "a convenience that had lost its usefulness."

Mrs. A. reacted to her mother's death with considerable sadness and social withdrawal. These feelings were heightened by the accusatory attitude of her middle brother who berated her for "taking advantage of mother and using up all her money." After settling her mother's affairs, Mrs. A. moved closer to her oldest brother. After his death, she traveled for the last time to another continent and had what she described as "my final fling." It was at that point that she had her heart attack.

Diagnostic Formulations

My initial evaluation of Mrs. A. indicated that she was suffering from a depression with hypochondriacal features and alcoholism, which was now in remission. (She had stopped drinking approximately two years prior to starting therapy.) In addition, there were the obvious problems related to intimacy, marriage, and parenthood. When Mrs. A. entered midlife, she reacted symptomatically to the aging process in herself and to her mother's death, becoming hypochondriacal and later obese.

I believed that Mrs. A. had not come to grips with issues from multiple levels of development, particularly those from young adulthood. However, I was intrigued by her keen intellect and curiosity. She was a woman who suddenly recognized that her itinerant lifestyle had caused her to "race through life" without experiencing many of its most significant pleasures—particularly a lasting (and sustaining) relationship with children and grandchildren. How could that have happened, she asked? Was it too late to do anything about it? Here was an introspective bud that might blossom in a conducive therapeutic setting. Could it happen in one so old? I decided to try.

The Therapy

For the first three years of treatment, Mrs. A. was seen once or twice per week. Thereafter, treatment continued every other week (except for occasional weekly visits when periods of crisis arose) to the present. Because the patient had no financial resources of her own, the treatment was paid for by Medicare and Medi-Cal.

Opening Phase. The initial psychotherapy sessions were dominated by Mrs. A.'s hypochondriacal concerns about her dizziness, blurred vision, weakness, and anxiety. This soon led to consideration of the major change that had occurred with her life following the heart attack. Never having experienced any physical limitations, Mrs. A. now tired easily and found herself occasionally short of breath. She lamented: "I haven't adapted to old age . . . old age is ugly . . . I'm on my way down and out; this is just an anticlimax to an interesting life, and there is nothing left for me anymore."

She did not believe that there was any way that she could adapt to these new limitations, and she felt at the end of her "lifeline." Besides her failing health, Mrs. A. was confronted with a bleak financial picture. She had always had what appeared to be an endless supply of money from her parents, but as her mother's illness lingered, these resources were used up, leaving her feeling abandoned and nearly destitute.

A number of sessions during the first six months of

therapy revolved around her initial lack of reaction to the heart attack and subsequent recognition of its staggering impact. She would say, "I'm a different person now; I'm so vulnerable and helpless." Mrs. A. was especially bothered by the sense that her condition was permanent. Increasingly, she felt that she had lived her life and had no future.

Gradually, we reconstructed the experience during the heart attack. Mrs. A. described the crushing pain that took her breath away as a very frightening experience—this was in sharp contrast to her response at the time of the attack. Then she ignored the pain, believing it to be due to indigestion. In the hospital she was "the ideal patient" (according to her cardiologist), who never complained and went along with all procedures and recommendations. I interpreted that her current hypochondriacal symptoms were in part a defense against the terror, panic, and loss she sustained at the time of the heart attack. Subsequently, as the hypochondriacal symptoms subsided, Mrs. A. was better able to accept the limitations imposed by the heart condition.

As she came to see herself as someone who had, indeed, had a heart attack, the patient began to work on her sense of "getting old." She began to read extensively about psychotherapy, psychiatry, and psychoanalysis. During the second half of her first year of therapy, her introspective curiosity grew by leaps and bounds. "I've always wanted to find out more about myself, but I was afraid that no one would ever be able to figure me out. I never could, before this." Mrs. A. expressed fear that I would tire of her and get rid of her like the other men in the recent and distant past.

By this time, the patient was thoroughly enjoying the therapy sessions and began reporting dreams and memories about her past relationships with parents, siblings, and husbands. She became fascinated with the idea that there were "hidden meanings" that had motivated her over the years.

As she spoke of her pattern of "being on the move," I pointed out that her wandering appeared to be precipitated in part by "strong emotions" from the past. When I suggested that we might be able to understand this more clearly, she responded with a flood of thoughts about her father who dominated every action and thought, and many memories of strict, at times vindictive, teachers. I was eventually able to interpret that one of the "strong emotions" that motivated her frequent moves was repressed anger toward her father that was stimulated in situations (marriages) in which she felt dominated. Mrs. A. responded with further memories of rebelliousness but then focused, mournfully, on how shocked she was by the realization that this option was no longer open to her. She realized she had never taken time to reflect on her impulsive behavior, let alone control it for any length of time, until she was forced to do so by the heart attack.

Middle Phase. Slowly, Mrs. A. began to idealize me as a caring, stable, knowledgeable father who could be trusted with her innermost thoughts. I became a father-protector. Mrs. A. would bring me medical questions about her physical status that had been "inadequately explained" by other physicians. For instance, whenever the internist would advise her to stop smoking or go on a specific type of diet, she would immediately come to me and try to find out "the real truth" about why this might or might not be indicated. She began bringing me baked goods in various shapes and forms, especially at holidays or other times when she was feeling particularly close to me. Initially, I felt surprised that this older woman would see me in a paternal role because I was thirty years her junior.

At the beginning of the second year of treatment, however, I was perplexed by her frequent self-berating and self-critical comments. Only after a period of time did I realize that she was expecting me to be much like her critical, dominating, father who would punish her for her rebellious and free-wheeling attitudes and behavior. When I did not respond like him, she unrelentingly attacked herself until her harsh conscience had been assuaged. After I interpreted her expectation that I would attack her much as her father had done, especially during her teen years, she felt both surprised and relieved; she was grateful that this masochistic pattern of behavior could be understood.

Gradually, Mrs. A. became more outgoing, slept better, and began to lose weight. At this point in the therapy, she began the quest to have her institutionalized younger brother moved from his board-and-care facility in another city so that she could visit him regularly and deal with the injustices that she imagined were being inflicted upon him. When Mrs. A. ran into the resistance of the board-and-care operator, who did not want him transferred, she enlisted my aid to learn more about patients on conservatorship and their rights as well as the treatment facilities that might be available for her brother locally. Over a period of six months, the patient's attentions and activity were mobilized and directed toward the goal of having her brother transferred. I wrote a letter to the conservator indicating that Mrs. A. was competent and interested in her brother's welfare and could serve as a suitable conservator.

After the bureaucratic haggling was finished, her brother was transferred, and I saw him in consultation to help my patient understand how to best meet his needs. He had a chronic organic brain syndrome, which was apparently secondary to repeated insulin shock treatments with prolonged coma. Filtering through the organicity were paranoid ideation on a fixed, grandiose delusional system. In general, he had the appearance of a backward state hospital patient. I educated Mrs. A. on the proper care and treatment of someone with a chronic organic brain syndrome (the need for structural predictability and clarity of information, etc.) and maintained him on the psychoactive medications that had been started some years ago.

As the years passed, his condition deteriorated progressively to the point that he could no longer be managed in an open board-and-care home. I therefore facilitated his transfer to a longer term, locked facility where he died.

When her brother was the center of Mrs. A.'s attention, an ample opportunity was available for the reworking of feelings toward her mother and next-younger brother with whom she had similar relationships—albeit with more intact people. The ambivalence experienced toward her brother caused much distress; Mrs. A. feared that her anger would have a devastating effect. This led to a discussion of similar wishes toward her mother whom she both loved and wished dead, particularly during the long final illness. This burden of unresolved guilt and grief for her mother and brothers was repeatedly worked through in therapy, resulting in Mrs. A.'s feeling less conflicted about her own aggressive, hostile impulses toward those she loved and outlived. She was thereafter more able to tolerate her ambivalence and accept her longevity.

Thus, a major therapeutic focus, as Mrs. A. watched her brother's downhill course, was a continuing adaptation to, acceptance of, and working through feelings about growing old. Through his death, she confronted her own advancing age and mortality. For example, several years earlier, when Mrs. A. had thought of caring for her brother, she felt "strong and secure, the big sister." Now, she had "shot [her] wad" and felt incapable of confronting the entrenched bureaucracy surrounding his transfer. Becoming "too angry" might precipitate another heart attack and death. I helped the patient see that, whereas previously she had enjoyed strong feelings, she now saw them as dangerous and life threatening. Again, her life had been dramatically changed by this sense of fragile emotional equilibrium, due to her cardiac condition and advancing age.

Another layer of the overdetermined nature of her fear of strong emotion, especially anger, was related to her living longer than her next younger brother who died at age sixty. Mrs. A. experienced survivor guilt; he had died from his heart attack and she had not. "Fate must have missed me. I should have died. I lived such a bad life," she said. Thus, not only aggression and hostility might lead to another heart attack; she might be punished for allowing her emotions such free rein throughout her adult life.

When her brother was moved to a local facility, Mrs. A. was surprised by his debilitated state. "He's old. So am I. We're both ugly. It's all finished." We explored the equation she had made between youthful beauty and expensive clothes on the one hand and strength and power on the other, particularly the power to attract men. Now, overweight and poorly dressed, she felt powerless and hopeless. This led to further associations about being old and weak and having to depend on others, such as myself. Mrs. A.'s dependence on me became a major aspect of the treatment. When I went away on vacation that year, she developed symptoms of staggering and lightheadedness. We began to explore her feelings that I was now the major source of power in her life; through an alliance with me she could borrow my strength and protect her brother and herself from life's insults and the ravages of old age.

In a dream, later in the second year of therapy, I was represented as the hated middle brother, a successful professional, who had decided to try a new fountain-of-youth drug on the senile brother. In her reaction, the patient described her own fears of dying. In her youth she had tempted death by living a wild, adventuresome life. Now, in old age, death had the upper hand. Perhaps, like her brother in the dream, I had a magic potion to restore youth. Although Mrs. A. wished me to have such power so she could survive, she hated me for possessing it.

Our intense work began to produce adaptive changes. Toward the end of the second year of treatment, Mrs. A. decided to take a genealogy course. As she discovered unknown ancestors, in a sense gaining thereby new loved ones and conquering time and death, her attitude toward her known relatives softened. In Eriksonian terms, Mrs. A. was coming to terms with the relationship between her own lifecycle and those who had preceded her. Later, after taking all the genealogy courses that were offered at the various adult schools, the patient returned to an earlier interest, painting. In an attempt to gain my love and approval, she began to bring her paintings to our sessions, acting in some ways like a five-year-old trying to seduce her father.

As time passed, Mrs. A. became increasingly aware of another complication of aging, arthritis of the hands, knees, and hip joints, described by an internist as degenerative. She feared that she would become crippled and bedridden, then placed in a nursing home like her mother. In addition, she berated herself for being less active but soon saw this as a defense against accepting the reality of another limitation that had come with age.

At the beginning of the third year of treatment, the patient related an upsetting dream in which she was busy packing for "a final trip" to visit her mother whom she knew was dead. She awoke in an anxious state with a sense of loss and finality. How could she go on any trip, feeling the way she did? If only she could travel again, as she did so easily for most of her life, she would go out of the country and find her abandoned children. Like the mother in the dream, they too were "dead," lost to her. The wish to seek out her children began to increase in urgency. In another dream, Mrs. A. went to a doctor's office and was told that she would have to scream before she could see her children. She wondered what price she would have to pay for a reunion. Was she being deprived of this possibility as punishment for abandoning them?

On Turning Age Sixty-Five. During the third year of therapy Mrs. A. turned sixty-five. Now she was "officially designated as old," a "certified old lady." Reaching this milestone heightened her feelings of insignificance and inadequacy because her "grand plan for life" had not produced any money, friends, or substantial material possessions. At times Mrs. A. felt angry and cheated, discontent and unhappy with her lot in life. There was no one but me to turn to for support and solace. In part, her complaint was a wish for greater attention from me. She had become friends with an older woman who was unfamiliar with the complexities of American life, and their friendship continued to the present.

My efforts in psychotherapy were directed toward helping Mrs. A. recognize the magical thinking surrounding turning sixty-five. She realized that it was quite unreasonable to believe that "the bottom would fall out" just because she had a birthday, but she had always believed that people aged sixty-five were "finished." As we focused on her capabilities, Mrs. A. became more accepting of her status. After all, now that she had been "declared old," she was entitled to certain rights and privileges. In addition to being freed from the obligation to work because sixty-five was the official retirement age, Mrs. A. noted that she "knew a thing or two about life" and could advise the young and foolish (as she now saw her youth) about the pitfalls ahead. Being younger, I, too, could benefit from her wisdom, particularly about life in foreign countries.

During the fourth year of treatment, Mrs. A. continued to be concerned about her aging, as was manifested by her tiring more easily and a new concern—"I'm getting forgetful," particularly about names and dates. As the patient's sixty-sixth birthday approached, time was "speeding by" and her age was "hard to believe."

Soon after her birthday, Mrs. A. related a dream in which I was talking with her debilitated brother. In the dreams, Mrs. A. resented my firm statement that I did not have to explain to her what was going on; her brother would do so. Reactions went from being disappointed and angry with me for not giving her useful answers to questions about her brother and herself. She wanted to be "cradled" and taken care of like him. She was not getting enough from me. I interpreted this dream as containing a wish to be taken care of in the present, like her brother, and at the same time to be a child, young again, "cradled" in a loving, protecting, parent's arms. She tearfully nodded in agreement, but then stated with resolve, "But it can't be so; I'll do the best I can with what I have." Not much later, her brother deteriorated to the point that I placed him in a long-term, closed geriatric center. Mrs. A. mourned her brother's progressive deterioration and deeply missed the opportunity to take him out of the hospital on weekends.

Becoming a Mother and Grandmother. Later, in the fourth year of treatment, Mrs. A. received a letter from an old friend in a foreign country. Its arrival further stimulated her curiosity and concern about her children, who were still there. She was quite reluctant to find out more about her daughters and eventually, after much procrastination, did write a letter to this friend, asking about them. This occurred after we had focused extensively on the overdetermined nature of her reluctance to "open up the old wounds." It was my belief that on one level she again feared punishment for sexual and aggressive impulses expressed through "flings with men" and the eventual abandonment of her children. Such retribution might take the form of another heart attack or a stroke. Further, she feared that her daughters would reject her overture with abuse and ridicule. Another layer of this reluctance was exposed when Mrs. A. thought of the ambivalent relationship she had with her own mother. "What if I turn out to be as terrible a mother as she was?" As Mrs. A. worked through her fears of motherhood via identification with her own mother, she felt comfortable enough to write again to her friend to ask about her daughters.

This process took about a year. In the fifth year of treatment Mrs. A. summoned her courage and wrote to her children. To her amazement, she received an immediate reply; they wanted to meet her! Within two weeks both daughters came for an anxiety-filled but joyous reunion. Because I saw growth along the adult developmental lines of parenthood and grandparenthood as essential to the patient's mental health, I accepted her invitation to meet the family. Her older daughter, age thirty-two, a bright, interesting woman, was very supportive of her mother. Unfortunately, the thirty-year-old daughter suffered from emotional problems. Again, I took the role of advisor and resource person, reviewing the daughter's care over the past ten years during which she had been recurrently hospitalized and treated with various medications. I gave Mrs. A. and her daughter a list of board-certified psychiatrists in her country, one of whom eventually saw the daughter.

Mrs. A.'s life was now significantly changed. Overnight

she became a mother with one successful child and another with major problems. Contact between mother and daughters was continuous—the children called frequently and visited four to five times a year. When the grandchildren came to see her, Mrs. A. again proudly brought them to meet me. They were active, inquisitive children who enjoyed being pampered. Mrs. A.'s newly found happiness was marred by the death of her brother. She mourned his death but felt that he had really died for her when his dementia had become so severe that meaningful communication ceased. "I found my daughters again just in time. Now that my brother is gone I'd be completely alone if it weren't for them."

Turning Age Seventy. Mrs. A. approached her seventieth birthday with a considerably more positive attitude than she had on her sixty-fifth. Although feeling "old and on my last lap," she energetically engaged her daughters and grandchildren on their frequent visits. Her role as mother and grandmother—"I feel needed again. I have a purpose in life"—was clearly energizing and tended to put psychosomatic preoccupations into a more manageable perspective.

Discussion of the Clinical Presentation. Mrs. A. sought treatment at age sixty-two for the relief of psychosomatic symptoms (and obesity) that developed after a heart attack. The symptoms were similar to ones the patient had experienced approximately twenty years earlier that were related then to failure to master a number of midlife developmental tasks. Then Mrs. A. had responded to two failed marriages, the abandonment of her children, and a dawning awareness of the limitations incumbent in the aging process by a regressive return to mother. In a sense, the developmental process up to that time had been dominated and skewed by unresolved, intensely ambivalent feelings toward her mother that blocked adult separation and individuation. The infantile surrender to her mother was initially punctuated and modulated by the well-established patterns of frequent travel, involvements with men, and excessive use of alcohol. Thus, for several years, Mrs. A.'s conflicted feelings about dependence versus independence were managed through alternating periods of caring for her mother and abandoning her.

The adaptation worked until time and reality finally caught up with the patient in her early sixties. Then the heart attack, obesity (another expression of the wish to be nurtured), death of mother, and limited financial resources blocked the previously utilized means of obtaining gratification. A depression with somatic ruminations followed. The presenting symptoms were thus understood to be the culmination of a lifetime of pathologic development and a response to the difficult developmental tasks of late adulthood.

As Mrs. A. entered old age, she sought to reestablish, through her chronically disabled brother, ties to the family of childhood. Because I understood the importance of this developmental process, I facilitated the transfer of her brother to this community and took on an educational and caretaking role for both. Mrs. A.'s reinvolvement with her long-lost brother produced feelings of wholeness and well-being and a sense of longitudinal connection with her "roots." The relationship with her brother stimulated her to analyze conflicts about being a mother and led eventually to greater acceptance of that adult role. The resumption of a meaningful relationship with her children and grandchildren was seen as a resolution of a major developmental task of late adulthood.

Much work was done on the issues of aging. As Mrs. A. mourned the loss of her youthful beauty, physical endurance, and past lifestyle, she came to understand the neurotic components of her fear of mortality, particularly the idea that she would become "too emotional" and cause her own death. As Mrs. A. turned age sixty-five and then seventy, we explored the magical connections between birthdays and death. As feelings about aging became less conflicted, they were sublimated into interests in genealogy and painting. Not surprisingly, the developmental task of accepting aging was deeply connected with these other themes. For instance, the pastoral scenes that Mrs. A. chose to paint were of the countryside around her mother's childhood home. As death approached she had turned despair into integrity and filled her remaining years with feelings of love, fulfillment, and contentment. Life can begin at seventy!

References

1. *Fulfillment Through Maturity*

1. *The American Heritage Dictionary of the English Language* (New York: American Heritage Publishing Co., 1969), p. 807.
2. Erik Erikson, *Childhood and Society,* 2nd ed. (New York: Norton, 1963), p. 124.

2. *The Importance of Childhood Experiences*

1. Sigmund Freud, 1905, "Three Essays on the Theory of Sexuality," in *The Standard Edition,* ed. J. Strachey (London: Hogarth Press, 1958), 7:125–243, p. 176.
2. Sigmund Freud, 1909, "Analysis of a Phobia in a Five-Year-Old Boy," in *The Standard Edition,* ed. J. Strachey (London: Hogarth Press, 1958), 12:213–218.
3. Rene Spitz, *Hospitalism: An Inquiry into the Genesis of Psychiatric Conditions in Early Childhood,* Psychoanalytic Study of the Child, vol. 1 (1945), pp. 313–342.
4. Anna Freud, *Normality and Pathology in Childhood: Assessments of Development* (New York: International Universities Press, 1965).

5. Ibid., p. 59.
6. Calvin Colarusso, *Mother, Is That You?*, Psychoanalytic Study of the Child, vol. 42 (1987), pp. 223–237.

3. *Early Childhood*

1. Rene Spitz, *The First Year of Life* (New York: International Universities Press, 1965).
2. Erik Erikson, *Childhood and Society*, 2nd ed. (New York: Norton, 1963).
3. Ibid., p. 252.
4. Margaret Mahler, Fred Pine, and Annie Bergman, *The Psychological Birth of the Human Infant* (New York: Basic Books, 1973).
5. David Winnicott, "Transitional Objects and Transitional Phenomena," in *Playing and Reality* (New York: Basic Books, 1953), pp. 1–25.
6. Robert Stoller, *Sex and Gender: On the Development of Masculinity and Femininity* (New York: Science House, 1968).
7. Anna Freud, *Normality and Pathology in Childhood: Assessments of Development* (New York: International Universities Press, 1965).
8. Ibid., pp. 74–75.
9. Erikson, pp. 255–256.
10. Sigmund Freud, 1909, "Analysis of a Phobia in a Five-Year-Old Boy," in *The Standard Edition*, ed. J. Strachey (London: Hogarth Press, 1958), 10:3–148.
11. Ibid., p. 7.
12. Ibid., pp. 9–10.
13. Ibid., p. 19.
14. David Guttman, "Psychological Development and Pathology in Later Life," in *New Dimensions in Adult Development*, ed. Robert Nemiroff and Calvin Colarusso (New York: Basic Books, 1990), pp. 170–185.
15. Phyllis Tyson and Robert L. Tyson, *Psychoanalytic Theories of Development* (New Haven: Yale University Press, 1990), pp. 217–218.

4. *Latency and Adolescence*

1. Elizabeth Bremner Kaplan, *Reflections Regarding Psychomotor Activities during the Latency Period*, in Psychoanalytic Study of the Child, vol. 20 (1965), pp. 220–238, p. 220.
2. Sigmund Freud, 1921, "Group Psychology and the Analysis of the Ego," in *The Standard Edition*, ed. J. Strachey (London: Hogarth Press, 1958), 18:67–143, pp. 90–91.

3. Erik Erikson, *Childhood and Society*, 2nd ed. (New York: Norton, 1963), p. 260.
4. Lili Peller, *Libidinal Phases, Ego Development, and Play*, Psychoanalytic Study of the Child, vol. 9 (1954), pp. 178–198.
5. Erikson, p. 261.
6. Peter Blos, *The Second Individuation Process of Adolescence*, Psychoanalytic Study of the Child, vol. 22 (1967), pp. 162–186.
7. Calvin Colarusso, "Psychoanalysis of a Severe Neurotic Learning Disturbance in a Gifted Adolescent Boy," *Bulletin of the Menninger Clinic* 44(6), (1980), pp. 585–602.

5. It All Begins with the Body

1. Marcia K. Goin, "Emotional Survival and the Aging Body," in *New Dimensions in Adult Development*, ed. Robert Nemiroff and Calvin Colarusso (New York: Basic Books, 1990), pp. 518–531, p. 524.
2. Carl Eisdorfer and Robert Raskind, "Aging and Human Behavior," in *Hormonal Correlates of Behavior, Vol. 1. A Lifespan View*, ed. B. E. Eleftreriois and R. L. Spatts (New York: Plenum Press, 1975), pp. 369–387, p. 380.
3. William Masters and Virginia Johnson, *Human Sexual Response* (Boston: Little, Brown, 1966), pp. 241–242.
4. Ibid., pp. 203–204.
5. David Wechsler, "Intellectual Changes With Age," in *Mental Health in Later Maturity* (Supplement 168, Federal Security Agency: U.S. Public Health Service, 1941), p. 46.
6. Lucy Jarvik, Carl Eisdofer, and J. E. Blum, *Intellectual Functioning in Adults* (New York: Springer, 1973), p. 67.

6. Creating New Life

1. Calvin Colarusso, *The Third Individuation: The Effect of Biological Parenthood on Separation-Individuation Processes in Adulthood*, Psychoanalytic Study of the Child, vol. 45 (1990), pp. 170–194.
2. Judith Kestenberg, "Regression and Reintegration in Pregnancy," *Journal of the American Psychoanalytic Association Supplement, Female Psychology #5*, 24 (1976), pp. 213–250.
3. Calvin Colarusso and Robert Nemiroff, *The Race Against Time: Psychotherapy and Psychoanalysis in the Second Half of Life* (New York: Plenum, 1985).

4. David Guttman, "Psychological Development and Pathology in Later Adulthood," *New Dimensions in Adult Development*, ed. Robert Nemiroff and Calvin Colarusso (New York: Basic Books, 1990), pp. 170–184.
5. Bertram J. Cohler and Robert M. Galatzer-Levy, "Self, Meaning, and Morale Across the Second Half of Life," in *New Dimensions in Adult Development*, ed. Robert Nemiroff and Calvin Colarusso (New York: Basic Books, 1990), pp. 214–263.

7. The Quest for Sexual Intimacy

1. George Vaillant, "Natural History of Male Psychological Health, XII: A Forty-Five-Year Study of Predictors of Successful Aging at Age 65," *American Journal of Psychiatry* 147 (1990), pp. 31–37, p. 32.
2. Helen Singer Kaplan, "Sex, Intimacy, and the Aging Process," *Journal of the American Academy of Psychoanalysis* 18(2) (1990), pp. 185–205, p. 185.
3. Ibid., p. 187.
4. Ibid., p. 191.
5. Eli Miller, "The Development of Intimacy at Age 50," in *The Race Against Time: Psychotherapy and Psychoanalysis in the Second Half of Life*, ed. Robert Nemiroff and Calvin Colarusso (New York: Plenum, 1985), pp. 121–141.

9. Play in Adulthood

1. Albert Solnit, *A Psychoanalytic View of Play*, Psychoanalytic Study of the Child, vol. 42 (1987), pp. 205–222.
2. Anna Freud, *Normality and Pathology in Childhood: Assessments of Development* (New York: International Universities Press, 1965), p. 81.
3. Eric Plaut, *Play and Adaptation*, Psychoanalytic Study of the Child, vol. 34 (1979), pp. 217–232, p. 219.
4. Robert Waelder, 1932, "The Psychoanalytic Theory of Play," *Psychoanalysis*, ed. S.A. Guttman (New York: International Universities Press, 1976), pp. 84–100.
5. Lili Peller, *Libidinal Phases, Ego Development and Play*, Psychoanalytic Study of the Child, vol. 9 (1954), pp. 178–198.
6. Mortimer Ostow, *Play and Reality*, Psychoanalytic Study of the Child, vol. 42 (1987), pp. 193–204, p. 200.

7. Solnit, p. 214.
8. Ostow, p. 194.
9. David Winnicott, "Transitional Objects and Transitional Phenomena," *International Journal of Psychoanalysis* 24 (1953), pp. 89–97, p. 94.
10. George S. Moran, *Some Functions of Play and Playfulness*, Psychoanalytic Study of the Child, vol. 42 (1987), pp. 11–29.
11. Solnit, p. 209.

10. Work

1. Anna Freud, *Normality and Pathology in Childhood: Assessments of Development* (New York: International Universities Press, 1965), p. 77.
2. Erik Erikson, *Childhood and Society*, 2nd ed. (New York: Norton, 1963), p. 255.
3. Ibid.
4. Judith M. Bardwick, *The Plateauing Trap* (New York: American Management Association, 1986).

11. The Power of Time

1. Robert J. Lifton, *History and Human Survival* (New York: Random House, 1970).
2. Robert J. Lifton, *Home from the War* (New York: Simon & Schuster, 1973).
3. Robert J. Lifton, *Death in Life* (New York: Touchstone Books, 1976).
4. Robert J. Lifton, *The Life of the Self* (New York: Simon & Schuster, 1976).
5. Robert J. Lifton, *The Broken Connection* (New York: Simon & Schuster, 1979).
6. Ibid., p. 5.
7. Erik Erikson, *Childhood and Society*, 2nd ed. (New York: Norton, 1963), p. 268.
8. Elliot Jacques, "Death and the Midlife Crisis," *International Journal of Psychoanalysis* 46 (1965), pp. 502–514.
9. Calvin Colarusso and Robert Nemiroff, *Adult Development* (New York: Plenum, 1981), ch. 7.
10. Daniel J. Levinson, C. N. Darrow, and E. B. Klein, *The Seasons of a Man's Life* (New York: Knopf, 1978).

11. Bernice L. Neugarten, "Time, Age and the Life Cycle," *American Journal of Psychiatry* 136 (1979), pp. 887–894.
12. Judith M. Bardwick, *The Plateauing Trap* (New York: American Management Association, 1986).
13. Allison Lurie, *The War Between the Tates* (New York: Warner, 1975), p. 12.
14. John Hassler, "Turning Forty in Analysis," in *The Race Against Time: Psychotherapy and Psychoanalysis in the Second Half of Life*, ed. Robert Nemiroff and Calvin Colarusso (New York: Plenum, 1985), pp. 97–115.

12. Wisdom, Maturity, and Fulfillment

1. Gary Levinson, "New Beginnings at Seventy: A Decade of Psychotherapy in Late Adulthood," in *The Race Against Time: Psychotherapy and Psychoanalysis in the Second Half of Life*, ed. Robert Nemiroff and Calvin Colarusso (New York: Plenum, 1985), pp. 171–188.

Index